Global Warming and the Political Ecology of Health

Advances in Critical Medical Anthropology
Series Editors: Merrill Singer and Pamela Erickson

This new book series will significantly advance our understanding of the complex and rapidly changing landscape of health, disease, and treatment around the world with original and innovative books in the spirit of Critical Medical Anthropology that exemplify and extend its theoretical and the empirical dimensions. Books in the series address topics across the broad range of subjects addressed by medical anthropologists.

Global Warming and the Political Ecology of Health

Emerging Crises and Systemic Solutions

Hans A. Baer and Merrill Singer

Walnut Creek, CA

LEFT COAST PRESS, INC.
1630 North Main Street, #400
Walnut Creek, California 94596
http://www.LCoastPress.com

Hardback ISBN 978-1-59874-353-1
Paperback ISBN 978-1-59874-354-8

Library of Congress Cataloging-in-Publication Data

Global warming and the political ecology of health : emerging crises and systemic
solutions / Hans A. Baer and Merrill Singer.
    p. ; cm. — (Advances in critical medical anthropology ; v. 1)
Includes bibliographical references and index.
ISBN 978-1-59874-353-1 (hardback : alk. paper) -- ISBN 978-1-59874-354-8
(pbk. : alk. paper)
  1. Global warming--Health aspects. 2. Medical anthropology. I. Baer, Hans A.,
1944- II. Singer, Merrill. III. Series.
  [DNLM: 1. Greenhouse Effect. 2. Environmental Exposure. 3. Environmental Health--economics. WA 30.5 G562 2009]
RA793.G565 2009
363.738'7--dc22
2008032124

Printed in the United States of America

♾™ The paper used in this publication meets the minimum requirements of American
National Standard for Information Sciences—Permanence of Paper for Printed Library
Materials, ANSI/NISO Z39.48—1992.

08 09 10 11 5 4 3 2 1

Cover design by Cheryl Carrington

Contents

Introduction

Our world is changing in dramatic and consequential ways. From melting glaciers to rising seas, and from increases in violent storms to emergent and spreading diseases, many of these changes reflect a pattern of planetary warming. While some have called into question whether the changes we are seeing around us are the outcome of something more than cyclical patterns, the sheer volume of mounting data of diverse sorts has convinced most climate scientists that the global warming is real, that it is increasingly threatening to human life and well-being, and that it is largely the result of human or anthropogenic activities, particularly since the Industrial Revolution. According to Dessler and Parson,

> Of all the environmental issues that have emerged in the past few decades, global climate change [or global warming] is the most serious, the most difficult to manage. Many aspects of human society and well being—where we live, how we build, how we move around, how we earn our livings, what we do for recreation—still depend on a relatively benign range of climate conditions, even though this dependence has been reduced and obscured in modern industrial societies by their wealth and technology. [Dessler and Parson 2006:1]

In short, there is little doubt any more that global warming will have severe economic, social, political, and health consequences as the 21st century unfolds. Even though these consequences will not be equally distributed nor will they arrive all at once, it is clear that collectively human societies have never faced an environmental problem on this scale and complexity before. Despite such observations, most anthropologists, including medical anthropologists, as well as other social scientists, have been slow in coming to grips with the impact that global warming is presently having and will continue to have upon humanity for decades and possibly even centuries to come.

This book seeks to develop both a critical anthropology and a critical medical anthropology of global warming, one that moves beyond the emphasis of most anthropological and other social scientific studies with their limited focus on adaptation of human societies to global warming. As a few world systems theorists and critical environmental sociologists have done, we argue that global warming ultimately is rooted in the capitalist world system with its orientation to ever-expanding production and consumption, both of which contribute to the emission of various greenhouse gases into the atmosphere. Likewise, it is our perspective that health should not be seen through a narrow medical lens or as a series of isolated problems. Rather, health is fundamentally rooted in sociocultural and political-economic systems, and thus intertwined with the world system and with anthropogenic climate change.

While climate scientists have done humanity a tremendous service by calling attention to the seriousness of the consequences of global warming or climate change, the solutions that they propose in terms of how societies can adapt to and mitigate global warming fail to call for the paradigm that an authentic program of mitigation requires. As critical medical anthropologists, it is our contention that if humanity is going to respond adequately to global warming, it will have to make a transition from the capitalist world system to a global democratic order based upon ecosocialist principles. This book examines the gravity of global warming; its manifestation as yet another contradiction of global capitalism; changes in human health, including settlement patterns, subsistence, nutrition, and disease, as fundamentally intertwined with the effects of climate change and global capitalism; the inadequacies of the emerging climate regime and "green capitalism" as a strategies of mitigation; and ultimately the need to create a democratic ecosocialist world system as a strategy of genuine mitigation.

A number of years ago, before the full magnitude and accelerating pace of global warming became clear, the British social epidemiologist Peter Townsend argued that to significantly improve world health we must address structural barriers that create illness and death among poor and socially marginalized groups within and across nations. To achieve health equity, he argued (Townsend 1986:29), "the only long-term remedy is to restrict the power and wealth of the rich, to dismantle the present structures of social privilege, and to build social institutions based on fair allocation of wealth and on social equality." To this profound proposition, we would add, we must also address the present structures of production and associated ideologies of consumption based on sound principles of environmental preservation. Further, because structures of social inequality, environmental degradation, and human health are inexorably linked, in the contemporary world social justice must include environmental justice and health equity.

Anthropological Examinations of Global Warming

There is a strong tradition in anthropology of analyzing systemic forms of social injustice, including the sociopolitical conditions under which the greatest burdens of ecological degradation are borne inequitably by specific groups. Until recently, however, only a small group of anthropologists had examined aspects of global warming or climate change. The field of global warming is now moving very quickly and the number of anthropologists working on the issue has grown accordingly. This volume is intended to contribute to this growing body of work as well as to strengthen linkages between the anthropology of climate change and the political ecology of health.

In an early study, Willet Kempton, James S. Boster, and Jennifer A. Hartley (1995) examined U.S. environmental values by conducting semi-structured interviews with 43 informants (20 laypeople, 21 environmental specialists, 2 pilot subjects) as well as surveys of 42 respondents (30 Earth First members, 27 Sierra Club members, 29 laypeople, 30 dry cleaners, and 26 sawmill workers) from New Jersey and Maine. They investigated their informants' perceptions of three major local environmental changes, namely ozone depletion, species extinctions, and global warming. Many laypeople, they found, confounded global warming as a subset or a consequence of ozone depletion.

Subsequently, Brown (1999) published an article on "climate anthropology," which, she argues, includes an examination of the impact of global warming on societies. Roncoli and Magistro (2000) argued that anthropologists need to examine "global climate change" as part and parcel of the anthropology of climate variability, a phenomenon that includes droughts, hurricane, and other instances of erratic weather pattern. While archaeologist Brian Fagan (1999:76) is correct in his assertion that "global warming is nothing new for humanity," the magnitude of the warming that the planet has been experiencing, and is predicted will continue for decades to come, is on a magnitude never experienced before by humanity. Fortunately, in his more recent book, *The Long Summer: How Climate Change Changed Civilization*, Fagan acknowledges this grim and imminent reality:

> We live within the capsule of a global economy, seemingly oblivious to climate events with the potential to kill thousands [or, more accurately stated, millions], in a time when human populations have exploded and cities are the dominant form of human settlement. With the Industrial Revolution, we took a giant stride into an era in which we are frighteningly exposed to potential cataclysm, enhanced by our own seeming ability to warm the earth and increase the probability of extreme climate events. [Fagan 2004:250]

Various climate anthropologists have been working for some time on the impact of specific climate events, such as droughts, torrential rains, hurricanes, El Niños, and earthquakes, on human societies (e.g. Andrus et al. 2008). Many climate scientists argue that these localized and regional climate events may be manifestations of broader patterns of climate change. In the introduction to their anthology *Weather, Climate, Culture*, Sarah Strauss and Ben Orlove (2003:10–11), however, refer to "climate change" only in passing, and none of the essays included in their volume focuses specifically on climate change or more specifically global warming. In other publications, however, Orlove, along with various colleagues, has examined several local climatic events related to global warming, especially El Niño in the Andean area and in southern Uganda (Orlove 2003; Orlove et al. 2000, 2002; Orlove and Kabugo 2005). In their contribution to the Strauss and Orlove anthology, West and Vasquez-Leon (2003), in an essay about farmers' and ranchers' perceptions of climate variability in the Sulphur Springs Valley of Arizona, examine their informants' (N = 71) views about climate change in the local area. They note: "A few participants expressed a strong belief in local climate change. Most of the interviewees, however, believed that any change was just part of a cycle and not permanent—e.g., observed changes were examples of climate variability" (West and Vasquez-Leon 2003:243). Many informants sensed that the area was becoming drier or that droughts had become more commonplace, but they did not link these changes with others being reported elsewhere in the world.

With respect to the specific impact of global warming on human health, in his medical anthropology textbook, Cecil Helman (2007:449), while noting that global warming "is one of the most important features in modern life," only very briefly discusses the issue as one of a series of anthropogenic forces affecting human health. Even John Bodley, in his book *Anthropology and Contemporary Human Problems* (2008:7–8, 307–309), refers only in passing to "global warming" or "global climate change," despite the fact that he deals in great depth with the global environmental crisis. In "Climate Change and Severe Weather," Greg Guest and Paul R. Epstein provide a short overview of the effects of global warming on health (Epstein and Guest 2005:242–243). Elsewhere, Epstein (2002a, 2002b, 2005), who is the associate director of the Center for Health and the Global Environment at Harvard Medical School, has published extensively about the impact of global warming on human health, and with Evan Mills edited an anthology titled *Climate Change Futures: Health, Ecological and Economic Dimensions* (Epstein and Mills 2005).

To date, only a few anthropologists have dealt with global warming or climate change at length. One exception is Celeste Ray's (2002) book chapter titled "Cultural Paradigms: An Anthropological Perspective on Climate Change." Ray (2001:90) argues that policies about global warming "must employ cross-cultural knowledge of benign environmental practices while maintaining consciousness of traditional family and community structures, labour division, and localized subsistence strategies". While Ray is to be commended for bringing the anthropological lens to the study of climate change, her analysis does not discuss the relationship between local sociocultural dimensions of climate change and the treadmill of production and consumption that we believe is critical to understanding the social engine driving global capitalism. A number of other anthropologists also have began looking at the impacts of climate change on diverse human subsistence strategies (e.g. Little et al. 2001, Morton 2007).

As part of the extensive Arctic Climate Impact Assessment project, Nuttall and his colleagues examined the impact of global warming on subsistence patterns and the adaptive strategies of indigenous Arctic peoples to climate variability in the past and present. They argue that "as the climate changes, the indigenous peoples of the Arctic are facing special challenges and their abilities to harvest wildlife and food resources are already being tested" (Nuttall et al. 2004:685). Also of note, Myanna Lahsen (2005a), an anthropologist based at the Center for Science and Technology Policy at the University of Colorado at Boulder, has conducted ethnographic research on how climate models and atmospheric scientists deal with issues of certainty and uncertainty associated with general circular computerized models that seek to project possible global climatic changes emanating from greenhouse gas emissions. She also has written about U.S. climate politics and discusses the role that "conservative and financial elites" have played in supporting campaigns to counter growing concern among Americans about global warming (Lahsen 2005b).

Emilio F. Moran (2006), one of the few anthropologists on the Intergovernmental Panel on Climate Change, refers to global warming in various places in his recently published book *People and Nature: An Introduction to Human Ecological Relations*. He cites the impact of what he prefers to term "climate change" upon the spread of various infectious diseases, plant growth, and animal migration and poses questions about the seriousness of the problem as follows:

> Once we begin to operate well above any recorded levels [of greenhouse gas emissions] not just for one but more many measurable parameters, the question has to be asked if we have begun to play a reckless game with the survival of our species on planet Earth. Do we recognize that business-as-usual threatens the end of life as we know it? Are we willing to use the considerable mental capacity, and exercise our political will, to ensure our survival and that of our children? Or are we so self-satisfied in our own material success that we cannot recognize overwhelming evidence when we see it? Is the evidence above sufficient? What else might one need to know? In the answer lies our likelihood of having a future in a world worth living in. [Moran 2006:21, 23]

Our own interest in global warming emerged in the process of writing a recent textbook titled *Introducing Medical Anthropology* (Singer and Baer 2007). While researching materials for the chapter on "Health and the Environment: Toward a Healthier World," Hans Baer reviewed published material on the impact of global warming on health which was incorporated into a section titled "The Impact of Global Warming on Health" (Singer and Baer 2007:189–193). He also wrote a working paper on the need to develop a critical anthropology of global warming (Baer 2007) which prompted further discussions with Merrill Singer, leading eventually to the writing of this book. Baer subsequently was invited to write op-ed pieces on global warming for the *Australian Journal of Anthropology* and *Medical Anthropology* (Baer 2008a, 2008b). Meanwhile, Singer began elaborating on the role of global warming on syndemics for his forthcoming book *Introducing Syndemics:Toward a New Biosocial Synthesis in Public Health* (Singer, in press) and in the chapter "Ecosyndemics: Global Warming and the Coming Plagues of the 21st Century" in the forthcoming book *Plagues: Models and Metaphors in the Human "Struggle" with Disease* (Singer, in press). He also was able to expand this examination through a series of invited lectures at McMaster University, Simon Fraser University, University of Calgary, Auckland University, and the University of Connecticut.

In furthering this work, Hans Baer and Megan Jennaway, a medical anthropologist in the School of Population Health at the University of Queensland, co-organized a session on "Anthropological Perspectives on the Impact of Global Warming on Human Societies: Processes of Adaptation and Mitigation" that occurred at the Australian Anthropological Society conference in Canberra on October 30– November 2, 2007. Baer and Singer presented together on "Production and Consumption as Sources of Global Warming: Beyond Capitalism and Toward an Alternative World System" at the Climate Justice seminar sponsored by the Development Studies program at the University of Melbourne along with several grass-roots organizations, including Friends of the Earth, the Western Regional Environmental Centre, and the Socialist Alliance on August 2, 2008.

The *Australian Journal of Anthropology* has also entered the discourse on global warming. The first issue of 2008 (volume 19, issue number 1) includes a Soapbox Forum devoted to "Anthropological Perspectives on Climate Change." Kay Milton has written the introduction to this series of short essays, which includes contributions by herself, Megan Jennaway, and Hans Baer. These essays address similar themes to those addressed at the AAS session described above: the role of fear in shaping people's responses to global warming (Milton), the need for an alternative to the capitalist system that has contributed to global warming (Baer), and the millenarian frenzy in debates about global warming (Jennaway). The collection also includes an article by Simon Batterbury (University of Melbourne), which argues the case for anthropologists' engagement with the issue of global warming, and three more ethnographically based essays by Monica Minnegal and Peter Dwyer (University of Melbourne), Deborah Bird Rose (Australian National University), and Sandy Touissant (University of Western Australia). These contributions discuss, respectively, the responses of fishermen in the Gippsland region of Victoria to the climatic uncertainties in their region, and the contemporary experiences of Aboriginal communities whose everyday preoccupations do not include global warming but whose futures might be shaped by it. At the same time, in North America, the 2007 American Anthropological Association meeting included a session titled "Witnessing, Communicating, Acting: Substantiating Anthropology's Role in Confronting Climate Change."

Additionally, Susan A. Crate and Mark Nuttall are in the process of editing an anthology titled *Anthropology and Climate Change: From Encounters to Actions* that is slated to be published by Left Coast Press in 2009. Their edited volume will consist of 24 chapters that are divided into three parts: climate and culture, anthropological encounters that focus upon how local populations around the world are responding to climate change or global warming, and anthropological actions in response to climate change.

Ultimately, the critical anthropology and critical medical anthropology of global warming will be a multidisciplinary endeavor, one that draws from not only anthropology but climate science, sociology, political economy, political science, human geography, epidemiology, public health, and probably even other disciplines, such as psychology. A critical anthropology of global warming must seek to be part and parcel of what Glantz (2003:97) terms "climate affairs," an endeavor that he sees as drawing insights from several academic disciplines in the physical, biological, and social sciences and the humanities. In that anthropology focuses upon the holistic study of human societies from their very beginning and into the future and in all parts of the globe, it has a unique contribution to make to the study of the impact of global warming on human societies.

In this light, this book is guided by an *integrated ecosocial perspective* that is informed by three theoretical currents: greenhouse gas theory, political ecology theory, and critical medical anthropology, each of which is defined below.

- **Greenhouse gas theory:** A multidisciplinary understanding of the nature and effects of greenhouse gases that recognizes the substantial sociogenic origin of increasingly accelerated and socially disruptive global climate changes.
- **Political ecological theory:** An approach to understanding the factors that impact and result from environmental-society interaction that recognizes the fundamental importance of political economy, including capitalist production, market-driven distribution of resources, urbanization, and population growth.

- **Critical medical anthropology:** An approach to understanding human health at the local, regional, national, and international levels that emphasizes the central role of interaction between structural factors (like the distribution of power in society and the structuring of social inequality), biological factors (like human biological evolution and pathogenic adaptation to human hosts), and cultural patterns (like social beliefs systems, practices, and organization) on human health and health-related behaviors.

Our integration of these three approaches suggests a theoretical framework that: 1) links structures of control and social inequality (as seen in the underlying social relations and processes driving capitalist production) to increasingly powerful forces of economical globalization, human population growth, and urbanization; and 2) ties these structures and processes to the production of greenhouse gases and resulting global climate changes, as well as to environmental degradation and significantly increased human sickness, suffering, and death. Further, the perspective on global warming and its consequences presented in this book is framed by an *engaged praxis orientation* that merges theory and social action based on the following premises:

1. Social systems do not last forever, whether at the local, regional, or global level;
2. The capitalist world system or global capitalism has been around for about 500 years but has come to embody so many inherent contradictions that it must be transcended to ensure the survival of humanity and animal and plant life on a sustained basis;
3. There is a need for an alternative global system, one that is committed to meeting people's basic needs, social equity and justice, democracy, and environmental sustainability. Proposals for such an alternative system have come under various terms, including *global democracy, Earth democracy, eco-anarchism,* and *ecosocialism.*
4. Anthropologists and other progressive social scientists are too small a group to act as a vanguard in the struggle against global warming and capitalism. They must form links not only with climate scientists on whose findings they rely but also with anti-systemic movements, including the labor, anti-corporate globalization or social justice, peace, indigenous and ethnic rights, and environmental movements, and a growing climate or anti-global warming movement. In essence, a critical anthropology of global warming must be both an engaged anthropology and an anthropology of the future.

In sum, this book seeks to develop a critical anthropology, and more specifically a critical medical anthropology, of global warming—one that moves beyond the emphasis of most anthropological and other social scientific studies to date, which tend to focus on adaptation of human societies to global warming. Given the adverse health consequences of global warming, we can speak of the diseases of global warming.

These include any "tropical disease" that spreads to new places and peoples, but also include deteriorating nutrition and fresh-water supplies because of desertification of pastoral areas or flooding of agricultural areas. Taken together, the diseases of global warming will have enormous an impact on human health and well-being. In light of the existing patterns of health disparities, the health impacts produced by global warming are not likely to be equally distributed but will tend to fall disproportionately on the poor and otherwise marginalized populations and groups within and between societies. In other words, as we show in this book, those least responsible for causing global warming will bear most of the health consequences it produces.

While climate scientists have done humanity a tremendous service by calling attention to the seriousness of global warming and some of the problems associated with it, the solutions that they generally propose both in terms of how humanity can "adapt" to and "mitigate" global warming fail to come to grips with the realities of the capitalist world system. As Grimes and Kentor (2003:261) argue, most climate scientists lack training in social scientific analysis that is essential in comprehending the "political, economic, and social forces" that drive global warming. Global capitalism has so many inherent contradictions, including ones that contribute to increasing social disparities and population growth, environmental degradation, and armed conflict, that ultimately it must be transcended if humanity and the planet are going to survive. A comprehensive program of mitigation will require the development of an alternative global system, one committed to meeting people's basic needs, social equity and justice, democracy, and environmental sustainability.

1

Global Warming

A Grave Contradiction of the Capitalist World System

After years of debating and gathering new information, climate and environmental scientists, with few exceptions, now agree that global warming is a grim reality, one that is largely due to human-related or anthropogenic activities. This is the view of bodies such as the Intergovernmental Panel on Climate Change (IPCC, a United Nations organization consisting of some 2,500 climate scientists around the world), the American Geophysical Union, the U.S. National Academy of Sciences, the Union of Concerned Scientists, and various international organizations. Global warming and its repercussions have become topics of increasing public awareness (Cox 2005:2). Recognition and concern about abrupt climate change has found its way into popular culture and even the mainstream media. In the United States, the generally sedate Public Broadcasting Service (PBS), which has come to rely heavily upon corporate funding and in the process has blunt its historically critical stance, ran a television special on November 2, 2005, titled "Global Warming: The Signs and the Science," with the following message:

> [H]uman activities are provoking an unprecedented era of atmospheric warming and climate change. We're seeing more drought, more wildfires, more flooding, bigger storms and more variable weather. Tropical diseases are moving north, childhood respiratory illness is skyrocketing, and in the last three decades over 30 diseases new to science have emerged.

Feature stories are now regular fare on National Public Radio (NPR), but on more mainstream U.S. media as well.

Down under, in Australia, *The Age*, a liberal Melbourne-based newspaper, now regularly runs articles on the issue. The government-owned Australian Broadcasting Corporation (ABC) presents regular television newscasts and documentaries on global warming or climate change, stressing its impact on Australia and various regions of the country, particularly the southeastern portion, which has been adversely affected by a severe drought for about a decade.

Concern about global warming can be found at both ends of the political spectrum. The socialist left around the world has become increasingly vocal about the dangers to the planet and humanity as a result of global warming. At the same time, several evangelical Christian groups have joined in the chorus decrying global warming and proclaiming that it constitutes a violation of humanity's stewardship over God's creation.

In particular, at the popular level, Al Gore's movie *An Inconvenient Truth* (see Gore 2006) and the *The Stern Review*, authored by former World Bank chief economist Nicholas Stern (2007), have helped to propel global warming/climate change into the public consciousness around the world. As a result, a growing number of business leaders, such as the CEO of British Petroleum, have come to embrace a form of "green capitalism" that asserts that while global warming poses a serious threat to the existing global economy, capitalism has the capacity to reform itself, adopt new forms of energy and environmentally sustainable technologies, and continue to sustain economic expansion and profit-making.

Despite broad concern voiced about global warming, leaders of several rapidly developing countries, particularly China and India, maintain that advocates calling for curtailment of greenhouse gases across the globe are engaging in a double standard that does not recognize the need for the developing world to undergo the same processes of industrialization and modernization that the developed countries have undergone. The late Anil Agarwal (n.d.a:6) argued that developed countries "have been emitting carbon dioxide in the Earth's atmosphere for years before developing countries" and many poor people in the latter "will need their share of ecological space to increase what could be termed **survival emissions.**" As a result, people in developed countries will need to decrease their per capita greenhouse emissions, thereby permitting poor people in developing countries to increase theirs as they improve their material standard of living.

The Tipping Point in Public Awareness of Global Warming

Awareness and concern about global warming is not new. In 1896, the Swedish scientist Svante Arrhenius predicted that the burning of coal would double atmospheric carbon dioxide over the course of the next 3,000 years, resulting in an increase of about 9°F (5°C) in the average global temperature (Hardy 2003:55). In 1938, Guy Stewart Callender, an engineer with an amateur interest in climate issues, presented a lecture before the Royal Meterological Society in London in which he displayed various weather statistics that he interpreted as an indication that the earth's temperature was increasing (Weart 2003:2).

A few climate scientists made similar assertions during the 1950s. Charles Keeling of the Scripps Institute of Oceanography reported the first direct measurements of changing carbon dioxide concentrations in the environment. He had measured carbon dioxide concentrations from a laboratory atop Mauna Loa in Hawaii, and detected a rise of carbon dioxide from 312 parts per million (ppm) in 1958 to 330 ppm in 1972. Roger Revelle lectured about the planet's future in 1966 to students at Harvard University, one of whom was Al Gore, Jr., who became alarmed when he learned about Keeling's evidence indicating a rising carbon dioxide rise in the atmosphere (Weart 2003:142). Gore famously went on to become a U.S. Congressman from Tennessee in 1977, a U.S. Senator in 1985, and later Vice President during the Bill Clinton administration (1993–2001). Some environmentalists and many climate scientists had expressed concern about global warming as far back as the 1970s, and the IPCC was formed in 1988. Over the next 15 years, there was a steady rise, year by year, in the extent of public, academic, and political discourse on global warming.

During the 1980s, concern about the atmosphere focused more on the dangers inherent in the depletion of the ozone layer that encircles the planet than on global warming. In 1985, 20 nations signed the Vienna Convention for the Protection of the Ozone Layer. This was followed by the Montreal Protocol on Substances That Deplete the Ozone Layer, which contributed to the reduction of chlorofluorocarbons (CFCs) in the stratosphere, and the World Conference on the Changing Atmosphere: Implications for Global Security, better known as the Toronto conference, in 1988. The latter event called on world governments to set strict targets for reducing greenhouse gas emissions (Weart 2003:154).

Ironically, the summer of 1988 also witnessed a series of record-breaking heat waves and droughts in many U.S. regions. In response, congressional hearings on planetary weather were held in Washington, DC, at which renowned climate scientist James E. Hansen, along with other scientists, testified that a century-long trend of global warming had resumed after a period of levelling off during the 1950s, 1960s, and early 1970s (Stevens 1999:131). At the hearings, Hansen stated "with 99 percent confidence" that the planet was undergoing a significant and long-term warming trend and suggested that the greenhouse effect was the culprit (quoted in Weart 2003:155). These developments prompted the environmental movement, which until then had only expressed passing concern about global warming, to take closer notice and ultimately to engage in greater action. Also in 1988 the World Meteorological Organization and other United Nations environmental agencies established the Intergovernmental Panel on Climate Change, a body that has played a key role in creating international awareness of the inescapable reality of global warming and its implications for both the environmental and humanity.

It appears that Gore was one of the first politicians to understand the seriousness of global warming and to publicly call for a reduction in greenhouses gas production. He also held congressional hearings on carbon dioxide emissions during the late 1970s. Despite his highly touted 1992 best seller *Earth in the Balance: Ecology and the Human Spirit*, in his capacity as vice president, Gore functioned as a rather muted voice on environmental matters, including on the issues of global warming. Furthermore, he did not particularly emphasize environmental issues generally, or the growing danger of global warming specifically, during his 2000 bid for the U.S. presidency. Nonetheless, as journalist David Remnick (2006) noted in a *New Yorker* essay:

> In the 1992 campaign against Bill Clinton, George H. W. Bush mocked Gore as "ozone man" and claimed, "This guy is so far out in the environmental extreme we'll be up to our necks in owls and outta work for every American." In the 2000 campaign, George W. Bush cracked that Gore "likes electric cars. He just doesn't like making electricity." The younger Bush, . . . demanded that Gore "explain what he meant by some of the things" in his 1992 book, "Earth in the Balance"—and then unashamedly admitted that he had never read it. A book that the President did eventually read and endorse is a pulp science-fiction novel: "State of Fear," by Michael Crichton. Bush was so excited by the story, which pictures global warming as a hoax perpetrated by power-mad environmentalists, that he invited the author to the Oval Office.

A few years into the beginning of the 21st century, however, a tipping point was reached in which many politicians and ordinary people came to believe that global warming is real and potentially threatening. The issue began appearing as a regular feature in the global mass media, and it showed up on government policy agendas in numerous countries. These dramatic changes even finally forced U.S. President George W. Bush and Australian Prime Minister John Howard, both of whom vigorously opposed their respective countries ratifying the Kyoto Protocol, to admit that global warming, or what they prefer to term "climate change," is a reality. There appear to have been three driving engines behind these remarkable developments:

1. A rapidly mounting body of scientific evidence from diverse disciplines (climatology, geology, virology, glaciology, etc.) all pointing to the same conclusion: that global warming was not only happening but doing so at a rapid pace and with growing effects;
2. The image evidence, such as pictures of how much glaciers had retreated, and direct experience of the increasing number of severe storms and serious heat waves that began impacting people's lives; and

3. The emergence of increasing numbers of prominent spokespersons, scientists, environmental activists, and science-aware politicians, which brought global warming to the attention of the mass media.

Other factors, including the efforts of some social scientists, also contributed to the growing awareness that global warming constitutes a serious threat to the environment and, as a result, to humanity as well. Conversely, despite this heightened consciousness, we are still living in an era of continued denial by ultra-conservatives and business interests who profit enormously from the status quo, as well as public resistance to radical lifestyle changes needed personal sacrifices. Table 1 depicts our model of the stages of global warming recognition that encapsulates the preceding discussion.

Humanity as a whole has not yet entered the fifth stage of our model, namely panic, although some individuals may at times experience this response to global warming. Nevertheless, in the likely event that global warming's impact on human societies and the planet will continue to worsen over the course of the next decade or two, such a scenario is very possible. Conversely, a potential alternative to the fifth stage of our model is Concerted Action, involving dramatic changes in global carbon emissions and related ameliorative efforts. Thus far, however, progress toward this alternative has been agonizingly slow. We explore this issue in some detail later in the book, but suffice it to say at this point that vested interests in "business-as-usual" play a very significant role in undercutting serious efforts to mitigate global warming.

We turn now to addressing a fundamental question that helps to clarify the nature of resistance to the grave seriousness of thorough-going global mitigation efforts, namely: what is driving anthropogenic global warming?

Table 1. The Stages of Global Warming Awareness

	Stage	Characteristics
1	Open Denial	Public attacks by special-interest groups and conservative pundits on those who call attention to global warming
2	Waiting for Undeniable Proof	Questioning the data, arguing it is insufficient, and stressing that scientists don't agree
3	Eager Minimalism	Acceptance of the reality of global warming but calling for minimal actions (celebrated publicly as adequate to solve the problem)
4	Awakening to Crisis	Shocked realization that we are far passed the tipping point and damages will be severe
5	Panic	Public expressions of dread and terror (riots, etc.)

The Political Ecology of Global Warming

In this book, we posit that global warming is primarily a product of global capitalism, which is characterized by a constant drive for profits and ever-increasing emphasis on production and consumption. From the perspective of political ecology, capitalism is inherently at odds with the environment, which it views as a bottomless pit of resources and as a receptacle for the waste products of production—the quantity of which tends to grow because of the intrinsic need of capitalism to relentlessly expand and increase profits. Environmentalist Clive Hamilton (2003) has called this capitalism's "growth fetish." Capitalism is inherently "growth-oriented—growth [in the production of commodities] ... resting on the exploitation of nature, including human labour, in production" (Pepper 1993:219). This productivist ethic has historically despoiled, and continues to despoil, an ecologically fragile biosphere and channels its limited resources to the privileged few, particularly in developed societies but also in developing societies, at the expense of the masses. This is not to say that capitalism has been the only social system that is destructive to the environment. Societies ranging from foraging to horticultural villages to agrarian states have had adverse impacts on the environment, probably on an increasing scale. Foragers contributed to the creation of grasslands; pastoralists overgrazed their lands; and peasants caused deforestation. In addition to the role of class conflict and warfare, the demise of agrarian and feudal state societies was also due to, as Hughes (1975:29) observes, "their failure to maintain a harmonious balance with nature." However, capitalism has exerted a negative impact on the environment on a much broader and profounder scale than any previous social systems. Under capitalism, as Foster argues, the

> cash nexus has become the sole connection between human beings and nature. With the development of the capitalist division of nature, the elements of nature are reduced to a common denominator (or bottom line): exchange value. In this respect it does not matter whether one's production is coffee, furs, petroleum [the single greatest contributor to greenhouse gas emissions], or parrot feathers, as long as there is a market. [Foster 1994:121]

Industrial capitalism brought with it unprecedented rates of resource utilization and waste release. From its emergence in Europe, capitalism has expanded into a world system of unequal exchange between developed and developing societies.

Further, as noted, it is environmentally destructive, as the economists Robert Chernomas and Ian Hudson (2007) argue in their book *Social*

Murder and Other Shortcomings of Conservative Economics. This status and the economic power on which the modern multinational corporation is founded have allowed corporations to wreak environmental havoc in the pursuit of profit. According to Chernomas and Hudson, conservative economic theory, which has become the dominant ideology of modern capitalism, asserts that any interference in the business of business—such as controls on carbon emissions—is inherently wrong (because it provides no benefit to society), socially unnecessary (because corporations can be counted on to police themselves to protect their reputations), and economically inefficient (because the increased costs to corporations outweigh any benefits to consumers). All of these premises are wrong because sound environmental and health regulations have made an important contribution to public health, corporations have a dismal record of self-control, and the benefits to consumers of strong government regulation of corporations has been freedom from social murder from injurious and environmentally destructive killer commodities (Singer and Baer 2008).

In addition to anthropogenic sources, of course, natural forces, such as periodic atmospheric-ocean interactions, cyclical ocean currents, volcanic eruptions, sunspots and solar activity, tidal forces, and orbital variations also contribute to global temperature changes (Burroughs 2001:204–225). As Burroughs (2001:237) notes, however, compared to anthropogenic forces, "these are subordinate issues." Moreover, as John Bellamy Foster, a critical sociologist, observes:

> The ecological crisis engendered by the capitalist economy ... threatens the collapse of world civilization, and irreparable damage to the entire biosphere from which human society and the planet as we know it may never recover—if current trends are not reversed. The latest scientific reports indicate that global warming is, if anything, increasing faster than we previously thought, leading to fears of unpredictable and cumulative effects and of abrupt climate change .... The removal of environmental regulations as part of neoliberal economics has only served to heighten this ecological crisis. [Foster 2005a:14–15]

The term *neoliberalism* has come to refer to a philosophical perspective (which, to complicate matters, is neither new nor liberal) that is embraced by conservative economists, policy makers, and corporate officials who urge the minimization of government regulation of the "free market," including allowing the free flow of goods and services across national borders and the removal of domestic or international environmental regulations that hinder production. Despite opposing government restrictions on markets or the ability to sell their products anywhere and everywhere, corporations strongly demand government support for their own needs, such as the development of the military-industrial complex or assistance in cleaning up environmental damage incurred by their own productive activities. Western governments, international lending institutions, and even components of the United Nations have adopted the philosophy of neoliberalism and promoted it through their policies and actions.

One expression of neoliberalism is the notion that all problems, from poverty to pollution, are fixed through market activities. Activities that appear to counter this approach have tended to elicit doubt and disdain from economic and political sectors that are wedded to a neoliberal perspective. Private multinational corporations and state-owned corporations in both capitalist- and socialist-oriented societies have created both a global factory and a new global system characterized by extensive motor vehicle pollution, acid rain, toxic and radioactive waste, deforestation, desertification, and, of particular concern in this book, global warming and associated climatic changes.

In considering the complex interaction of political economy and the environment, particularly under capitalism, we draw upon the field of *political ecology*. As Howard L. Parsons argues, "Economy is a matter of ecology: it has to do with the production and distribution of goods and services in the context of human society and nature . . . . [It recognizes that] under the ecological practices of monopoly capitalism, the natural environment is being destroyed along with the social environment" (Parsons 1977:xii). As critical medical anthropologists, we seek to contribute to a larger interdisciplinary initiative that can be termed the *political ecology of health* (Baer 1996; Singer 1998).

Expanding upon the work of historian Alfred W. Crosby (2004), who explores the impact of European diseases, flora, and fauna that accompanied military conquest and colonialism in the displacement of indigenous peoples in the Americas and Australasia, Foster and Clark examine other manifestations of ecological imperialism, particularly in the context of the present-day capitalist world system, including:

> The pillage of the resources of some countries by others and the transformation of whole ecosystems upon which states and nations depend; massive movements of population and labour that are interconnected with the extraction and transfer of resources; the exploitation of ecological vulnerabilities of societies to promote imperialist control; the dumping of ecological wastes in ways that widen the chasm between centre and periphery; and overall, the creation of a global "metabolic rift" that characterizes the relations of capitalism to the environment, and at the same time limits capitalist development. [Foster and Clark 2004:187]

The "metabolic rift" refers to a break in the metabolic relationship between humans and the natural environment which occurs in various economic activities, such as industrial agriculture, tropical monoculture, and mining in which the soil becomes depleted of its nutrients, contaminated with chemicals, or ripped open in order to extract natural resources such as gold, copper, and petroleum. Furthermore, global capitalism contributes to the creation of long-distance trade networks, which require enormous quantities of energy to sustain, and massive metropolitan areas, which provide the labor force of concentrated capitalist industrial production and become rationalized in the interests of the economics of scale (Clark and York 2005).

We will return to this discussion of the economic factors driving global warming by way of a discussion of the capitalist world system below. Before doing so, however, we turn to a review of the complex and entwined climate and environmental changes associated with global warming that are currently reshaping our world. As we will assert, these drastic changes are tied to specific contradictions of the capitalist world system.

An Overview of the Impact of Global Warming on the Planet

As previously indicated, despite debate about regional and temporal variations in temperature, the vast majority of climate scientists now believe that a global technology that relies heavily upon fossil fuels—namely coal, petroleum, and natural gas—plays a significant role in atmospheric emission of carbon dioxide. Today, the carbon dioxide level is apparently at its highest in the past 600,000 years or so (Henson 2007:154), having increased from about 280 parts per million (ppm) in the atmosphere before the Industrial Revolution to 379 ppm in 2005 (IPCC 2007a:2). With respect to the argument that global warming is largely a natural phenomenon, climate scientist William F. Ruddiman argues:

> As human emissions of [greenhouse] gases have increased over the last few thousand years [particularly since the Industrial Revolution], so too have combined impact on climate. Had nature been in full control, Earth's climate would naturally have grown substantially cooler. Indeed, greenhouse gases produced by humans caused a warming effect that counteracted most of the natural cooling. Humans have come to rival nature as a force in the climate system. [Ruddiman 2005:63–64]

In addition to carbon dioxide, other greenhouse gases include methane, nitrous oxide, the chlorofluorocarbons, and ozone. Of the various sources of greenhouse gas emissions in 2000, 59 percent came from fossil fuel carbon dioxide, 18 percent from carbon dioxide derived in land-use activities, 14 percent from methane, 8 percent from nitrous oxide, and 1 percent from several other highly active greenhouse gases (Pittock 2005:158–159). Methane (CH_4) comes from biomass decomposition, coal mining, natural gas and oil system leakages, livestock, wastewater treatment, cultivation of rice, burning of savannah and some from burning of fossil fuels. Nitrous oxide (N_2O) comes from agricultural soils.

Modern agriculture relies very heavily upon fossil-fuels energy. Cleared land, including forests, appears to constitute the second largest source of carbon dioxide emission, only surpassed by fossil-fuels combustion, and has been estimated to account for 10 to 30 percent of total global carbon dioxide emissions (Hardy 2003:118). In addition, some agricultural practices result in methane emissions, such paddy rice farming (accounting for about 40 percent of global methane emissions) and livestock production (accounting for about 15 percent of global methane emissions). Other forms of land destruction derive from overgrazing (often resulting in desertification), dam construction, industrial expansion, and urban sprawl, in large part related to population growth.

In terms of its impact upon the planet, global warming has contributed to rising sea levels, the melting of glaciers, erratic weather patterns, shifts in animal and plant life, reductions in biodiversity, and the possibility of irreversible events. These striking effects are described in turn.

Rising Temperatures: From Global Dimming to Global Warming

The mean temperature of the earth has increased about 1.37°F (0.76°C) between 1850–1899 and 2001–2005 (IPCC 2007a:5). A period of cooling, however, from 1945 to 1970 may have been linked to a process called *global dimming* that was caused by an increased output of aerosols in the atmosphere from both volcanoes and industrial activity, such as the burning of coal, oil, and wood, but also tiny airborne particles of soot, ash, sulphur compounds, and other pollutants (Victor 2004:10). Aerosol particles and other particulates given off by industrial activities absorb solar radiation and reflect it back into space. Other sources of global dimming include the burning of tropical grasslands and forests and desert dust storms. Global dimming produces a cooling effect that may have partially masked the impact of greenhouse gases on global warming. It is important to note that aerosols are not the same as greenhouse gases, which consist of carbon dioxide, methane, nitrous oxide, near-surface ozone, water vapour, and CFCs and related compounds that also have been a major in stratospheric ozone depletion. The risks associated with ozone depletion, as, for instance, manifested in increase skin cancer rates, have diminished as a result of the passage of the Montreal

Protocol, which called for CFCs to be replaced by substitutes such as halochlorofluorocarbons (HCFCs), which have appreciably shorter lifetimes and are far less likely to damage the ozone layer.

According to Henson (2006:182), "most of the world's highly industrialized nations began cleaning up their smokestacks and tailpipes by the 1970s, and the economic downturn of the 1990s across the Eastern bloc further reduced aerosol production." Rapid industrialization in China and India has contributed to global dimming over the past several decades while at the same time contributing to greenhouse gas emissions. About 90 percent of sulphate aerosols are produced in the Northern Hemisphere, thus in part explaining why the Southern Hemisphere, where there is less industrial activity than there is in the North, has been experiencing more global warming (Sturman and Tapper 2006:474–475). While some might argue that global dimming serves to curtail global warming, at least for the short term, the impact of aerosols in terms of quality of air and depletion of the ozone layer hardly constitute a justifiable rationale for allowing for their ongoing emission into the atmosphere.

Various studies indicate that the earth experienced a rapid warming trend beginning around 1910, a levelling off between the early 1940s and early 1970s, and another rapid rise to the present (Firor and Jacobsen 2002:104). For example, scientists at the NASA Goddard Institute for Space Studies (GISS) gather data from a global network of some 800 climate-monitoring stations to measure changes in earth's average temperature with records going back to 1880 (Brown 2003:60). Their data show that temperatures began to climb in 1977 and have been above the norm every year since. They averaged 0.47°F (0.26°C) above the norm during the 1980s and 0.40°C above the norm during the 1990s. The 20th century was the warmest century in the past millennium, and the period from 1990 to 2000 was the warmest decade of the past millennium. In the first three years of the 21st century, temperatures were 0.99°F (0.55°C) above the norm. GISS reports that 2005 was the warmest year ever on record. The World Meteorological Organization and the U.K. Climatic Research Unit at the University of East Anglia, however, concluded that 2005 was the second warmest year, behind 1998. These differences reflect varying ways of measuring global temperature, but ultimately the conclusion is the same: the planet is growing ever warmer in measurable and consequential ways.

Recently, the IPCC (2007a:5) reported that "eleven of the last twelve years (1995–2006) rank among the 12 warmest years in the instrumental record of global surface temperature (since 1850)." Even if greenhouse gas emissions were to be drastically cut back now, a completely hypothetical scenario under present circumstances, there would still be a *thermal time lag* that would result in an average temperature rise of between 2.78°F (0.5°C) and 5.56°F 1°C (Lynas 2007:264).

Warming over the past several decades has tended to be greater at higher latitudes and in some midcontinental regions. Over the past three decades, Barrow, Alaska, underwent an average temperature rise of 4.16°F (2.31°C); Juneau, 3.54°F (1.97°C); and Anchorage, 2.26°F (1.26°C). On the West Antarctic Peninsula, the average temperature increase since 1950 has been 8.8°F (4.49°C) in winter and 4.5°F (2.5°C) annually. Global warming is expected to further accelerate oceanic evaporation and to increase overall global average temperature (Hardy 2003:77). Furthermore, as a result of global warming, higher temperatures are becoming increasingly common during the winter months and nights. Over the course of the 20th century, "winters warmed more than summers did, and over land the nighttime lows warmed almost twice as much as did the daytime highs" (Henson 2007:157). While some might argue that warmer winters are a benefit of global warming—because of lower heating bills—it may also spell a trend toward hotter summers, which may have serious implications for both agricultural activities and health.

Rising temperatures are contributing to the thawing of peat bogs, which are wetlands situated in cold, temperate areas primarily in the Northern Hemisphere, resulting in the release of methane into the atmosphere. The West Siberian bogs cover over 600,000 square kilometers but other bogs are found in Ireland, northern Germany, Scandinavia, Canada, Alaska, and the northern areas of Minnesota and Michigan. In August 2005, scientists reported that the western Siberian peat bog is thawing at an incredible rate. Furthermore, as Lohmann (2006:11) notes, "Some scientists fear that if the oceans are warmed beyond a certain degree, there may also be sudden, catastrophic releases of methane from methane hydrates on the sea floor previously kept quiescent through high pressures and low temperatures." In other words, the increasing release of methane sets off a feedback mechanism in which warming releases methane, and more methane in the atmosphere further heats the earth, which releases even more methane. Feedback mechanisms of this sort appear to have played a significant role in the increasing pace of global warming.

Rising Sea Levels, Warming Oceans, and Melting Ice Caps and Glaciers

The IPCC (2007a) reports that due to a rise in the average global surface temperature, sea levels around the world increased an average of 0.07 inches (1.8 mm) per year between 1961 and 2003. The IPCC projects a sea level rise of another 7 to 23 inches (18 to 59 cm) over the course of the current century. The melting of glaciers and the projected melting of the much larger Greenland and Antarctic ice caps will also contribute significantly to a rise of sea levels (Whyte 1995:118–119). A NASA study in late 2002 found that the ice pack covering the Arctic Ocean is vanishing at the rate of about nine percent per decade, about three times more rapidly than scientists had previously predicted (Gelbspan 2004:21). Indeed, in August 2000 no ice existed at the North Pole (Hillman 2004:22). Some scientists predict that the Arctic Ocean could be ice-free during summers by 2100. In contrast to the past, when explorers unsuccessfully sought a Northwest Passage, freighters can now sail across the top of the North American continent in open water during the summer months. At a more microscopic level, melting ice will leave a greater absorptive surface that will reflect less heat back into the atmosphere. Furthermore, the melting of permafrost could release large quantities of trapped methane, a process that has already begun.

A rise in global sea levels as a result of snow and ice melting (and rising water temperature) poses dangers of flooding and coastal erosion in densely populated low-lying coastal plains and river deltas that already are barely above or even below sea level. Rising sea levels threaten much of the Netherlands, Bangladesh, the U.S. Eastern Seaboard, the coast of the Gulf of Mexico, many low-lying Pacific Islands, the Maldives in the Indian Ocean, the deltas of the Nile and Mekong Rivers, coastal and riverbank cities of the United Kingdom (including London), and the coastal areas of India, Japan, and the Philippines. For example, a sea level rise of 34 inches (83 cm) would produce floods that would displace millions of people in heavily populated low-lying areas in China's Pearl River Delta, Bangladesh, Thailand, and Egypt (Gelbspan 2004:6).

Oceans presently absorb much of the carbon dioxide from fossil fuel emissions. Unfortunately, the warming of the oceans may result in their decreased absorption of carbon dioxide; unabsorbed carbon dioxide remains in the atmosphere, where it contributes to a speeding up of global warming (Hossay 2006:8). The oceans have been absorbing much carbon dioxide but may be reaching a saturation point, resulting in rising land temperatures.

In many mountain ranges, snow is becoming confined to higher altitudes during summer, which was not the case in the past. Glaciers, which are flowing ice sheets being drawn downstream due to the pull of gravity, are in retreat all over the world, including the Andes, the Himalayas, the Alps, the mountains of New Guinea, and in Africa. Glacier National Park in Montana, for example, contained over 150 glaciers in the late 1800s but has only 35 left; it is predicted that it will not have any glaciers by 2030 (Diamond 2005). The glaciers around Chacaltaya, the highest mountain in Bolivia, are shrinking by about 30 feet a year, producing grave concerns about water availability in future years. Similarly, glaciers in the Alps have lost more than half their volume since 1850 (Hardy 2003:39). The glacier on Mount Kilimanjaro in Kenya underwent a decline of about 80 percent between 1912 and 2000, and 95 percent of Alaskan glaciers have experienced a doubling of their thinning or reduction rate since the mid-1990s (Lynas 2004:218). The annual summer melt of the Hindu Kush and Himalayan glaciers are major water sources for China, India, and much of continental Asia. Increased melting would cause greater flow for several decades, after which some heavily populated regions are likely to run out of water. Glaciologists have discovered that glacial melting has resulted in the development of large rivers of meltwater, which are contributing to sea level rises, below the Greenland and Antarctica ice sheets (Pearce 2006:27).

Erratic Weather Patterns

Storms, floods, and droughts, depending upon the geographical location, may intensify due to global warming. As temperatures rise, more water tends to evaporate from the ocean, which means that overall more moisture is available in the atmosphere to produce rain. The U.S. National Oceanic and Atmospheric Administration's National Climatic Center concluded that growing weather extremes witnessed in recent years are due, by a probability of 90 percent, to rising levels of greenhouse gases. The burning of fossil fuels affects the world's oceans in at least three ways: 1) a changing pattern of El Niño-Southern Oscillation (which has two modes known as El Niño, in which the trade winds across the Pacific weaken or reverse, and El Niña, in which the trade winds become stronger than usual); 2) fallout from carbon emissions resulting in increased acidity of the oceans; and 3) the possibility of warming-driven disruptions in normal flow of deep-water currents that determine climatic conditions in much of the world. An extreme El Niño can afflict two-thirds of the globe with droughts, floods, and other extreme weather (Flannery 2005:85). Global warming over the course of the present century is expected to result in the following scenarios: 1) increasing precipitation in higher latitudes, leading to increased winter/spring runoff and flooding in some areas; 2) decreasing precipitation and increasing drought frequencies at lower latitudes; 3) increased summertime evaporation and decreasing surface flow and soil moisture at mid to high latitudes; 4) decreasing lake levels in some areas, with changes in wetland communities; and 5) decreasing per capita water availability, particularly in low-latitude countries with high population growth rates. Per capita water availability in Africa already has diminished by 75 percent over the past half century (Hardy 2003:81).

Animal and Plant Life

Another consequence of global climate change is that plants and animals are moving into regions closer to the poles because these regions are becoming warmer. Mammals, birds, butterflies, and fish are moving to new eco-niches in order to survive. Animals like polar bears, which are adapted to arctic conditions, however, cannot migrate and are in danger of extinction due to the contraction of the arctic ice pack and a reduction of animals, such as seals, upon which they feed (because their island breeding sites are sinking below the sea). A combination of overfishing and global warming has contributed to the reduction of cod stocks in the North Sea to one-tenth of what they were only 30 years ago (Hillman 2004:23). Since 1992, the Kenai Peninsula in Alaska has experienced an infestation of bark beetles due to higher temperatures (Hillman 2004:25). Coral reef damage is occurring all over the world, including the Great Barrier Reef in Australia (Henson 2006:117–120).

The Possibility of Irreversible Events or Amplifying Feedback

Notably, the IPCC distinguishes between Type I climate change, which is gradual, and Type II, which is much more abrupt and results in crossing *critical tipping points*. Possible irreversible events stemming from global warming include the West Antarctic ice sheet sliding into the ocean; changes in ocean currents; oceans becoming more acid as a result of more carbon dioxide being dissolved into them; and the melting of the Greenland ice cap (Diesendorf 2007:29–30).

Some climatologists fear that the Arctic may have already passed an irreversible tipping point. Notes Lynas:

> Since the 1990s, land areas have been warming at nearly half a degree per decade—double the previous rate. Earlier snowmelt means more summer heat goes into the air and ground rather than into melting snow, raising temperatures further in what is known as a "positive feedback" effect, where warming becomes a self-reinforcing spiral. The snowmelt feedback is not the only one: as more dark-coloured shrubs and forest encroach onto the once-white tundra, still more heat is absorbed by the new vegetation. [Lynas 2007:31]

Computer models developed by the Arctic Climate Impact Assessment Group indicate that one degree of global warming for the planet as a whole translates into two degrees of warming in the Arctic. Between December 2004 and December 2005, 14 percent of the Arctic Ocean's sea ice disappeared. Because of these changes, the Arctic Ocean may be moving into being ice-free from much of the year. The implications of such a development are mind boggling to say the least.

According to UNESCO:

> Studies have shown that ecosystems tend to respond to a warmer climate by releasing more carbon to the atmosphere and actually accelerating climate change. This change is expected to occur during this century because natural carbon pools containing hundreds of billions of tonnes of carbon might become vulnerable to turning into carbon sources as global warming and deforestation continue . . . . Preliminary analyses indicate that over the next 100 years the vulnerable carbon pools could release 200 ppm in atmospheric CO_2, on top of a CO_2 increase from fossil fuel combustion in the order of 200–550 ppm. [UNESCO 2006:3]

The warmth that has kept the climate of coastal North America and northern Europe hospitable to civilization for so long could in the future be replaced by a rapid freeze due to shutdown of the North Atlantic Ocean Conveyor, which presently allows the Gulf Stream to have a warming effect on Northwest Europe. James Hansen (2007b), probably the leading U.S. climate scientist, foresees the possibility of disintegration of West Antarctica and/or Greenland ice sheets in a "rapid, non-linear fashion," resulting in a "rise of sea level of more than 5 meters (16.4 ft) by 2095". Indeed, some 10,000 square kilometer of ice shelf have splintered from both sides of the Antarctic Peninsula, including the collapse of the Larsen B ice shelf in March 2002 (Lynas 2004:58).

In short, once various feedback chains, related in part to the long lifetime of some greenhouse gases and the long memory of the climate chain, get started, they may be self-perpetuating and need no further anthropogenic input to keep going. Thus it is imperative for humanity to invoke drastic mitigation efforts in order to reverse the feedback chains that could produce a global calamity. As Houghton (2004:190) so aptly observes, "because some of the impacts may turn out to be irreversible and also because of the time taken for human activities and ecosystems to respond and change course, it is important to have an eye on the longer term." While most projections of the impact of global warming only depict scenarios up until 2100, it is extremely important for both the sake of humanity and the planet to develop scenarios further into the future, to 2200, 2300, and beyond. Without wanting to sound like doomsday prophets, it is evident that more than ever humanity needs to invoke the *precautionary principle,* which maintains that it is better to err on the side of caution rather than permit the possibility of a more serious catastrophe than climate scientists have anticipated.

The Capitalist World System and its Contradictions

Immanuel Wallerstein, the principal proponent of world systems theory, maintains that capitalism "as a system of production for sale in a market for profit and appropriations of this profit on the basis of individual or collective ownership has only existed in, and can be said to require, a world-system in which the political units are not co-extensive with the boundaries of the market economy" (Wallerstein 1979:66). Capitalism is an economic system of production and exchange that exploits technology, natural resources, and labor in the pursuit of profit making. While the world system consists of some 185 nation-states and several thousand nations or ethnic groups, it has a unitary economic division of labor consisting of three units: 1) the core, 2) the semi-periphery, and 3) the periphery (Wallerstein 2004).

The core is the primary site of multinational corporations that are involved in technologically advanced, capital-intensive production, which in large part has shifted from heavy industry to a service/information technology economy. Core countries have wealthy, powerful corporate classes that exert a strong influence on state policies. States in core countries are strong and backed up by technologically sophisticated militaries and police forces. Core countries also tend to have a large managerial/professional class, a large relatively affluent working class, but often many semi-skilled, menial workers and underemployed and unemployed workers who constitute a surplus labor force that tends to suppress wages. The major core countries include the United States, Japan, Germany, the United Kingdom, and France; minor core countries include countries such as Sweden, Italy, Switzerland, Canada, and Australia.

Both the semi-periphery and the periphery constitute sources of cheap raw materials, agricultural resources, and cheap labor for the core. Semi-peripheral countries have a national capitalist class that tends to be economically dependent upon a transnational capitalist class based in the core. They have a moderately sized managerial/professional class and roughly an even mixture of a skilled labor force and a semi-skilled and unskilled labor force. States in the semi-periphery generally have relatively strong states that are backed up by relatively sophisticated militaries that obtain their weapons in large part from arms manufacturers based in core countries. While the semi-periphery is exploited by the core, it functions as a stabilizing mechanism in the world system by virtue of the fact that it exploits the periphery. Examples of semi-peripheral countries include Russia, Brazil, Mexico, China, Saudi Arabia, Indonesia, and South Korea.

Finally, the periphery, which is exploited by both the core and the semi-periphery, consists of the poorest countries in the world, such as Bolivia, Haiti, Zimbabwe, Namibia, Afghanistan, and Papua New Guinea. Peripheral countries have small national capitalist and managerial/professional classes, small working classes, and large numbers of semi-skilled and unskilled workers and peasants, many of whom may be landless. States in the periphery tend to be weak, unstable, inefficient, and corrupt and are propped up by openly repressive militaries. The capitalist world system is dynamic in the sense that countries may rise and fall in their status, such as rising from the semi-periphery to core, as the United States did between the 19th and 20th centuries. Over the course of the development of the capitalist world system, however, the gap in wealth and income between the rich and poor countries has tended to widen.

Bearing in mind the gravity of global warming, we argue that any effort to grapple with its anthropogenic sources must address the *contradictions of capitalism,* which have been touched upon in the discussion above. Conventional proponents of capitalism laud its technological achievements and assert that eventually economic growth will result in material prosperity for all. However, there is a great deal of evidence that contradicts these claims, such as the growing socioeconomic gap within and between nation-states, conflicts in many parts of the world in the aftermath of the collapse of the Soviet Union, the depletion of natural resources, environmental degradation, and ongoing population growth. Indeed, in keeping with this assertion, anthropologist John Bodley (2008) contends that the environmental crisis provoked by global capitalism produces many social problems, including overpopulation, overconsumption, poverty, war, crime, and many personal crises, including a wide array of health problems.

Over the course of the development of the capitalist world system, the gap between rich countries and poor countries has tended to widen (UNDP 1999). J. Watkins (1997), an Oxfam policy analyst, maintains that whereas in 1966, the richest fifth of the world's population earned an income 30 times greater than the poorest fifth, by 1997 the gap had more than doubled to 78.1 times. Even the World Bank (2001), a capitalist institution that claims to be committed to the eradication of global poverty (but which many social analysts see as significantly contributing through its lending policies to the further impoverization of underdeveloped countries), reported that whereas in 1960, per capita GDP in the richest 20 countries was 18 times greater than in the poorest 20 countries, by 1995 this gap had widened to 37 times. The poorest 20 percent of the world's population earns only about one percent of the world's income (Ponting 2007:337). Over three billion people, or about half of the world's population, lives on less than $2 a day. While there has been a tremendous amount of economic development in East Asia,

South Asia, and Southeast Asia, much of which has been accompanied by widening internal social stratification as well as environmental degradation, Africa, despite being rich in natural resources, has become the home of the poorest people in the world. According to Maddison (2001), 57 African countries were worse off in terms of per capita GDP in 1998 compared to 1950. Table 2 below shows that the number of people living on less than $2 per day increased in all developing regions, except East Asia.

Growing socioeconomic inequality is characteristic of many societies around the world, including developed nations. Whereas in the United States, the gap between average CEO pay and worker pay was 41 to 1 in 1982, by 2003 it had grown to 301 to 1 (Anderson and Cavanaugh 2005:56). This widening gap is the direct result of a shift in wealth from poor and working people to the rich. Holly Sklar notes:

> In today's corporate America, workers see gutted paychecks and pensions despite rising worker productivity, while CEOs get golden pay, perks, pensions, and parachutes. The pay gap between average workers and CEOs has grown nine times wider since the 1970s .... The number of billionaires is a record high, but the share of national income going into wages and salaries is at a record low. [Sklar 2006:A11]

CEO compensation comes in various forms. Lee Raymond, the former head of ExxonMobil, for example, received a $398 million retirement package, pushing his earnings over a 13-year period to $686 million or about $145,000 a day (Rumble 2006). Furthermore, in many developing countries,

> Many elites have gotten rich by snatching up state-owned enterprises at bargain rates when governments were forced . . . to privatize. In 2003, Asia (excluding Japan) and Latin America boasted seventy-six of the world's 587

Table 2. People Living on Less Than U.S. $2 a Day (in millions)

Region	1981	2001
South Asia	821	1,059
East Asia and Pacific	1,151	868
China	858	596
Sub-Saharan Africa	288	514
Latin America and Caribbean	99	128
Europe and Central Asia	8	93
Middle East and North Africa	52	70
Total	2,419	2,732
Total, Excluding China	1,561	2,136

Source: Adapted from Anderson and Cavanaugh (2005:50).

billionaires, up from only five in 1986. This doesn't even include Russian billionaires, who were nonexistent in 1986 but numbered twenty-four as of 2003. [Anderson and Cavanaugh 2005:56]

As Milanovic (2002) reports, a pattern of overall increasing inter- and intra-country inequality occurred between 1988 and 1993, with the richest one percent of people received as much income as the bottom 57 percent. He also reports that the top decile (10 percent) of the U.S. population earns an aggregate income that equals that of the poorest 43 percent of the world's population; and the ratio of the average income of the world's top 5 percent to the bottom 5 percent rose from 78 to 114 between 1988 and 1993.

Additionally, Cohen and Kennedy (2000:151) aptly observe, "a measure of income disparity may turn on such basic issues as the provision of clean water, access to shelter and health care and the chances of surviving infanthood."

Ongoing Conflicts in Many Parts of the World

War and genocide, along with trade competition and class struggle, have been integral components of archaic state societies, empires, and more recently global capitalism. According to anthropologist John Bodley,

> The elite-directed rise of commercially driven nations and empires since AD 1500, along with the corresponding construction of the global economic system by 1815, provided important new incentives for warfare and dramatically increased military sophistication and total casualties. Competition between major powers became periodic struggles for hegemonic power that were often focused on control over territories, colonies, markets, resources, and trade routes for the primary benefit of ruling elites. [Bodley 2008:244]

Despite the end of the Cold War following the collapse of the Soviet Union, ongoing conflicts in many parts of the world are ultimately related to states, such as the United States, United Kingdom, and Australia, doing the bidding of multinational corporations in their drive for resources and profits. As Kolko (1994:456) so astutely observes, since the end of World War I, the "logistical and planning mechanics of modern warfare have become the purvey of specialized companies and technicians." More recently, Kolko (2006:177) has argued that the 21st century has been marked by an exponential increase in the "destructive potential of weaponry" and "threats of war and instability unlike anything that prevailed when a Soviet-led bloc existed."

War often emanates from a competition for resources, such as in the conflict between the U.S. and Japan for oil resources in Southeast Asia, the Persian Gulf War of 1991, and ongoing conflicts in the Middle East and Central Area, a region that contains about 70 percent of the world's proven oil reserves and over 75 percent of the world's known natural gas deposits (Podobnik 2000:266). While recognizing that world wars "represent attempts to restructure political relations among states to correspond with changing realities," Chase-Dunn (1989:159) suggests that war may function as a "way in which states try to convert political-military strength into a greater share of world surplus value." Over the course of the 20th century and into the 21st, war has proven to be a profitable endeavor for various corporate interests, particularly in the case of the United States. Indeed, Cypher (2007) argues that the U.S. military-industrial complex has evolved from one characterized by *military Keynesianism* to one characterized by *global-neoliberal militarism*. Whereas the first scenario was exemplified during World War II, the Korean War, and the Vietnam War when military spending contributed both to profits for military contractors and to jobs and relatively high wages for workers, the latter scenario, as apparent in the War in Iraq, has entailed as much as possible the privatization of military functions, such as the serving of meals, the guarding of prisoners, the escorting of diplomats, and the building of bases. Many of these mercenary soldiers in the service of the U.S. military are not Americans but hired fighters from other lands (often former police or soldiers).

In terms of minor wars, in a study of the economic performance of 95 countries between 1970 and 1990, Sachs and Warner (1997) found that those countries with a higher dependence on natural resource exports have a lower economic growth rate, often due to associated internal conflicts. Elsewhere, Collier (2003) found that in the 54 large-scale civil wars that occurred between 1965 and 1999, a higher ratio of primary commodity exports to GDP significantly increases the risk of conflict. Collier and Hoeffler (2004) found that countries with one or two primary export resources, such as oil, diamonds, copper, cacao, coca, and bananas, exhibited a one in five probability of civil war in a given year. Countries lacking such primary products exhibited only a one in 100 probability of civil war. Tabb makes the following sobering observation about "resource wars":

> Indeed, the oil rich countries of Africa—Nigeria, Gabon, the Sudan, the Congo, Equatorial Africa, and Chad—have long histories of coups, military rule, and strongmen. Millions have died of hunger and disease as a result of wars over oil, diamonds, copper, and other resources as armed rebels steal, rape, and murder[,] making life-generating economic activity difficult if not impossible. In the Congo, one of the resource richest countries on the planet, a half dozen countries have armies deployed and countless rebel groups have fought to control rich deposits of gold, diamonds, timber, copper, and valuable cobalt and coltan in what is often referred to as "Africa's First World War." [Tabb 2007:34]

Historically, those developing societies that sought to make at least a partial break with the capitalist world system "through the growth of an oppositional state apparatus aimed at mobilizing the potential surplus for development either on democratic and authoritarian lines were faced with direct or indirect intervention by the United States and other center capitalist states" (Foster 2007b:8). Since the collapse of the Soviet Union, the United States has become the only nation with the political will, military might, and economic resources to intervene in virtually every corner of the globe. According to Kolko (2002:100), poverty, which is the downside of global capitalism, constitutes "one of the crucial root causes of every form of political instability, from religious fundamentalism to revolutionary movements, that pose challenges to the United States' goal of reorganizing the world to suit its own definitions—and interests." In the process of defending the economic interests of its multinational corporations and gaining access to vital resources like oil, the United States has transformed militarism into a multifaceted profit-making enterprise.

The U.S. share of the world arms market increased from 32 percent in 1987 to 43 percent in 1997 (Kolko 2002:111). While the United States often asserts that it seeks to spread democracy and counter terrorism around the globe, "of the 140 nations it gave or sold arms in 1995, 90 percent were not democracies or abused human rights" (Kolko 2002:111). During the Clinton administration, in 1995, the United States spent almost two-thirds of global expenditures on military research and development. Furthermore, its share of world military spending increased from 31 percent in 1985 to 36 percent in 2000. As the wars in Afghanistan and Iraq since September 11, 2001, particularly illustrate, in the words of Gabriel Kolko (2002:148), "wars, both civil or between states, remain the principal (but scarcely the only) challenge facing much of humanity in the twenty-first century." While some observers might posit that global warming and growing social inequality are equally challenging problems, ultimately both are manifestations of the contradictions of global capitalism and they are mutually reinforcing, with military production and conflicts contributing to greenhouse gas emissions and global warming promoting conflicts over increasingly precious resources (e.g., potable water).

With regard to causing global warming, the Pentagon is the single largest consumer of oil in the world. There are only 35 countries, in fact, that consume more oil than the Pentagon. The Pentagon's enormous energy demand stems from its control of a fleet of almost 200,000 passenger cars, buses, and trucks in addition to approximately 10,000 aircraft, almost 300 combat and support ships, 28,000 armored vehicles, and 140,000 high-mobility multipurpose wheeled vehicles (and these figures do not include the vehicles of private military contractors hired by the Pentagon). Notes Karbuz (2007), "except for 80 nuclear submarines and aircraft carriers, almost all military fleet (including the ones that will be joining in the next decade) run on oil . . . . [T]he US military is completely addicted to oil."

The U.S. Department of Defense oil budget more than doubled between 2005 and 2006 and has continued to rise since. Moreover, environmental activist Don Fitz (2007) points out: "Military production is unique. If it were halted, GHG [greenhouse gas] emissions would be reduced by (a) GHG from fixing up what's in the path of military attacks, in addition to (b) GHG produced during its regular activities of building bases, using weapons and transporting troops and equipment." The first Gulf War, for example, resulted in the release of 240 million tons of carbon dioxide (Resistance 1999:128). Further, other militaries around the world have been significant sources of pollution, including greenhouse gas emissions, due, in part, to heavy reliance on energy-inefficient equipment and vehicles (Timmons, Grimes, and Manale 2003).

The figures cited above do not include the amount of oil-based energy required for the manufacture of military hardware and construction of military facilities, roads, and air strips. Linda McQuaig (2004:3) observes that "[e]ven as the competition over dwindling reserves heats up and threatens to cause international conflict, we are faced with a still more devastating consequence of our addiction to oil—global warming." Unfortunately, most analyses of global warming tend not to factor in war's contribution to this phenomenon.

With regard to the consequences of global warming on warfare, the Pentagon and CIA have developed war scenarios in anticipation of the competition for natural resources and mass social displacements resulting from a possible worldwide cataclysm (see Webb 2007). Military analysts have begun to talk of global warming as a "threat multiplier," a force that intensifies global instability by creating health and social problems like food insecurity or flooding that causes mass migration, water shortages, and disease—issues that have a history of provoking social conflict. This was the message of the 35-page report "National Security and the Threat of Climate Change," issued in 2007 by a group of 11 retired U.S. generals and admirals issued by the CNA Corporation (2007). British defense secretary John Reid has predicted that global warming "will make scarce resources, clean water, viable agricultural land even scarcer" and thus "make the emergence of violent conflict more likely" (quoted in Klare 2006). As this discussion suggests, global warming and war are thus mutually reinforcing, with war and war production fueling global warming and global warming pushing countries to war.

Depletion of Natural Resources and Environmental Degradation

Capitalism, with its emphasis on economic expansion and ongoing production, operates on the assumption that natural resources are infinite, when in reality they are clearly finite. Indeed, some analysts, such as Andre Gorz, argue that capitalism is moving toward self-destruction because of its emphasis on ever-expanding production.

> Economic growth, which was supposed to ensure affluence and well-being for everyone, has created needs more quickly than it could satisfy them, and has led to a series of dead ends which are not solely economic in character: capitalist growth is in crisis not only because it is capitalist but also because it is encountering physical limits. [Gorz 1980:11]

In a similar vein, Foster (2007:7) argues that the current ecological crisis—one that is most dramatically illustrated by global warming—is a "product of a globalizing capitalist economy."

Table 3 depicts the ecological footprint of various categories of countries, regions, and specific countries. Following Wackernagel and Rees (1996), the term *ecological footprint* refers to the human impact upon the environment based on the productive land and marine area required to support the overall material standard of living of a particular region or country. It is calculated by measuring the consumption of energy, biomass (such as food and fiber), building material, water, and other resources and converting this into land area. The United States has the highest per capita ecological footprint of any nation in the world, considerably higher than that of many developed societies, particularly in Europe. Further, William E. Rees, a professor of community and regional planning at the University of British Columbia, asserts that the ecological footprint indices now in use tend to understate the ecological impact that human societies have on the planet:

> While we define the footprint comprehensively to include the land/water areas required for waste assimilation, our calculations to date do not account for waste emissions other than carbon dioxide. Accounting fully for this ecological function would add considerably to the ecosystem area appropriated by economic activity. Together these factors suggest that our ecological footprint calculations to date are more likely to be under-estimates than over-estimates. [Rees n.d.:1212]

It is important to bear in mind that within global regions and specific countries there are tremendous variations in the ecological footprints of specific individuals. Even in a developed country, a wealthy family with

Table 3. Ecological Footprint of World, Regions, and Selected Countries, 2003

	Population Per Capita (millions)	Ecological Footprint (global hectarces/person)
World	6,301.5	2.23
High-income countries	955.6	6.4
Middle-income countries	3,011.7	1.9
Low-income countries	2,303.1	0.8
Africa	846.8	1.1
Congo	3.7	0.6
Egypt	71.9	1.4
Ethiopia	70.7	0.8
Kenya	32.0	0.8
Nigeria	124.0	1.2
South Africa	45.0	2.3
Middle East & Central Asia	346.8	2.2
Afghanistan	23.9	0.1
Iran	68.9	2.4
Iraq	25.2	0.9
Israel	6.4	4.6
Kuwait	2.5	7.3
Saudi Arabia	24.2	4.6
Asia-Pacific	3,489.4	1.3
Australia	19.7	6.6
China	1,311.7	1.6
India	1,065.5	0.8
Japan	127.7	4.4
New Zealand	3.9	5.9
Pakistan	153.6	0.6
Latin America & Caribbean	535.2	2.0
Brazil	178.5	2.1
Cuba	11.3	1.5
Mexico	103.5	2.6
Peru	27.2	0.9
North America	325.6	9.4
Canada	31.5	7.6
USA	294.0	9.6
Europe (EU)	454.4	4.8
Finland	5.2	7.6
Germany	82.5	4.5
UK	59.5	5.6
Europe (non-EU)	272.2	3.8
Albania	3.2	1.4
Norway	4.5	5.8
Russian Federation	143.2	4.4

Source: Adapted from Living Planet Report 2006, pp. 28–34.

multiple residences and motor vehicles leaves a much greater ecological footprint than a slum dweller or homeless person does. Researchers at Oxford University, for example, surveyed almost 500 people living in Oxfordshire in the United Kingdom and found that a small sector of the population accounted for a disproportionately large share of the total carbon produced each year (Scenta 2007). The wealthiest 20 percent of people in their sample produced over 60 percent and those in the poorest 20 percent produced only one percent of the total carbon emissions. The highest emitters had incomes of £40,000 (US $74,000) or more a year. People in this group produced an average of 11.3 tons of carbon dioxide emissions per year, twice the national average and about four times the emission levels of the poorest sector in the study.

Poverty, Population Growth, and the Environment

Demographers have often observed that the greatest rate of population growth tends to occur among the poor. While upper- and middle-class people worldwide frequently are perplexed as to why the poor have more children—because the former realize that financially supporting children to adulthood and sometimes even beyond constitutes a massive expenditure—people in developing societies, both in rural and urban areas, commonly view children as breadwinners who add to the family coffers. Mamdani (1972) notes that peasants in India and other developing societies particularly welcome additional sons because they can help work the land. Even in urban areas, children are viewed as an asset among the poor. Boys in Mexican cities, for example, often work as shoe shiners, and both young boys and girls may sell items such as chewing gum, tortillas, or other foods prepared by their mothers. Ultimately, as Bodley (2008:218) asserts, "a more equitable distribution of economic resources would help slow population growth; however, it is crucial that improvements in the economic conditions of households be accompanied by policy changes that give women more control over fertility decision making."

Historically, capitalist penetration of pre-capitalist economies has contributed to population increases, as indigenous households struggle to meet the demands for taxes that were imposed by colonial states. In this context, having more breadwinners became part of an adaptive household strategy to remain solvent in a capitalist market economy. Rural household failure, a not uncommon occurrence in this context, pushed families into urban migration in search of a new means of livelihood. As a result, capitalism had a strong hand in both population increase and rural-to-urban migration, as well as the emergence of the megacity, including all of its consequent climatic impacts.

Global Warming as a Consequence of Capitalist Expansion

As previously stated, global capitalism as a system that is dependent on fossil fuels has played a significant role in the emission of carbon dioxide and other greenhouse gases into the atmosphere. UNESCO (2006) reports that fossil fuel emissions have increased by more than 1,200 percent over the past 100 years. As Newell (2000:9) observes, "More than most other environmental issues, global warming goes to the heart of the modern industrial economy . . . . Hence, unlike the issue of ozone depletion, with which it is often compared, global warming relates to basic patterns of production and consumption, and potentially their transformation."

Capitalism is an economic system of production, exchange, and consumption that exploits technology, natural resources, and labor in the pursuit of profit. Moreover, industrial capitalism has expanded into a world system of unequal exchange between developed and underdeveloped countries, and between the wealthy owners of productive resources and those who sell their labor as a means of survival. This has significant implications for global ecological destruction, of which global warming is a significant reflection. As Foster and Clark argue,

> Nowadays, the curse of oil has also come back to haunt the rich countries too—their environments and their economies—in the form of global warming, or what might be called a planetary rift in the human relation to the global commons—the atmosphere and oceans. This planetary ecological rift, arising from the workings of the capitalist system and its necessary companion imperialism, while varied in its outcomes in specific regions, has led to ecological degradation on a scale that threatens to undermine all existing ecosystems and species (including the human species). [Foster and Clark 2004:193]

Ideologically, global capitalism has been able to overlook the ecological damage it causes through its embrace of a worldview characterized by a powerful "productivist ethic," that is, a belief that continual economic expansion is necessary, socially beneficial, and natural, as summarized in folk sayings like "you can't stop progress."

Grimes and Kentor (2003:264) argue that "world system research on CO_2 production to date has found that the volume of energy consumption and thus CO_2 production continues to track [the] world-system position [of nations and regions], being greatest in the core, intermediate in the semi-periphery, and lowest in the periphery." In large part due to pressure from the environmental movement, however, which has at times formed alliances with the labor movement, governments in core countries have passed legislation demanding cleaner industries and more fuel-efficient motor vehicles. Furthermore, core countries have increasingly shifted toward a service/information economy and have had the financial resources to invest in more energy-efficient technologies (Dietz and Rosa 1997). Multinational corporations and governments in the core often export polluting industries to the semi-periphery and periphery rather than improving environmental standards in their own countries (Roberts and Grimes 1997:196). Furthermore, "since 1975 the production efficiency (as measured by the ratio of CO_2/GDP) within the core appears to be growing while that within the semi-periphery is falling, presumably due to the relocation of manufacturing away from the high wages of the core toward the lower and more politically repressed wages found in the semi-periphery" (Grimes and Kentor 2003:264). Dependence on foreign investments also tends to accelerate carbon dioxide emissions in developing societies, particularly those in the semi-periphery (Grimes and Kentor 2003:270). As Burns and coauthors (1997:439) note, "a strong semiperipheral state apparatus depends in the modern world economy on heightened industrial or agricultural production which, regrettably, frequently bypasses the health and environmental safeguards that commonly attend such production in core countries." Table 4 below indicates that while the total carbon dioxide emissions in the high-income (for the most part core countries) greatly exceeds the total carbon dioxide emissions in the high-middle income, middle-income, low-middle income, and low-income countries combined, the production efficiency in all of the latter countries is worse than that for the high-income countries.

Sadly, as Roberts and coauthors observe,

The highest polluters per unit GDP are expected to be in neither the richest nor the poorest countries, but instead those in the middle, roughly corresponding in world-system terms to the semi-periphery and upper periphery. These are the countries having enough fossil-fuel dependent technology to compete in the world market, but not enough sophisticated infrastructure to do so efficiently. [Roberts et al. 2003:288]

Table 4. Average Total CO_2 Emissions and CO_2/Per Unit GDP for Income Groups of Countries in 2000

Category of Countries	Average Total Emissions (million tons CO_2)	Average Cumulative CO_2 Per Unit GDP
High-Income Countries (24)	120,162	0.1479
High-Middle Income (20)	5,917	0.2710
Middle Income (33)	18,161	0.2960
Low-Middle Income (54)	20,155	0.5262
Low-Income Countries (61)	24,834	0.4066

Source: Adapted from Roberts and Parks (2007:147).

Under the unequal exchange relationships inherent in the capitalist world system, semi-peripheral countries also produce methane emissions from cattle production (such as in the Amazon Basin of Brazil), much of which is exported to the core, and engage in deforestation (such as in Indonesia and Brazil), thus depriving the ecosystem of an important mechanism for sequestering carbon dioxide (Burns et al. 1997).

Conversely, while the production efficiency has tended to improve in the core countries, there has been a tendency for total carbon dioxide emissions and per capita emissions to increase, as Clark and York (2005:411–412) demonstrated occurred in the United States, the Netherlands, Japan, and Austria between 1975 and 1996. They note, "Thus, gains in the efficiency of the use of fossil fuel have typically resulted in expansion of their use in industrialized capitalist nations. As a result, carbon emissions generally increase with modernization and it concomitant 'improvements' in technology and gains in efficiency" (Clark and York 2005:412). Of course, such a trend is not surprising given the need of global capitalism to continually expand.

The United States, with four percent of the world's population, produces 25 percent of the greenhouse gases. It emits more greenhouse gases than most of the developing countries in Asia, Latin America, and Asia combined (Lindsay 2001:228). According to Roberts and Parks, "the average U.S. citizen dumps as much greenhouse gas into the atmosphere as nine Chinese citizens, eighteen citizens of India, and ninety Bangladeshis, but even more startling is that each U.S. citizen on average pollutes as much as over five hundred citizens of Ethiopia, Chad, Zaire, Afghanistan, Mail, Cambodia, and Burandi" (Roberts and Parks 2007:146).

There is, however, considerable variation among U.S. states in terms of greenhouse gas emission in total and per capita (Rabe 2004:2). Australia has the highest greenhouse gas emissions per capita of any developed country, at almost 27 tons per person (Hamilton 2007:39). It also has a poor overall energy efficiency compared to other Organization for Economic Cooperation and Development (OECD) countries (Hamilton 2007:43).

Motor vehicles are an especially important source of greenhouse emissions. Worldwide, automobile ownership rose from 32 million in 1930 to 775 million in 2000. According to Ponting,

> Car production now consumes more resources than any other industry. It uses about 20 percent of world steel production, 35 percent of the zinc, 50 percent of the lead, 60 percent of all natural rubber and 10 percent of world aluminium production. In addition, over a third of the world's oil consumption is accounted for by vehicles. In parallel, the rise of the car has brought into being a whole range of subsidiary industries—road construction, petrol stations, car sales dealerships and service garages. [Ponting 2007:330]

The United States alone has some 225 million cars, over 40 percent of the world's total (Hillman 2004:50). Gonzalez (2005) argues that urban sprawl, particularly in the United States, has contributed to higher emissions of greenhouse gases, particularly carbon dioxide. Both motor vehicle companies (including vehicle manufacturers, tire manufacturers, and gasoline manufacturers) and land development operations have encouraged this pattern of urban sprawl. Kenworthy and Laube (1999) conducted a comparative study of carbon dioxide emissions from private motor vehicles in various types of cities around the world. Whereas in 1990, private motor vehicles in U.S. cities emitted five tons (4,609 kg) of carbon dioxide, those in Australian cities emitted three tons (2,774 kg), in Canadian cities 2.9 tons (2,675 kg), in European cities 1.9 tons (1,769 kg), in what they term "wealthy Asian" cities (such as Singapore and Hong Kong) one ton (997 kg), and in developing Asian cities 0.8 tons (739 kg) (Kenworthy and Laube 1999:603).

Notably, air travel constitutes the least energy-efficient form of transportation. In 2003, air transportation accounted for 1.6 billion travelers (People's Health Movement 2005:194). Various sources indicate that air travel may be contributing from three to eight percent of greenhouse emissions (Spence 2005:148). Hillman cites the following four reasons as to why air travel constitutes the fastest growing source of greenhouse gas emissions:

> First, it is highly energy-intensive; second, its speed enables and encourages people to travel long distances; third, its use is increasingly rapidly; and finally, its contribution to global warming is around three times greater than is indicated by the carbon dioxide emissions of a single flight. The additional damage occurs because other greenhouse gases are emitted from aircraft and the fact that this occurs more destructively in the upper atmosphere. [Hillman 2004:37]

In addition to carbon dioxide, aircraft emit nitrogen oxide and other greenhouse gases. While the airline industry has, since the mid-1970s, halved the amount of fuel it burns to transport each of its passengers, the expansion of the industry has more than offset these savings in fuel efficiency. Air travel has been projected to double by 2015 (Webster 2001). Transportation of foodstuffs and consumer products by ships, airplanes, railroads, and trucks around the world constitutes another significant source of greenhouse gas emissions (Sobhani and Retallack 2001:226–227).

National Development Efforts

One of the important contemporary tensions in the world today is between national development efforts and greenhouse gas emissions.

Most underdeveloped countries are committed to a program of national development intended to improve the standard of living of their populations and their overall technological capacities. Some developing countries, such as China and India, have embarked upon rapid programs of industrialization. As a result, it is expected that greenhouse emissions from developing countries will soon exceed those from developed countries. Raupach et al. (2007:5) report that the developing and least-developed countries (which include China and India) "accounted for 73 percent of the global emissions growth in 2004." In terms of greenhouse emissions, China is "predicted to overtake the US by 2030, with a 20-fold increase in car ownership. The IMF's World Economic Outlook for 2005 predicted that China's oil consumption would triple from 6.4 million barrels per day in 2004 to 18.7 million barrels per day in 2030. (Broinowski and Wilkinson 2005:188).

India, another growing giant in the developing world, now has a population of about a billion people. While in the past most Indians were reliant upon biomass energy resources, as a result of increasing industralization and commercialization India's GDP has been growing at a rate of more than six percent per annum and has been turning to greater and greater coal use, due to its greater availability (Shukla, Ghosh, and Garg 2003). Indian carbon dioxide emissions are rising 3 percent per year, and oil consumption is expected to hit 2.8 billion barrels per day by 2010 (Lynas 2007:85).

Anderson and Cavanaugh assert that the World Bank, which funds development, has been a major contributor to greenhouse gas emissions:

> The Institute for Policy Studies has calculated that between 1992 and 2003, the World Bank financed fossil fuel extraction and power plant projects that ultimately will release over 50 billion tons of carbon dioxide into the atmosphere .... Almost every project has benefited Northern fossil fuel corporations, especially those based in the United States. [Anderson and Cavanaugh 2005:82]

Global Warming as an Element within a New Global Ecosystem

Multinational corporations and state companies in both capitalist and postrevolutionary societies have created not only a global factory but a new global ecosystem characterized by industrial and motor vehicle pollution, toxic chemical and radioactive wastes, deforestation, desertification, and last, but not least, global warming. As a result of its emphasis on ever-expanding production, capitalism, Gorz (1980) argues, is on the verge of self-destruction. Sadly, the least developed countries, which produce comparatively small amounts of greenhouse gas emissions, have the most to lose from global warming because they have fewer resources to use in adapting to significant climate change and their economies are more dependent upon agriculture. Conversely, even with their affluence, developed societies cannot indefinitely adapt to an ever-warming planet with its associated climatic changes. While many corporate elites, elected politicians, government functionaries, and policy makers have come to recognize that mitigation will be necessary to curb global warming, as we argue later in this book, existing climate regimes and green capitalism are insufficient for to carry out this task.

2

Lifeways in Peril

The Impact of Global Warming on Settlement Patterns and Human Perceptions of Climate

New South Wales, in the southeastern sector of Australia, has been hard hit by a drought that began in 2002–2003 and is characterized by both low rainfall and higher-than-average temperatures. The economic impacts have been enormous, but so too have been the social effects of what Prime Minister John Howard (2002) described as "one of the most severe droughts in the last 100 years." A study by the Centre for Rural Social Research (Alston and Kent 2004:xiii) found that the social impacts "include erosion of income for farmers and small business, increased rural poverty, increased work loads . . ., the need [for farmers] to seek alternative income, health (including mental health) and welfare issues, problematic service access, overload of service providers, [and] declining education." The lived experience for farmers is dramatically expressed in their comments to researchers (Alston and Kent 2004:51):

- "One drought too many . . . . One more bit of hopelessness."
- "You've lost a bit of your heart . . . . You've lost a bit of yourself. It will never be quite the same. It will never be quite as good again."
- "It certainly makes you more cynical. It's harder to get up in the morning."
- "It just sends you mad."

As these painful comments poignantly reflect, the effects of global warming endanger human societies and cultures, and put whole lifeways at peril. As a result of increasing temperatures, rising sea level, and heightened turbulent weather, whether in the form of droughts or storms, global warming portends to have serious impacts upon many of the peoples, including foragers, horticulturalists, pastoralists, peasants, and city dwellers, whom anthropologists have historically studied. This chapter focuses primarily on the impact of global warming and related climate changes on sociocultural systems in general and more specifically on settlement patterns in various parts of the world. What happens to people's immediate habitats, however, is intimately intertwined with their subsistence patterns, access to water and food, and health, topics that are covered in more detail in Chapters 3 through 6.

49

Small indigenous communities in particular are finding themselves threatened by rising sea levels, loss of water supplies due to increased salinity or aridity, or decreased food availability as native plant and animal species are lost to global warming. The growing pattern of severe drought in certain regions, very possibly related in many cases to global warming (although also driven by past mismanagement and unequal distribution of water resources), is adversely affecting horticulturalists, agriculturalists, and pastoralists across the planet, particularly in sub-Saharan Africa. While obviously the poor are and will continue to be the ones most profoundly devastated by global warming–related droughts, even farmers and ranchers in developed countries are feeling their brunt. For example, over the course of the past several years, droughts and often accompanying bushfires have regularly hit various parts of the eastern Australian states of Queensland, New South Wales, and Victoria. Rural communities and suburban areas in the capital cities are being threatened by bushfires, and farms, crops, and grazing lands cannot be sustained due to water shortages. Some farmers are being forced to forfeit their operations and even committing suicide rather than facing financial collapse and threat to their lifestyle. Indeed, the Australian Capital Territory experienced a massive bushfire in the summer of 2003 that destroyed numerous homes and devastated surrounding bushland and large portions of the Brindabella Mountains. The fire was so severe and wide-ranging that firefighters from western North America were brought in to assist.

Both in Australia and elsewhere in the world, including the United States, coastal areas are being increasingly threatened by global warming–driven hurricanes, cyclones, and storm surges, while other areas are being hard hit by drought and water shortages. While the number of hurricanes worldwide has not increased since 1970, the percentage of Category 4–5 hurricanes has nearly doubled (Henson 2007:84–96). Rising sea levels threaten segments of populations in countries as widely scattered as Bangladesh, Egypt, China, the Netherlands, and the United States, and entire populations of island nations, particularly in the South Pacific and the some 1,200 Maldives Islands in the Indian Ocean. According to Hardy (2003:148), a sea level rise of 0.66 to 2.3 feet (0.2 to 0.7 m) would result in increased beach erosion and coastal flooding, the loss of various coastal ecosystems (e.g., mangroves, wetlands, and coral reefs, particularly the Great Barrier Reef), the displacements of millions of people from low-lying areas, and saltwater intrusion into aquifer water supplies, thus posing a danger to farming and human habitation. Over 300 million people live within three feet, or about a meter, of sea level (National Geographic 2004:28), putting all of them and their ways of life in peril. Farmers and pastoralists in drought-stricken areas are being forced to migrate to new places, including to already densely populated cities in developing countries as well as cities in developed countries, particularly those in Europe. There are presently an estimated ten million environmental refugees in the world, and it has been estimated that there could be 150 million by 2050 (Cowie 1998). A Commonwealth Scientific and Industrial Research [Australia] report released on October 8, 2006, indicated that "millions of people on low-lying islands and lands in the Asia-Pacific region will become environmental refugees in the next 40 years due to rising sea levels resulting from global warming."

One of the places in Asia that is beginning to feel the impact of rising ocean levels is Bangkok, the ever-expanding capital of Thailand, home to ten million people and one of 21 of the world's largest 33 cities on the risk list for ocean flooding (others are New York and Los Angeles). Bangkok, built about 200 years ago on swampy land at the northern edge of the Gulf of Thailand where the Chao Phraya River drains into the sea, rises only three to five feet (0.9 to 1.5 m) above gulf waters, which have been rising approximately one-tenth of an inch a year. Resting on a clay base that sits above the city's underground freshwater aquifers, Bangkok actually has been sinking at the rate of four inches per year (accelerated by the pumping of freshwater from the aquifers for the growing urban population and industrial base of the country). At this rate, the capital will be below sea level by 2030 (Gray 2007). In addition to the devastation visited upon Bangkok residents, the impact will be felt throughout Thailand. Alluvial plains formed by the Chao Phraya River that now host productive rice paddies will be inundated, as will factories and other vital resources concentrated in the capital that provide food and other necessities for the nation. In October 2007, the government of Thailand was forced to divert 350 million cubic feet of water from the river into rice fields north of the city to prevent flooding in the capital. The military was called in because of concern about protests from villagers whose homes and rice fields were destroyed. Within the last three decades, half a mile of shoreline has slipped below rising sea water, portending an alarming future for the city.

The Impact of Global Warming on Coastal Inhabitants

An estimated 23 percent of the world's population resides both within 60 miles (100 km) from the coast and around 300 feet (less than 100 m) above sea level (Small and Nicholls 2003). Coastal areas contain 12 of the world's 16 largest cities with populations over ten million people and are about three times as dense as inland areas. Various coastal cities, including Tokyo, Shanghai, Hamburg, Rotterdam, and London, are protected by dikes, levees, and other structures. New Orleans, a city well upstream from the Mississippi River Delta and the Gulf of Mexico, had an elaborate, but antiquated, system of levees that did not protect it when Hurricane Katrina struck on August 28, 2005. Over 80 percent of Australians, including those in all the state and territorial capitals and in the increasingly growing seaside towns, reside on or near the coast. The IPCC (2007a:520) reports: "About 711,000 addresses (from the National Geo-coded Address File) are within 3 kilometers of the coast and less than 6 meters above sea level, with more than 60 percent located in Queensland and NSW [New South Wales]."

Even without global warming, the hazards caused by unsettled weather affect more people and cause significantly more economic damage than any other type of natural danger. No better recent example of this can be found than the massive tsunami that rose up in the Indian Ocean on December 26, 2004, following an underwater earthquake. The colossal waves of the tsunami achieved landfall on the shores of 12 different countries along the ocean rim. Hardest hit was the Indonesian province of Aceh, home to 170,000 of the 230,000 people killed by the storm. The provincial capital of Banda Aceh alone suffered over 60,000 deaths, one-fourth of the city's population. Beyond lives lost, thousands were injured and the homes and worldly possessions of many more were washed out to sea. There were places in which hardly a single building was left standing at the sites of what had been thriving communities (World Watch Institute 2007). With global warming, storms of similar impact are expected to be more common than in the past, with dire consequences for the communities caught in harm's way.

Ground Zero: Places at Risk

Bangladesh, a densely populated country of some 120 million people, is often mentioned as being under immediate danger from rising sea levels since a large portion of its population resides in the delta formed by the Ganges, Brahmaputra, and Meghna Rivers. For example, the country experienced a devastating storm surge in November 1970 that resulted in over 250,000 deaths and another in April 1991 that caused well over 100,000 deaths (Houghton 2004:151). Storm surges that strike coastal Bangladesh generally move inland, resulting in massive flooding. According to Houghton (2004:150), "about ten percent of the country's habitable land (with about six million population) would be lost with a half metre of sea level rise and about twenty percent (with a population of about 15 million) would be lost with a 1-m rise." In addition to the inundation of people's homes and communities, rising sea levels endanger large expanses of rich agricultural land, the source of income for about 85 percent of Bangladesh's population. The country often is subjected to violent storms, including at least one major cyclone every year. Global warming, however, very likely will increase the frequency of such storms as well the impact of climate on numerous communities.

The Nile delta, one of the oldest intensely cultivated areas on earth, is heavily populated, with population densities of up to 1,600 inhabitants per square kilometer (0.6 miles). It is home to over seven million people, about 12 percent of Egypt's population. Like Bangladesh, it faces a serious threat due to rising sea levels (Houghton 2004:152). It is estimated that a one meter rise in the ocean level would drown the coastal sand belt that protects cultivated areas and flood large parts of the delta, putting the Egyptian city of Alexandria at severe risk. In addition to destroying agricultural land, flooding would lower water quality in the delta's lagoons, the source of one-third of Egypt's fish catches.

Other regions of the world facing threat due to rising sea levels include parts of Southeast Asia (such as Vietnam, Thailand, the Philippines, and Indonesia); the alluvial coast plains of eastern China; the Mississippi River Delta; the Netherlands; and the Norfolk coast of eastern England. Coastal cities in danger of flooding include Shanghai, Kolkata, Lagos, London, Rotterdam, New York, Miami, and New Orleans among others. As Johansen (2006a:414) reports, since 1900 "sea levels have risen 12.3 inches in New York City; 8.3 inches in Baltimore; 9.9 inches in Philadelphia; 7.3 inches in Key West, Florida; 22.6 inches in Galveston, Texas; and 6 inches in San Francisco." Hong Kong is also subject to flooding resulting from storm surges and heavy rains (Yim 1996). Portions of the Japanese cities of Tokyo, Osaka, and Nagoya are situated below sea level and are only protected from the open sea by dikes. In the case of the Philippines, poor squatter settlers living in the deltas of the Baataan and Bulacan Rivers and along Manila Bay in particular are at risk from a rising sea. Although they may "increase the height of house posts to accommodate an increasing sea level they are vulnerable to an increased threat of storm surges" (Perez, Feir, Carandang, and Gonzalez 1996:143). While Venice has been plagued by floods for hundreds of years, the rising Adriatic Sea (resulting from global warming) has also contributed to the city's growing water management problems, to the extent that it has lost two-thirds of its inhabitants since 1950, with only some 60,000 people remaining in this world-renowned tourist attraction (Johansen 2006a:438).

As Flannery (2006:204) observes, cities "constitute fragile entities vulnerable to stresses brought about by climate change." Major cities already suffering from water shortages possibly related to global warming include New York, Los Angeles, Atlanta, Chicago, Washington, DC, Tucson, Sydney, and Melbourne (Glantz 2003:58). Furthermore, cities act as "heat islands" in that they entrap considerable heat due to the presence of concrete roads, building structures, factories, parking lots, massive shopping centers, and motor vehicle exhausts.

The Impact Global Warming on Small-island Inhabitants

Various island nations, particularly in the South Pacific and Indian Oceans, are in danger of oceanic inundation. These include Tuvalu (which we discuss below in a short case study), Kiribati (pop. 78,000), the Marshall Islands (pop. 58,000), Tokelau (pop. 2,000 and a dependent territory of New Zealand), and the Maldives (pop. 269,000). The Carteret Islands, located 60 miles (86 km) northeast of Bouganville, are expected to fall below sea level by 2010. Residents of the coral atoll began a phased evacuation to Papua New Guinea in 2005, and as a result have been called the first refugees of global warming. Efforts to keep the sea at bay, through the building of a sea wall and the planting of mangroves, failed, leading to a continued pattern of storm surges washing over the island and pulling homes and trees back into the ocean, drowning vegetable gardens in saltwater, and contaminating drinking water.

As Ebi, Lewis, and Corvalan indicate, these locales

> share many features that constrain their ability to adapt to current climate variability and future climate change, including their small or very small physical size, remoteness from major land masses, limited natural resources (often with unique animal and plant life), vulnerability to natural disasters and extreme weather events, economies sensitive to external shocks, populations with high growth rates and densities, poorly developed infrastructures, and limited financial and human resources. [Ebi et al. 2006:58]

A World Bank (2000) study of the economic impact of global warming for several Pacific islands, for example, found that, barring mitigation or some kind of effective adaptation, changing climate will wreck havoc on both "high islands" (those that rise above sea level) and "low islands" (those that do not rise much above the level of the surrounding ocean). For a high island like Viti Levu, Fiji, the World Bank study concluded that damages of between $23 million and $52 million can be expected each year by 2050, equivalent to about three percent of Fiji's GDP in 1998. Low islands, such as Tarawa, Kiribati, in Polynesia (formerly part of the Ellice Islands with Tuvalu), could experience average annual damages of more than $8 million to 16 million each year, or about 18 percent of Kiribati's GDP in 1998. As the recognized rate of onset of global warming effects has changed, it is now believed that the World Bank assessment could be realized far earlier than 2050.

Mountainous South Pacific island nations such as Fiji, Vanuatu, the Solomon Islands, the Cook Islands, Samoa, and Tonga have been undergoing beach erosion of up to three feet (1 m) per year (Lynas 2004:112–113). Global warming will adversely affect the tourist industry on many of these South Pacific islands by destroying coral reefs, damaging beaches, creating increasingly uncomfortably high nighttime temperatures, and taxing the availability of freshwater. For instance, in Bega Lagoon, on the southern side of Viti Levu, a popular tourist diving site in Fiji, as much as 80 percent of the coral has been lost to lethal bleaching caused by warming seas. Conversely, as Becken (2005:381) observes, "there is increasing awareness that tourism is an important contributor to climate change through its consumption of fossil fuels and resulting gas emissions."

Tuvalu: An Icon of the Dangers of Global Warming

More than any other South Pacific island nation, Tuvalu, a former British colony known as the Gilbert and Ellice Islands that gained independence in 1978, has captured worldwide attention with respect to the dangers of rising sea levels. This remote country situated roughly midway between Hawaii and Australia had a population of 11,305 in 2003. Tuvalu means "Cluster of Eight," because one of the nine islands that comprise this state was uninhabited at the time of European contact. The bits of land that make up Tuvalu are spread across 420 miles (676 km) of sea. The people of Tuvalu live increasingly perilously on a chain of islands that together provide a landmass of only ten square miles (26 km). The fourth smallest nation in the world, with the smallest population of any member state of the United Nations, the country has very limited natural resources. Roughly 80 percent of Tuvaluans over age 15 engage in farming and fishing, with the remainder of the labor force working in wage jobs either in the public or private sector in the capital of Funafuti (Ralston, Horstmann, and Holl 2004:10). In addition to marine life, the population consumes *pulaka* or taro, coconuts, pandanus fruit, and bananas. Various health problems are prevalent on the islands, including diabetes, hypertension, acute respiratory infections, and tuberculosis, especially among women. Causes include overcrowding, poverty, and limited access to health care. For example, Tuvalu has a tuberculosis prevalence of 100 cases per 100,000 people, giving it the highest ranking as a place of risk for acquiring TB according to the World Health Organization.

Global warming is not a future event on Tuvalu. Already Tuvaluans are experiencing the erosion of their beaches, damaging tidal surges, and the intrusion of saltwater into cultivated areas. Saltwater destroyed many taro pits, thus transforming a staple crop into a luxury item (Lynas 2004:100). Like all small island nations, freshwater is at a premium on

Tuvalu,which has no rivers, and a significant decline in the availability of freshwater is life-threatening. Lower-than-average rainfall in 1997–1998 in Majuro Atoll, in the Republic of the Marshall Islands, for example, caused a drought and severe drinking-water shortage. Fresh water also is vital to cultivation on the islands. The main traditional staple crop in Tuvalu is taro, a tropical plant rich in vitamins and minerals as well as starch and dietary fiber, grown primarily as a vegetable food. In most of Tuvalu, taro is planted in depressions and excavated pits that are cut down to subsurface freshwater aquifers that have been partially refilled with decomposing organic matter. Pit cultivation of this sort is highly susceptible to changes in climate that impact freshwater quality. In Tuvalu, contraction of the freshwater aquifers on the nation's five atolls (a result of the combined effects of increasing water demand by a growing population and rises in the sea level caused by global warming) could severely reduce crop yields. The crop that is expected to be most immediately affected is pulaka, or giant taro. Reduced yields from pulaka pits are "likely to have significant cultural ramifications, given the central role of this crop in Tuvaluan society" (Secretariat of the Pacific Regional Environment Programme 1996: Section 6.4.1). Other varieties of taro are also at risk of rising sea levels.

Global warming is also eroding natural breakwaters, such as coral reefs. Ralston, Horstmann, and Holl report:

> As Tuvalu is near the cyclone belt, it is always at risk from the tropical storms and cyclones. The capital of Funafuti, for example, could be flooded as a result of a cyclone prompting a one-in-ten year's wave, the result of which the existing coastal infrastructure would not survive. Meanwhile, the chances of such an extreme event could be doubled if the sea were to rise only 0.5 meters. [Ralston, Horstmann, and Holl 2004:7]

In August of 2002, government leaders from 16 Pacific island nations held the 33rd Pacific Islands Forum in Suva, Fiji, at which they collectively expressed strong concerns about the extreme hardships global warming was already causing. Participants issued a communiqué to developed nations responsible for most greenhouse gas emissions petitioning them to begin addressing the global effects of disruptive environmental change. The following year, at the 58th Session of the United Nations General Assembly, Prime Minister Saufatu Sopoanga of Tuvalu declared that his people "live in constant fear of the adverse impacts of climate change. For a coral atoll nation, sea level rise and more severe weather events loom as a growing threat to our entire population. The threat is real and serious, and is [no different than] a slow and insidious form of terrorism against us" (quoted in TuvaluIslands.com 2007). Similarly, in response to discussions concerning relocating populations from threatened islands to safer locales (a process that is informally already under way as islanders have moved in growing numbers to New Zealand and elsewhere), Tuvalu's United Nations Ambassador, Enele Sopoaga, in an interview with Salon.com, sternly stated:

> There are a lot of places in the world you can relocate Tuvaluans to and then forget about the problem of climate change. I don't believe this is a responsible way to deal with the problem. . . . Tuvaluans want to live in their own islands forever. To relocate is a short-sighted solution, an irresponsible solution. We're not dealing here with Tuvalu only. All of the low-lying island coastal areas are going to be affected. You tell me whether the world is ready to evacuate everybody. There is a challenge to reverse and address climate change, to try to mitigate greenhouse gas emissions, and I think the world should focus on that. [Berzon 2007:3]

In the words of David Stanley (2007), "as ocean levels continue to rise, the entire population of Tuvalu may have to evacuate, third world victims of first world affluence." In contrast to Australia, New Zealand recognizes environmental refugees and has witnessed an increase in the migration of Tuvaluans, most of whom left their home islands because of the rising sea (Johansen 2006a:435). The New Zealand government has agreed to take in 75 Tuvaluans per year over the course of 30 years but requires that applicants be of "good character and health, have basic English skills, have a job offer in New Zealand, and be under 45 years of age" (quoted in Ralston et al. 2004:15). Over 3,000 Tuvaluans already have left their homeland, many of them now residing in Auckland.

Tuvalu is a member of the Alliance of Small Island States, an organization created in 1990 to lobby internationally on behalf of small island nations vulnerable to the effects of global warming. It has also joined the Pacific Island Climate Change Assistance Program and has implemented a five-point plan to address the impact of global warming on its land and people. The ability of any of these efforts to save Tuvalu from destruction as a habitable place remains in doubt.

Impact of Global Warming on Inhabitants of Mountainous Areas

Most mountainous areas have been experiencing accelerated patterns of global warming. An estimated 26 percent of the world's population reportedly live in mountainous areas (Nogues-Bravero et al. 2007:420). Mountains are ecologically fragile areas. The special nature of mountain ecology not only impacts the people living in them or immediately below them but also those living at considerable distances away in lowland areas that rely upon water from melting mountain glaciers and snowfall.

Mountainous areas are important sources of hydroelectric power and sites of tourist activities, such as skiing, hiking, camping, and boating. According to Nogues-Bravo et al.:

> In humid areas, mountains supply up to 20–50 percent of the total [water] discharge, while in arid areas this figure is 50–90 percent, with extremes of over 95 percent. A change from snow-fed to rain-fed regimes associated with climate warming (i.e., less winter precipitation falls as snow and the melting of winter snow occurs earlier in spring) implies increasing variability in discharge, possible modifications of reservoir management patterns, and the increased necessity for dams. [Nogues-Bravo et al. 2007:425]

Global warming will result in unstable patterns of hydroelectric generation and will adversely affect ski resorts, which unfortunately tend to be energy-intensive and ecologically destructive enterprises both in terms of the ski runs themselves and nearby, often luxury, accommodations (Scott et al. 2007).

The melting of glaciers associated with global warming has resulted in the creation of a large number of glacial lakes, some of which constitute a risk for downstream inhabitants. For example, Tsho Rolpha Lake, situated at 15,000 feet (4,580 m) above sea level in the Nepal Himalayas, has grown six times in size since the 1950s (Horstmann 2004:3). An outburst flood would endanger the inhabitants of village of Tibeni 67 miles (108 km) downstream, the surrounding countryside, livestock, farms, bridges, other structures, as well as the Khimti hydropower project about 50 miles (80 km) below the lake. In the Swiss Alps, the village of Sas Balen is home to 423 inhabitants who reside two miles (3 km) below the Gruben glacier, which has been melting for over a century and as a result losing 24–28 inches (60–70 cm) in height annually (Cowie 1998:273). The village was flooded in 1968 and again in 1970, eventually prompting its residents to drain one of the meltwater lakes in 1995 to prevent further flooding. Wilfried Haeberli, the director of the United Nations' Glacier Monitoring Service, linked the threat of the village being inundated by mud and rushing water to global warming. Permafrost and Climate in Europe, which monitors the impact of global warming on mountains, reports that melting glaciers have contributed to the increasing volume of the Rhine, Rhone, and Po Rivers in Europe (Johansen 2006a:368).

The rapid melting of glaciers in the Andes has forced people to grow their staple crops at even higher elevations, a practice that contributes to deforestation and soil erosion. The Working Group on Climate Change and Development reports:

> The native communities of the Imbakucha Basin in Otavalo, Ecuador, already feel the impact of climate change. Unexpected frosts and long drought periods affect all farming activities. The older generation say they no longer know

when to sow because the rains do not come as expected. Migration offers one way out but represents a cultural nemesis and the human and social price to pay is high. The same is true for other communities living in areas between 2,500 and 3,500 metres above sea level, who depend on rain for cultivation. Coastal communities are also affected. [Working Group on Climate Change and Development 2007:17]

The flight of highland or mountain people to cities often means that they have to cope with an atomistic existence in overcrowded and polluted slums or shantytowns and try to eke out a living at low-paying factory or low-status service jobs, or as street vendors. Particularly for Andean people, who are adapted with their large hearts and low heart rates to the *altiplano*, adjusting to life in coastal or lowland cities can be physiologically taxing. The health and social costs of crowding and urban poverty are no less stressful.

R. Parish and D.C. Funnell (1999), two human geographers at the University of St. Andrews in the United Kingdom, conducted an examination of the potential impact of global warming in the High Atlas Mountains of Morocco, especially in light of various studies indicating that North Africa is likely to experience reduced precipitation over the course of the next half century or so. In the next chapter, we comment upon the impact of global warming upon agricultural activities in the High Atlas. Here, we briefly comment upon the impact of global warming on the tourist industry in the region. French colonialists in Morocco often retreated to the High Atlas region in order to escape the sweltering summer heat of the coastal and lowland regions. While both domestic and overseas tourism presently is highly concentrated in coastal areas, Parish and Funnell foresee a tourist boom in the High Atlas as temperatures rise in the lowlands. At the present time, tourism consists primarily of pilgrims attending religious festivals honoring various Islamic saints, athletes participating in winter sports, and day bus excursions from large cities such as Marrakech. Of course, skiing and winter sports, which presently attract both more affluent Moroccans and foreigners between December and March, would very likely diminish as a result of fewer snowfalls.

Impact of Global Warming on Arctic and Subarctic Inhabitants

Indigenous peoples in arctic regions have also been the object of intense study in terms of the impact of global warming on their lifeways and settlement patterns. The Arctic is often portrayed as the "canary in the cage" in the literature on global warming and associated climatic changes. For example, winters in southern Alaska have been 3.6°F–5.4°F (2–3°C) warmer than they were 30 years ago. Indigenous arctic peoples will have to cope with loss of sea ice and its impact on traditional hunting and fishing activities, changed migration routes of animals, coastal erosion due to wave action on ice-free coasts, loss of permafrost, and changes in the abundance of traditional food sources on land and in water. The Arctic Climate Impact Assessment, sponsored by nations with an interest in the region, includes two chapters that discuss the impact of global warming on arctic indigenous peoples and their perceptions of it. Chapter 3, authored by Henry Huntington et al. (2004), summarizes arctic peoples' perceptions of the climatic changes and shifts in animal and plant life associated with global warming. They present brief case studies of several communities, including Kotzebue in northwest Alaska, four communities in Nunavut, Qaanaaq in Greenland, and four Saami communities. In the case of Kotzebue, the tribal government conducted interviews with village elders about their perceptions of environmental changes in the region since the 1950s (Huntington et al. 2004:72–76). The elders reported that extreme climatic variability started during the 1970s, and spoke in particular of the impact of later freeze-ups of the ice. While the late freeze-up has contributed to better whitefish harvests, better clamming, better spotted seal hunting, and easier access to caribou and arctic fox, it has also resulted in a shorter ice-fishing season, poor access to the village for people living in outlying areas, rough ice conditions, greater danger when walking on the ice, and increased flooding and erosion. The elders felt that the deaths of two experienced hunters who fell through the ice while hunting was related to global warming.

In Chapter 12 of the Arctic Climate Impact Assessment, anthropologist Mark Nuttall and his colleagues examine the ways various indigenous arctic communities have adapted to global warming (Nuttall et al. 2004). They present case studies of the Inuvialuit community of Sachs Harbour in the Canadian Western Arctic, the Canadian Inuit in Nunavut, the Yamal Nenets of northwestern Siberia, and the indigenous peoples of the Russian North. In the case of Sachs Harbour on Banks Island, the team found that global warming has resulted in less sea ice during the summer, making the water rougher; more rain in summer and autumn, making travel difficult; unpredictable sea-ice conditions during the colder months, making both travel and hunting hazardous; and greater infestations of mosquitoes during the summer months (Nuttall et al. 2004:666–670). These conditions have resulted in more restricted access to seals and polar bears, which are served traditionally as important food resources. According to the report:

> One major impact of climate on the local perception is the issue of loss of predictability. Land-based livelihoods in the Arctic depend on people's ability to predict

the weather . . ., read the ice . . ., judge the snow conditions . . ., and predict animal movements and distributions. A hunter who cannot predict the weather or read the ice would be limited in mobility; one who cannot decide what to hunt and where cannot bring back much food. [Nuttall et al. 2004:670]

Many arctic coastal communities in Greenland, Canada, Alaska, and Siberia are found in extremely remote areas that are endangered by rising seas. Shishmaref, an Inupiat village of some 600 residents on Sarichef Island in northwest Alaska, finds itself besieged by a rising sea and increasingly violent storms (Lynas 2004:45–51). The encroaching sea has been threatening rusty fuel tanks containing 80,000 gallons of gasoline and stove oil (Johansen 2006a:308). Sea water also has at times inundated Shishmaref's water supply and washed a few homes out to sea. According to Gunter Weller, director of the University of Alaska's Center for Global Change and Arctic System Research (quoted in Willis 2004), "Shishmaref is an indication of what to expect in the future in other parts of the world."

As Cruikshank (2001, 2007) has shown, narratives of climate change and its impact on indigenous communities has a long history. This process is happening anew with contemporary weather-related environmental changes. Alaskan native and executive director of the Alaska Native Science Commission Patricia Cochran, for example, reports:

We are losing the lives of our people . . . . Primarily these are people who are traveling and falling through the ice because ice conditions are no longer the same. Experienced hunters, experienced travelers, whalers—every year we are losing more and more people because of the inability to read ice conditions as we've done in the past . . . . Summers are much hotter than ever before. Its warmer, drier, we're losing our lakes that are drying up. [Quoted in Wall 2007:1]

Similarly, Inuit activist and Nobel Peace Prize nominee Sheila Watt-Cloutier argued, in her presentation to the Inter-American Commission on Human Rights of the Organization of American States, that for indigenous communities being protected from the effects of anthropogenic global warming was a human rights issue. She quoted a hunter in Barrow, Alaska, to summarize the impact climate change has had on Inuit life: "There's lots of anxieties and angers that are being felt by some of the hunters that no longer can go and hunt. We see the change, but we can't stop it, we can't explain why it's changing . . . . Our way of life is changing up here, our ocean is changing" (quoted in Zabarenko 2007).

Elsewhere, in Siberian Russia, permafrost has rapidly been melting in numerous locations, resulting in the buckling and cracking of roads, the fracturing of airport runways, and serious structural damage to buildings and houses. A quarter of the inhabitants of the diamond-mining town of Mirny had to be evacuated because their houses were falling into the melting permafrost (Johansen 2006a:319). Similarly, a section of an apartment building in Cherskii collapsed due to the melting permafrost. This was not a singular event; as Robert Strom (2007:178) reports: "300 apartment buildings in Norilsk and Yakutsk have been damaged so far. If the permafrost keeps warming at the modest rate of just 0.075°C per year, all the five-story buildings in the city of Yakutsk (Population 193,000) will be destroyed by 2030."

Sections of the Trans-Siberian Railroad's track have collapsed and sunk into the melting permafrost as well. Additionally, the world's highest rail line linking Xining, the capital of Qinghai province in northwest China, and the Tibetan capital of Lhasa, has been subjected to serious problems due to the melting permafrost (Johansen 2006a:377). The same pattern has been witnessed on the slopes of the famous Matterhorn, in Switzerland. Permafrost holds the mountains pillars and rock faces together, and provides the anchor in which the set of manmade cable-car stations and pylons are rooted. With global warming, however, the permafrost is melting, resulting in alpine disasters, including the avalanches that killed more than 50 people at the Austrian resort of Galtur in 1999. At the International Permafrost Association meeting in Zurich in 2003 (McKie 2003), climate scientists and civil engineers reported findings on the growing effects of climate change. According to Michael Davies, a civil engineering professor at Dundee University and conference organizer:

> What happened on the Matterhorn . . . was the result of the Alps losing its permafrost. We have found that the ground temperature in the Alps around the Matterhorn has risen considerably over the past decade. The ice that holds mountain slopes and rock faces together is simply disappearing. At this rate, it will vanish completely—with profound consequences. [Quoted in McKie 2003]

A test borehole that was dug in Murtel in southern Switzerland found that frozen subsurface soils have warmed by more than a degree Celsius since 1990.

As these cases suggest, in artic and subartic areas, the foundations of many building and transportation systems rest on surfaces put at risk by global warming, thereby creating significant challenges to continued habitation of many areas.

Seeing Global Warming: Public Perceptions

Research on public awareness and perceptions of the risks to health of global warming suggests somewhat limited but growing concern. In a 24-country "Health of the Planet" survey, for example, Mertig and

Dunlap (1995) found that large majorities (ranging by country from 64 to 92 percent) reported that they felt that environmental problems would affect the health of their children and grandchildren. A longer form of this survey was administered in six countries (Canada, United States, Mexico, Brazil, Portugal, and Russia) (Dunlap 1996) and found that in all but Russia the majority of participants selected "very harmful" to characterize the expected impact of global warming on agricultural production and survival of animal species. Both Canada and the United States had smaller minorities, 27 to 31 percent, expecting harmful economic and lifestyle impacts. Turning to the issue of the relative ranking of perceived risk, a U.S. study by Bord, Fisher, and O'Connor (1998) found that people ranked heart disease, cancer, and car accidents as the greatest threats to their lives, while global warming was ranked lowest in terms of perceived personal threat.

As a consequence of significantly expanded press coverage and other attention paid to global warming by governments, schools, and other entities, the ranking of global warming as a perceived personal threat jumped considerably in recent years, especially in places already suffering from one or more of the many diseases of global environmental change. In June 2005 ABC News, for example, conducted a poll that queried Americans on their views about the gravity of global warming. Strom reports:

> In that poll 59 percent were convinced that global warming was underway, but only 33 percent thought it would affect their lives. Only 38 percent favored immediate government action to deal with the problem. A majority (67 percent) thought that global warming posed no serious threat in their own lifetime, but 79 percent thought it posed a "serious threat to future generations." A more recent Gallup poll in April 2006 gave similar results and found that Americans were more worried about water pollution, air pollution (not greenhouse gases), and toxic waste than they were about global warming. [Strom 2007:246]

Similarly, the second annual "America's Report Card on the Environment"—based on a telephone public opinion survey using a representative national sample of 1,001 American adults conducted by the Woods Institute for the Environment (2007) in collaboration with the Associated Press—found that Americans are now quite pessimistic about the state of the environment and, further, they want prompt action taken to improve environmental quality. The survey found that 52 percent of Americans expect the natural environment to deteriorate over the next ten years. An additional eight percent of survey participants reported that they believe the environment is in "poor" to "very poor" condition and not likely to improve. Moreover, the study reported that pessimism about the state of the natural environment is closely tied to beliefs about global warming and that almost all Americans agree that environmental damage is at least partly attributable to the actions of American businesses.

Anthony Leiserowitz elucidates the rather contradictory views that Americans hold about the seriousness of global warming. Based upon a national survey consisting of 551 subjects weighted by sex and age that he conducted from November 2002 to February 2003, Leiserowitz (2005) found that while 68 percent of his respondents expressed serious concerns about the impact of global warming on people around the world and the planet, only 13 percent viewed it as having serious consequences for themselves, their families, and their local communities, and only 22 percent viewed it as having serious consequences for the United States. In a later study Leiserowitz (2006:44–45) reports that 90 percent of his respondents believed that the United States should reduce its greenhouse gas emissions, 88 percent supported the Kyoto Protocol intended to achieve this goal, 77 percent supported government regulation of carbon dioxide emissions, and 71 percent supported a transition of the fossil fuel industry into a renewable-energy industry. Conversely, while 54 percent of the study participants supported restrictions on "gas guzzler" engines in cars, 74 percent opposed a gasoline tax and 60 percent opposed a business energy tax to pay for curbing greenhouse gas emissions. Not surprisingly, Democrats and liberals exhibited stronger support for anti–global warming policies than Republicans and conservatives, but the majority of Republicans and conservatives supported most anti–global warming policies as well. Nonetheless, various ultraconservative pundits continue to rail against taking global warming seriously and efforts to mitigate its effects. Nationally syndicated radio host Rush Limbaugh, for example, regularly asserts on his radio program and website that global warming theory is unsupportable by the facts.

Despite variegated perceptions of the gravity of global warming among many Americans and others, most people have not elected to become involved in environmental and, more specifically, climate politics. Despite a growing international climate justice movement, which we discuss in greater detail in the final chapter, the "naysayers" (a category composed of only seven percent of the participants) in the national survey reported by Leiserowitz who perceive global warming as a very low or nonexistent hazard tend to be more politically active, are more likely to vote, and have a strong representation in the federal government, including having influential connections with corporate elites. According to Leiserowitz (2005:1439) this group is "predominantly white, male, Republican, politically conservative, holding pro-individualism, pro-hierarchism, and anti-environmental attitudes, distrustful of other institutions, highly religious, and . . . rely on radio as their main source of news."

We discuss climate regimes and the politics of global warming at length in Chapter 7, but suffice it to say at this point that powerful conservative social forces and a pro-business mass media have played a significant role in increasing complacency about the gravity of global warming. In this effort, conservative think tanks, such as the American Enterprise Institute, the Cato Institute, the Competitive Enterprise Institute, the Heritage Foundation, the Hoover Institution, and the Marshall Institute, have had a hand in persuading influential politicians to oppose ratification of the Kyoto Protocol in the U.S. Senate (McCright 2000; McCright and Dunlap 2003).

Anthropologist Myanna Lahsen (2005b:155) maintains that "while the environmental movement grew out of broad-based grassroots mobilization, the anti-environmental [including the anti–global warming] movement, has largely been mobilized and paid for by conservative financial elites, joined by industry groups with vested interests in fossil fuels." In terms of the mass media, Boykoff and Boykoff (2004:125) argue that in their efforts to be "balanced," the leading U.S. newspapers, namely the *New York Times*, the *Washington Post*, and the *Los Angeles Times*, have until relatively recently downplayed the overwhelming evidence presented by climate science on the gravity of global warming. In the past, these media trendsetters systematically have given greater credence to the arguments of the global warming skeptics than either their numbers or evidence would otherwise warrant (Antilla 2005). Under the avalanche of evidence of diverse sorts that now points not only to the reality of global warming but to its growing pace, as well as to its dire potential to damage communities and their ways of life, major news organs have begun to more fully and even urgently report on the nature and risks of global environmental change.

On "Winners" and "Losers" in the Context of Global Warming

Ironically, some of the discussion on the impact of global warming on human societies is framed in terms of neoclassical microeconomics or the neoliberal language of *winners* and *losers*. While it is generally recognized that people in much of sub-Saharan Africa and on small island nations will be among the losers, various mainstream economists and businesspeople assert that people in what are generally low-density populated areas, such as much of Canada, Siberia, Tasmania, and New Zealand, will be among the winners in terms of longer growing seasons, such as for wine vineyards, and increasingly habitable lands. Real estate developers—perhaps even some who contributed to the crowding of communities along vulnerable coastlines—undoubtedly are eyeing remote areas in terms of potential future profits. While formerly inaccessible parts of Siberia, however, may be available for farming in the future, the melting of the permafrost could result in large portions of the region becoming swampland (Johansen 2006a:321). Similar, less than ideal outcomes may face other areas that some believe will become more habitable because of global warming. The nature of this debate is reflected in the remarks of Robert W. Coreil, the chairperson of the Arctic Climate Assessment, to the U.S. Senate Committee on Commerce, Science, and Transportation on November 16, 2004:

> Climate change is . . . projected to result in major impacts inside the Arctic, some of which are already underway. Whether a particular impact is perceived as negative or positive depends on one's interests. For example, the reduction in sea is very likely to have devastating consequences for polar bears, ice-dependent seals, and local people for whom these animals are a primary food resource. On the other hand, reduced sea ice is likely to increase marine access to the region's resources, expanding opportunities for shipping and possibly for offshore oil extraction (although operations could be hampered initially by increasing movement of ice in some areas). [Coreil 2004:3]

While Coreil recognizes that reduced sea-ice shipping and resource extraction could damage the environment and marine life, and thus adversely affect the health and cultures of indigenous arctic peoples, he fails to note that oil extraction would ultimately contribute to even more carbon dioxide in the atmosphere; nor does he even come close to suggesting that, if left unchecked beyond 2100, global capitalism could very possibly result in the ultimate destruction of most human, animal, and plant life on the planet.

Even the highly respected IPCC frames its discourse in various documents in terms of the "winners and losers" paradigm, such as when it argues that cold-water fisheries in North America will be adversely affected by global warming, whereas warm-water fisheries will benefit from it. Similarly, the IPCC argues that the tourist industry in southern European coastal areas will suffer due to global warming whereas it will prosper in the mountainous area of Italy, Spain, and France (IPCC 2007b). In its overview of the impact of global warming on small islands, such as those in the South Pacific and the Caribbean, the IPCC (2007b:689) report, which recognizes that tourism constitutes a major contributor to GDP and employment in these areas, observes that while higher temperatures could hamper tourist travel to small islands in low latitudes, such as those in the Caribbean and the South Pacific, it could stimulate tourist travel to mid- and high latitudes, presumably places such as Vancouver Island in British Columbia, Iceland, and Greenland.

Another example of the cost-benefit analysis employed by the IPCC is expressed in the following statement:

> Development, to a large extent, is responsible for much of the greenhouse gases emitted into the atmosphere that drives climate change. On the other hand, development contributes to reducing vulnerability to climate change and in enhancing the adaptive capacity of vulnerable sectors. [IPCC 2007b:488]

Under such a scenario, for example, most people in developed countries and the affluent in developing countries could cope with higher summertime temperatures by turning on their air conditioners, a practice that, ironically, serves to further exacerbate global warming and deplete energy resources.

In seeking to develop a critical anthropology of global warming, we urge a move beyond the limitations of the cost-benefit or winners-losers analysis that is part and parcel of a conventional approach to the impact of global warming on human societies. The reasons for this approach, as subsequent chapters in this book are intended to clarify, have to do with the extensive health consequences for people everywhere of global warming. In this regard, we find ourselves in basic agreement with the following observations made by Leichenko and O'Brien on the limitations of the winners and losers perspective:

> Under a binary approach, nations, regions, and populations are simply categorized as either winners or losers based on a series of biophysical measures such as changes in mean temperatures and rainfall amounts, with little attention to socially and politically generated differences in vulnerabilities to these changes. By the same token, adaptation strategies based on a winners and losers framework may tend to emphasize technological solutions. [Leichenko and O'Brien 2006:113]

As we argue in our concluding chapter, both adaptation to and mitigation of global warming will require nothing short of a global social transformation.

3

An Age of Weather Extremes

Consequences for Human Subsistence, Water, and Nutrition

Global warming may result in detrimental effects on food supply and security, especially in developing countries. Even if developing countries adapt to climate change, they will not be able to completely avoid the problems associated with climate change. Furthermore, these harmful outcomes of climate change in developing countries and potentially positive outcomes in developed countries will probably increase the gap in wealth, access to food, and health between rich and poor countries.

Lauren Sacks and Cynthia Rosenzweig 2007

Global Warming, Human Subsistence, and Health

We live at a time in which more is known about the quality of human life on planet earth and the state of the world's health than ever before. A flood of new information appears daily in the form of news reports, scientific studies, professional conference proceedings, and government documents. One lesson of this growing body of knowledge is recognition of the importance of building a broad understanding of the social and contextual factors that underlie health and overall well-being. This recognition was spurred in the late 1960s when the first extraordinary photographs of earth from outer space were sent back to us by the Apollo spacecraft. Seeing earth impressively hanging alone in dark space helped to modify how we think about our world, its limits, and various threats to its viability as a habitable environment. This new way of thinking about the world and human life on the planet was furthered by the World Health Organization in 1978 when it brought together representatives of many nations in the Russian city of Alma Ata (now Almaty, the largest city in Kazakhstan) to set universal standards and benchmarks for achieving "Health for All" people by the year 2000. The statement issued by this international forum emphasized the fundamental importance of going beyond overcoming disease or improving access to health care to addressing basic human-environmental interactions, including the status of living spaces, patterns and contexts of subsistence, the quality of diets, and access to breathable air and potable water. Reflective of this progressive attitude, Global Health Watch (2005), a collaborative international health-monitoring initiative launched by several popular health movements, nongovernmental organizations, and health workers and scholars, has expressed increasingly grave concern about global environmental degradation as a primary threat to human health. Among the key concerns raised by Global Health Watch are the direct and indirect effects of global warming, including:

- The impact of increasing regional droughts and changing patterns of rainfall on agriculture, food production, and food security, especially in already poor and lesser developed areas of the world like sub-Saharan Africa.
- The growing loss of viable habitats, producing notable consequences for planetary biodiversity, which, in turn, is expected to significantly shape human access to food sources.
- Rising sea levels and the threat they create for coastal and island populations as well as to drinkable, unsalinated, and unpolluted water for inland populations.
- More frequent environmental emergencies caused by extreme weather events like hurricanes and tsunamis.
- Increased civil unrest and resulting violence provoked by forced migration, increasingly scarce resources, demands for access to basic necessities, and efforts to exploit vulnerable migrant populations.
- Climbing rates of morbidity and mortality linked to rising temperatures, including heat exhaustion and related respiratory and other disorders.
- Spreading disease vectors and pathogens.

As summarized by the World Health Organization:

> Our increasing understanding of climate change is transforming how we view the boundaries and determinants of human health. While our personal health may seem to relate mostly to prudent behaviour, heredity, occupation, local environmental exposures, and health-care access, sustained population health requires the life-supporting "services" of the biosphere. Populations of all animal species depend on supplies of food and water, freedom from excess infectious disease, and the physical safety and comfort conferred by climatic stability. The world's climate system is fundamental to this life-support. [McMichael et al. 2003:2]

There is little doubt any longer among environmental and health scientists that intensifying climate change will have significant impacts on human subsistence, health, and well-being; indeed, climate change already is having consequential effects of various kinds around the planet. As a result, as Anthony McMichael (2003:15), the director of the Centre of Epidemiology and Population Health at Australian National University, and his coauthors emphasize, "this topic is likely to become a major theme in population health research" in the coming years. It is our contention that this is unavoidably so because the quality of life on earth is likely to be severely impacted by global warming.

With regard to health impacts, these concerns are not unwarranted. A recent study by the World Health Organization (2002) concluded that over 150,000 people a year are already dying from the diverse effects of global warming, and this number is expected to go up, doubling by 2020, if not earlier. The majority of these deaths are in developing nations in Africa, Latin America, and Southeast Asia. But these numbers are based on only a partial list of outcomes resulting from flooding, malnutrition, changing access to potable water, and spreading infectious diseases, and are seen by many public health activists as representing a conservative accounting of climatic effects (Patz et al. 2005). Given the accelerated rate and wider geographic distribution of the subsistence and health effects of global warming that have been recognized in recent years, far higher assessments may be needed. In light of growing evidence of the significant health consequences produced by global warming, scientists and health care providers are debating the details of which health effects, suffered by which populations, their degree of severity, and when they will occur. This discussion reflects an essential aspect of climate change, namely, that while the process is global, its specific effects will be local.

What is Health?

A starting point for assessing the range of human consequences of global warming is with a foundational examination of the nature of health. A widely accepted, if perhaps overly ideal, definition of health was developed by the World Health Organization (1978), which maintains that "health is a state of complete physical, mental and social well-being and not merely the absence of disease or infirmity." It is generally recognized that health is a reflection of the complex interrelationships that exist among biology, society, and the surrounding physical environment. Thus, the oft-cited LaLonde Report (LaLonde 1974) asserted that the four primary determinants of health are "human biology," "environment," "lifestyle," and "healthcare organization." In our efforts to develop a critical alternative to this and other conventional understandings of health, one that is keenly sensitive to biosocial interaction and the effects of human inequality on health status, access to health care, and human/environmental interactions, we (Baer, Singer, and Susser 2003:5) have defined health as "access to and control over the basic material and nonmaterial resources that sustain and promote life at a high level of satisfaction. Health is not some absolute state of being but an elastic concept that must be evaluated in a larger sociocultural context." In light of global warming, it is evident that the interaction of sociocultural systems and the physical environment—including the many ways human actions impact the environment and humans, in turn, are affected by environmental change—is a critical process in the determination of health. Consequently, control over the processes and structures that contribute most directly to global warming are of vital importance.

Fundamental to the assessment of the role of global warming in determining health around the world is *vulnerability*, a concept that unites ideas from epidemiology, comparative statistics in economics, risk mapping of hazards, and various approaches to health assessment. Vulnerability is a characteristic of individuals, households, and populations and has somewhat different, although interconnected, components and determinants at each of these levels (McCarthy et al. 2001, Turner et al. 2006). At the individual level, vulnerability is influenced by factors like age, sex, fitness, and pre-existing health status (and hence involves both personal attributes and social status), as well as what has been called "adaptive capacity," or the body's ability to recover following a climatic (or any other) threat to health (Comrie 2007). At the population level, vulnerability is an aggregate measure of underlying social conditions, such as the availability of access to health care or emergency response resources. Within and across populations, attention must be paid to issues of power, wealth, and social status because the toll of climate change is likely to be far harsher for some social strata than others. Adaptive capacity to cope with a flooding event, for example, varies considerably across populations and locations (Dawdy 2006). As Comrie notes, structural factors are critical:

> . . . consider the city of Nogales that straddles the US–Mexico border in the states of Arizona and Sonora. For a heavy rainfall event, exposure to extreme precipitation is the same on both sides of the border; sensitivity to floods and waterborne disease will differ because of drainage infrastructure, land use patterns, and sanitation systems; adaptive capacity will differ because of socioeconomic status and other factors such as access to health care. [Comrie 2007:237]

Household vulnerability provides a linkage between population and individual vulnerability. Access to resources varies by households, as does capacity to handle climatic or other threats to health (e.g., the number individuals capable of contributing to family well-being or of responding when a key household provider falls ill). Household failure (e.g., loss of access to reproductive resources like land or death of a key provider) puts all household members at heightened health risk. Vulnerability to a threat like hunger, for example, involves the interaction of exposure to chronic or episodic malnutrition, physical predisposition to the consequences of inadequate diet, and both household and social infrastructural capacity to respond to food shortages (Downing 1991, 1992, Liverman 1990, Messer 1989). Vulnerability to famine is likely to be highest among impoverished, undernourished, or otherwise stressed individuals, households, and populations, as is vulnerability to a range of other threats to health that are exacerbated by climate change.

Michael McGeehin (2007) of the National Center for Environmental Health at the U.S. Centers for Disease Control and Prevention has identified the primary areas in which global warming will take a toll on human morbidity and mortality, as listed below.

- Weather- and climate-related injuries, morbidity and mortality
- Lack of access to drinkable water
- Food insecurity and malnutrition
- Pollutant-related respiratory problems
- Disease linked to storms and flooding
- Spread of infectious diseases
- Injury from climate-triggered civil conflict

As this list suggests, there are at least seven major ways in which global warming influences health, each of which will be examined either in this or subsequent chapters. Consideration of the myriad ways global warming affects health suggests the need for a dynamic understanding that effectively captures the "mega-interaction" of three interfaces in light of historic and prevailing patterns of social inequality. Each of these interactions are examined below.

The first interaction is between human biology and our physical and social environments, all of which have been shaped over time by human activity and hierarchical social relationships. As a result of these interactions, contemporary health within a human population (which is the starting point for assessing the health effects of global warming) can be understood as a reflection of its evolutionary development in particular physical environments under changing sociocultural and sociostructural conditions. Shaping the critical approach to understanding this interface is the recognition that human history, including the history of social inequality, is embodied—that is, it is literally written "under the skin." For example, in assessing the causes of the high rate of hypertension found among African Americans, Nancy Krieger (2001), who has developed an ecosocial model of health, argues that it is the physical embodiment of a synergistic interaction of a set of factors. These include life-long exposure to racial discrimination, segregation, and economic deprivation (producing a chronic triggering of the body's natural "fight or flight" response); consumption of a high fat and salt and low vegetable diet (a product not of traditional dietary patterns but of historic and contemporary food access under conditions of domination); high rates of preterm birth (which can impair renal development and is itself a reflection of health disparities); exposure to hazardous environmental conditions in low-income neighborhoods (e.g., toxic wastes, lead paint, fumes from freeways and streets); targeted marketing of alcohol, tobacco, and other drugs by licit and illicit drug capitalists (e.g., the high frequency of advertisements for malt liquor and menthol cigarettes in Black neighborhoods); and inadequate access to quality and culturally sensitive health care. Hypertension among African Americans, in short, reflects an historic structure of social inequality across multiple life dimensions (e.g., living conditions, working conditions, social treatment, and access to health care) (Brink 2007). Comparison of blood pressure levels among various groups of African descent (people in West Africa, Afro-Caribbeans, Afro-Brazilians, Afro-Europeans, and African Americans in the U.S.) by Dressler (1993), for example, found that the latter group had significantly higher levels, suggesting the importance of social rather than genetic causes.

The second interface of concern is between human society and the physical environment and the ways that this either facilitates or retards the survival, spread, and lethality of pathogens or otherwise impacts the conditions under which humans live, such as the development of highly concentrated, densely packed populations in megacities or the impact of fossil fuel consumption on global warming, air quality, and exposure to toxins. Here too, as seen in previous chapters, this interaction is shaped by social inequality and the unequal distribution of power within and across communities and nations. As a result of this interface over many generations and during a historically growing capacity for human societies to directly and indirectly restructure the nature of nature, the physical environment to which human societies must adapt is a product of past human-environment interactions.

The third interface is between pathogens that evolve to target humans (which historically and with ever-greater frequency jump from other species to humans as we penetrate and reshape and rereshape diverse physical environments) and other health problems (e.g., diabetes, drug addiction, malnutrition), including social conditions and relationships that impact body systems like the immune system (e.g., stress, discrimination, stigmatization, exploitation), as well as access to disease prevention/health promotion services and medical care. This complex of factors drives the emergence of *syndemics*—that is, two or more diseases or other health conditions acting in tandem and which can have greater adverse health impact than the sum of their individual contributions. Syndemics are having increasing effects on human health internationally, especially the health of poor and socially marginalized populations that come to serve as reservoirs of human pathogens.

In addressing the multifaceted consequences of global warming for health, in this and the following three chapters we examine the three interactions described above by considering: 1) the range of risks to health created or enhanced by changing climatic conditions; and 2) the synergistic interactions among diseases produced by a changing climatic, physical, and social environment—which in this volume is termed an *ecosyndemic*—that have the potential for significantly increasing the total disease burden, including both morbidity and mortality, suffered by human populations worldwide.

Assessing the Diseases of Global Warming

Specific questions concerning the consequences of global warming for overall human health and social well-being include the following:

1. What are the subsistence, drinking water, and dietary consequences of global warming generally, including extreme climatic events, such as storm surges, flooding, and drought (addressed in this chapter)?
2. What are the health effects of changing air quality and the extent of air pollution, as well as increasingly frequent heat waves, on respiratory health and related health conditions (addressed in Chapter 4)?
3. What are the health effects of the spread of disease vectors and pathogens caused by global warming (addressed in Chapter 5)?
4. What are the health effects of new disease interactions (addressed in Chapter 6)?

Before beginning this examination, we first speak to the issue of social inequality as a determinant of the differential impact of global warming on human health and disease burden.

Social Inequality, The Diseases of Global Warming, and Social Change

Taken together, the various diseases of global warming appear likely to have a colossal and, barring effective mitigation, ever-increasing impact on human health and well-being. In light of the existing patterns of health inequality, however, the adverse health changes produced by global warming will tend to fall disproportionately on the poor and other disparity populations and groups within and between societies. Some public health experts concerned with health disparities have even cautioned against placing undue attention on the potential health problems associated with global warming as this will detract from a needed focus on the health consequences of existing social inequalities. Such concern, while understandable, is misplaced, as poverty, injustice, and global warming are not exclusive forces; they are likely to interact and worsen the plight of subordinated populations. As Jonathan Patz, a professor at the Gaylord Nelson Institute for Environmental Studies, argues, "climate change is making a bad situation even worse" (quoted in Monastersky 1996:1). Moreover, efforts by people within wealthier countries to adapt (individually) to global warming (e.g., through greater use of air-conditioning) may only exacerbate climate change, increasingly the likelihood that "in developing nations and poor communities [in wealthy countries], the health impacts [will] be significant" (Epstein and Rogers 2004:11).

Moreover, not only is the distribution of disease influenced by social structures, so too is access to knowledge about effective responses to the risks posed by spreading diseases, as well as the resources required to mount successful public health interventions. As Paul Farmer (1995:265), a physician and medical anthropologist, observes, "Those most at risk for emerging . . . diseases generally do not, in fact, have the benefit of cutting-edge scientific knowledge. We live in a world where infections pass easily across borders—social and geographic—while resources, including cumulative scientific knowledge, are blocked at customs." Further, as Farmer (1995:266) stresses, "The study of borders qua borders means, increasingly, the study of social inequalities." Exemplary is the U.S.–Mexico border, which, as Warner (1991) notes, has sharply contrasting patterns of health status, entitlements, and utilization reflecting stark disparities in wealth and resources north and south of the border. In the poignant words of Chicana writer Gloria Anzaldúa (1987), the U.S.–Mexico border is "an open wound where the third world grates against the first and bleeds." Death rates associated with infectious and parasitic diseases, for example, are far higher on the Mexican side of the border. With global warming, spreading infections like dengue and cholera have become major issues of concern along the border (Brandon et al. 1997).

The Food We Eat: Impact of Global Warming on Foraging, Horticulture, Pastoralism, and Agriculture

As stressed by Martin Mittelstaedt (2007), "the place where most of the world's people could first begin to feel the consequences of global warming may come as a surprise: in the stomach, via the supper plate." This is because extreme climate changes are beginning to contribute to deteriorating nutrition and freshwater supplies as a result of the desertification of crop and pastoral areas and the flooding of agricultural zones. Already over three billion people in the world are believed to be malnourished, the largest number and proportion of humans in desperate need of food and nutrients in human history. Inadequate nutrition is the single most important cause of illness and death, contributing annually to 16 percent of life years lost by the world's population and to 12 percent of all deaths (Global Health Watch 2005). Every day almost 800 million people in underdeveloped countries (just under one-fifth of the world's population) go hungry, and food insecurity (the hovering threat of inadequate diet) is widespread across the planet. Southern Asia and sub-Saharan Africa account for a significant proportion of this malnutrition. Moreover, the number of people in the world who are undernourished has been increasing by almost five million a year since the 1990s. A consequent of the growing food challenge faced by the world is that approximately 175 million children are estimated to be underweight. Yet, as Epstein (2000) notes, this number is likely to go up significantly as a consequence of global warming:

> Floods and droughts associated with global climate change . . . could damage crops and make them vulnerable to infection and infestations by pests and choking weeds, thereby reducing food supplies and potentially contributing to malnutrition. And they could permanently or semipermanently displace entire populations in developing countries, leading to overcrowding and the diseases connected with it, such as tuberculosis.

More broadly, Downing (1992) points out,

> The nature and extent of [local food security] risk must be located between the poles of global catastrophe and local resiliency . . . . Climate change is caused by local emissions of greenhouse gases, but embedded in a global economy. The pathways of climate change are clearly global. Equally apparent, unmitigated climate change would have global consequences—adverse impacts on agroecological potential, water resources and health would fuel increased resource conflicts, environmental migration, and international food crises triggered by drought.

Food in Fragile Zones

Global warming has already been having dramatic consequences for the hunting patterns of arctic peoples, perhaps more than any other traditional foraging people. According to Johansen,

> The Arctic's rapid thaw has made hunting, never a safe or easy way of life, even more difficult and dangerous. Hunters in and around Iqaluit [an Inuit community in Nunavut] said that the weather has been seriously out of whack since roughly the middle 1990s. Simon Nattaq, an Inuit hunter, fell through unusually thin ice and became mired in icy water long enough to lose both his legs to hypothermia, one of several injuries and deaths reported around the Arctic recently due to thinning ice. [Johansen 2006a: 289]

In contrast to the past, hunters now tend to hunt in pairs and take extra precaution to test the ice with their harpoons before venturing out in either fall or spring. Inuit hunters report that ivory gulls in the far north Canadian Arctic are disappearing, very likely because the diminishing ice cover has disturbed the gull's habitat (Johansen 2006a:292). The Inuit of western Greenland and Canada's arctic islands who hunt Peary caribou during the summer months have seen a decline in these herds from 26,000 in 1961 to 1,000 in 1997 (Flannery 2005:100). Other mammals, including polar bears, seals, and walruses, upon which the Inuit have long relied, have also become endangered species due to global warming. Indigenous arctic peoples will have to cope with loss of sea ice for hunting and fishing, changed migration routes of animals, coastal erosion due to wave action on ice-free coasts, loss of permafrost, and changes in abundance of traditional food resources on land and in water (Pittock 2005:114–115).

Remote inland foraging communities in the Arctic and subarctic are also under threat from global warming. For example, the Athabaskan village of Huslia, about 200 miles (320 km) west of Fairbanks, has experienced the disappearance of nearby lakes, an important source of fish, due to rising temperatures (Lynas 2004:52–57). Droughtlike conditions have resulted in a decline in the number of ducks, beaver, and muskrat, which traditionally have been importance subsistence items.

Cereal Foods: The Instability of Staples

A particular nutritional threat of global warming is a significant drop in cereal production at lower latitudes, offset only slightly by possible increased cereal crop productivity at mid- to higher latitudes. Cereal crops, like corn, wheat and rice, are particularly sensitive to high temperatures. In tropical and subtropical areas, these crops already are grown at the maximum temperatures that they are able to endure. A rise in temperature associated with global warming is likely to push past their zone of tolerance. Wheat plants that are subject to heat stress lose their capacity to engage in photosynthesis. Computer simulation models programmed with information on changing weather patterns indicate that the richest wheat-growing areas in the fertile zone stretching from Pakistan through Northern India and Nepal to Bangladesh may be decimated by the year 2050, if not sooner. Much of this area will become too hot and dry for wheat production, eliminating a primary food source for 200 million people and putting them at grave nutritional risk. In that wheat is an important part of the diet of one-fifth of the world's population, the potential consequences are momentous. According to Louis Verchot, the lead ecologist at the World Agroforestry Centre in Nairobi,

Kenya, which teaches poor farmers sustainable ways to improve their livelihoods, "The impacts on agriculture in developing countries, and particularly on countries that depend on rain-fed agriculture, are likely to be devastating" (quoted in Mittelstaedt 2007). Already global warming effects have been reported for many developing nations. In 1991 and again in 1994, global warming was responsible for widespread rice crop failures in Indonesia (Buan et al. 1996). During this same period, half of the rice and corn crop losses in the Philippines were due to climate variability (Ebi et al. 2006).

At special risk are subsistence farmers. Worldwide, in the last decade of the 20th century, cropland diminished by 20 percent, while per capita fertilizer production fell by 23 percent and per capita supplies of irrigation water diminished by 12 percent. Moreover, top soil is being lost at a rate that is 10 to 40 times more rapid than the rate of soil renewal. Improvements in biotechnology and other agricultural technologies notwithstanding, available per capital cereal grain levels have been dropping for several decades. As a result, a growing number of researchers believe that global warming will soon lead to a significant net loss of available food (Pimentel et al. 2000). Additionally, flooding and storms can introduce plant diseases that damage food crops. Soybean rust (*Phakopsora pachyrhizi*), a fungal disease of plants, for example, is believed to have been brought to the United States by Hurricane Ivan and was first identified in U.S. soybean fields in 2004. Spread of this blight on a major food cultigen is favored by the warmer, wetter conditions ushered in by global warming. Further, Castello et al. (1999) report finding a virus that attacks tomatoes (*Mosaic tobamovirus*) in 17 ice-core samples taken from glaciers in Greenland. Although entombed in ice for almost 150,000 years, the virus, which has a tough protein coating, was found to be viable upon defrosting. Subsequently, this team (Smith et al. 2004) found other pathogens in ice samples from Greenland, Antarctica, and Siberia, raising concern that the melting of glaciers caused by global warming will unleash ancient plant, animal, or human disease species for which there are no contemporary immunities.

Through its impact on weather extremes, such as the frequency of tropical cyclones and hurricanes, global warming is taking another toll on subsistence farmers. In 1990, for example, Tropical Cyclone Ofa slammed into the Pacific island of Niue and turned a food-exporting nation into a food importer for several years. In 2004, Tropical Cyclone Heta further damaged production on Niue. Similarly, the Caribbean island of Grenada lost ten percent of its gross domestic production to Hurricane Ivan, affecting not only production for local use but export production as well. Because the two main crops exported from Grenada, nutmeg and cocoa, have long gestation periods, even with restoration of cultivated areas, these crops will not begin producing until about 2014. With global warming threatening to accelerate the frequency of violent weather, storm-damaged islands may be hit a second and third time before they can recover from earlier weather events, prolonging and magnifying the damage to subsistence and ways of life (Easterling et al. 2007).

Drought is another treacherous risk to health on island nations. In 1997–1998, for example, Pacific nations faced severe drought conditions. On Palau and Pohnpei in the Federated States of Micronesia, for example, at the height of the drought drinking water was available for only two hours a day. By March of 1998, Palau was reporting the lowest rainfall on record for more than 100 years. Water supplies were almost completely depleted, agricultural production dropped by over 50 percent, there was total destruction of taro patches in several parts of the country, and a number of wildfires burned out of control. In the aftermath of the drought, Tropical Storm Utor caused an additional several million dollars of damage. Other affected nations in the region also suffered significant agricultural losses as well as damaged farmlands and disrupted ecosystems. Moreover, during the drought, pregnant women in Fiji were found to be suffering from drought-related micronutrient deficiencies, particularly in sectors of the island where the lack of water was most intense.

As this account suggests, "the potential impacts [of global warming] are complex and far-reaching [and] the true health burden is rarely appreciated" (Ebi et al. 2006:1959). Aside from the issue of how global warming will affect agricultural productivity, other contemporary factors negatively impacting global agriculture include the conversion of much land to residential, industrial, and commercial uses; the loss of arable land due to soil erosion; and the conversion of much land from the production of grains, much of which is consumed directly by humans, to the production of soybeans, which are converted into soy meal that functions as a protein supplement for livestock and poultry. Of course, the creation of additional agricultural land results from the processes of deforestation and breaking the sod of grasslands and irrigating them, as the latter are generally located in semi-arid areas. Further, as people around the world become more affluent, they tend to consume more and more meat and fish. Conversely, a small but growing segment of people in developed countries are becoming aware that vegetarianism leaves a smaller ecological footprint than does an omnivorous diet. At any rate, an estimated 20 percent of anthropogenic greenhouse emissions come from crop and livestock production, not only from carbon dioxide generated by industrial agriculture but also methane emitted by livestock (Pearson 2002:307).

Hardy (2003) delineates the following agricultural trends as resulting from global warming:

1. an overall shift of growing areas by several 100 kilometers per 1°C (1.8°F) temperature rise, resulting in increasing agricultural productivity in some areas and dramatic decreases in other areas;
2. little negative impact on agricultural production in developed countries of the temperate zone (other evidence, however, does not entirely support this argument and production could vary by location, frequency of storms, and pest abundance); and
3. the most severe negative impact in semi-arid agricultural regions (e.g., sub-Saharan Africa, northern Mexico, the Middle East, Northeast Brazil, and Australia), to the point where agriculture may have to cease in many of these regions.

The UN Food and Agriculture Organization (FAO) has warned that in the 40 poorest developing countries, home to approximately two billion people (450 million of whom are already undernourished), global warming could drastically increase malnourishment (Monbiot 2006:6–7). Researchers at the University of Florida, for example, conducted a study of the impact of rising temperature on rice plants. While rice is extremely hardy, these researchers found that yields of grains declined appreciably with temperature increases (Fountain 2000). Modest temperature increases would result in reduced rice yields of 20 to 40 percent by 2100, whereas larger rises in temperatures could completely halt rice production in many areas. Similarly, the U.S. Academy of Sciences released a research report by a team of nine scientists from China, India, the Philippines, and the U.S. who had measured the impact of rising temperatures on rice yields (Brown 2005). They concluded that yields typically fall by 19 percent for each 1°C rise in temperature during the growing season. Numerous heat waves have lowered grain harvests in key food-producing countries in recent years. This is illustrated by the effects of the record-breaking summer heat wave in Europe in 2003, which shrank harvests in every country from France eastward to Ukraine.

Case Study: Sub-Saharan Africa

Sub-Saharan Africa, a region composed of nearly 50 sovereign states, is particularly at risk for the adverse agricultural effects of global warming. Over 600 million people live in sub-Saharan Africa, and the vast majority of them depend directly on the land and food production for their sustenance. Yet only about six percent of the total landmass is cultivated at any point in time as shifting horticulture is the dominant pattern. According to Lennart Båge, president of the International Fund for Agricultural

Development, "Increasing crop failures and livestock deaths are already imposing high economic losses and undermine food security in parts of sub-Saharan Africa, and they will get far more severe as global warming continues" (quoted in Kenya Environment and Political News 2007).

In its *Special Report on the Regional Impacts of Climate Change: An Assessment of Vulnerability* (Watson et al. 1997), the Intergovernmental Panel on Climate Change emphasized that in this region especially vulnerable populations are small landholder horticulturalists who lack adequate resources, pastoralists, landless rural laborers, and the urban poor. The effect of climate change on small landholders and pastoralists varies depending on how much surplus they are able to produce and the prevailing terms of trade (e.g., between other types of food and livestock) at particular points in time and in specific locations. Subsistence farmers, most of whom are women, currently produce three-quarters of household food, through both field crops and home gardening. Under the impact of climate change, as well as other factors (e.g., soil erosion, fuel wood shortages), per capita food supplies have been steadily dwindling. As Myers and Kent (2001:41) warn, "there could eventually arrive a stage when much larger numbers of people would succumb to terminal malnutrition, precipitating a human tragedy of unprecedented proportions."

Currently, an estimated 200 to 250 million sub-Saharan Africans depend on maize as their staple food. Commonly it is grown in a mixed crop-and-livestock farming system. To assess the effects of global warming on maize production, Peter Jones and Philip Thornton used the most advanced climate-simulation models and data from the IPCC and the FAO to simulate the growth, development, and yield of maize crops over sub-Saharan Africa, Central America, and South America. The results showed an aggregate ten percent decline in yield by 2055 for smallholder rain-fed maize production, representing an annual economic loss of about $2 billion. Even more critical for the poor, this figure masks significant regional and local variation in subsistence farming systems, particularly in the many settings where cured maize stalks are fed to livestock during the dry season. Follow-up research specifically for sub-Saharan Africa, based on projected temperature increases and changes in rainfall patterns (Thorton et al. 2006), indicates that within 50 years the cropping season will shorten. Under one of the study's worst-case scenarios—one in which rapid economic growth and globalization continue to drive significant jumps in temperature—drought will become increasingly more likely by midcentury, causing crop failure and making maize farming untenable in the core maize production areas of eastern and southern Africa. Total annual losses could reach an average of ten million tons, or enough maize to feed 140 million people. According to

Carlos Sere, director of the International Livestock Research Institute in Nairobi (quoted in Hoff 2003), "Less maize means less grain for poor people, less feed for farm animals, and less milk and meat for hungry households. In Africa, animals contribute as much as 80 percent of farm cash income and provide draught power, fuel and credit." As a result, subsistence farmers who are dependent on maize are at grave risk from global warming.

Similarly, pastoralists are at significant risk because of global warming. In northern Kenya, for example, pastoralists lost ten million herd animals to a drought that began in 2003, leaving two-thirds of the population in the Turkana region without a livelihood. Left behind was a barren landscape dotted with the bleached white skeletons of cows and goats. Those who survived were forced to move their shrinking herds great distances to find water, but with dwindling resources inter-group conflicts among herders increased. Pastoralists have little other than their animals to rely on; when their animals die, whole populations are put at risk for survival. As a result, willingness to resort to violence to protect scarce and diminishing resources is high and creates yet another way in which global warming damages human health and well-being.

Reduced food supplies and resulting higher food prices have immediate impact on landless workers as well, individuals and households that are never able to develop much in the way of savings to protect them during difficult times. The IPCC (Watson et al. 1997:189), for example, notes that "a serious impact of climate change might be a decrease of 20 percent in local maize yields," sharply diminishing food supplies for farm laborers. Also at risk are the urban poor, a population that has seen dramatic increases in sub-Saharan Africa in recent years. Global warming is likely to significantly raise the price of food for this population. Many governments in the region, are already weak and staggering under the dual pressures of market globalization and lender-imposed structural adjustment programs, have limited ability to aid the rural or urban poor with food supplies. There are no stored surpluses in many areas nor infrastructural means of distributing them if there were.

Faulty Fixes

One of the technological fixes that has been recommended in some quarters in response both to the carbon dioxide emissions from motor vehicles and the diminishing supply of oil around the world is conversion to ethanol, a mixture of diesel fuel and vegetable products such as corn or sugarcane. More than 70 percent of automobiles sold now in Brazil can operate on ethanol. However, a major shortcoming with using ethanol as a fuel substitute is the incredible amount of land that it requires, meaning less food resources for already malnourished peoples in developing countries, including Brazil. In 2004, 12 percent of the U.S. domestic corn crop went into ethanol production (Working Group on Climate Change and Development 2007:30). Additionally, tropical forests, which play a vital role in reducing carbon dioxide levels, are being cut down to grow fuel crops, while fuel crop production itself adds considerably to the release of further quantities of carbon dioxide into the atmosphere.

Protein at Risk

Beyond direct impact on food crop and animal production capacity, global warming has a direct effect on nutrition through its impact on available protein sources. Thus, it is not only infectious anthroponotic, or human, diseases that are spreading as a result of global warming; zoonotic, or animal, diseases are spreading as well. For example, a devastating, virus-caused African livestock disease has been moving northward since 1998. In 2006, cases of bluetongue were found in the Netherlands, Belgium, Germany, and Luxembourg, contributing to the list of 12 European countries now reporting this disease. During the 1987 Rift Valley fever epidemic in Mauritania, the disease affected sheep, cattle, and other domestic animals, causing both abortions and fatal hepatitis infections (Shope 1992). Other animal diseases, such as Chikungunya, Mayaro, Oropouche, and Rocio, also are spreading to new areas as a result of global warming (Purse et al. 2005).

Another impact of global warming on protein supplies involves ocean and freshwater fish. Fish constitute a vital component of the human diet internationally, although varying considerably by location. Each year, people consume approximately 100 million metric tons of fish, and this food source comprises the primary access to protein for billions of people, including some of the poorest populations. As Brander (2003:43) notes, however, "Most commercial fish stocks are declining globally, due to excessive levels of fishing. In some cases climate change may be a contributory factor." To date, research on this issue has been limited, and findings are not clear-cut because it is difficult to partition the contributions of various causes of the decline of commercial fisheries. What is known is that fish are particularly sensitive to water temperature because, unlike mammals, they cannot regulate their internal body temperature which reflects that of the water around them. Increases in water temperature of as little as 1.8–3.6°F (1–2°C) has been found to cause massive fish kills in tropical aquaculture ponds and shallower pools in both the Amazon River area of South America and the Mekong River of Southeast Asia (Combes 2006). Additionally, as water temperature rises, pathogens that infect fish tend to develop faster and to become more virulent. As a result, fish that are already stressed by warmer water are placed at high risk for disease and death.

Fisheries constitute an especially important food source for island populations and as a consequence "the socio-economic implications of the impact of climate change on fisheries are likely to be important and would exacerbate other anthropogenic stresses such as over-fishing" (Easterling et al. 2007:700). Aaheim and Sygna (2000) examined the possible economic impacts of global warming on island-based tuna fishing and concluded that there is likely to be a decline in the total tuna stock and a migration of tuna species eastwards, making them harder to be reached by smaller boats and less well-funded fishing fleets. Coral reefs and other coastal ecosystems, which are already being severely affected by global warming, are also expected to have a significant impact on fisheries because of their role as breeding grounds (Graham et al. 2006). Moreover, in the South Pacific, rising sea-surface temperatures have been linked to increases in dinoflagellates, tiny organisms that can poison fish, a process known as ciguatera, causing widespread death as well as illness to people who consume infected fish products. In the Indian Ocean, ciguatera poisoning is associated with coral bleaching and dieoff of fish that make their homes in coral environments, known dire products of global climate change.

Additionally, fish that are adapted to living at cooler temperatures, such as salmon, trout, catfish, whitefish, bass, and sturgeon, are unable to reproduce if water temperatures are too high. At warmer temperatures fish become more active, their metabolism speeds up, and they experience an increased need for oxygen intake. Greater oxygen intake increases exposure to pollutants in the surrounding water. While warmwater fish are able to eliminate some pollutants from their bodies, this capacity is less developed in cool-water fish. Thus, fish like artic char that have been exposed to higher temperatures as a result of global warming tend to have heightened body levels of toxins like cadmium and lead. Moreover, available oxygen is used by fish in warmer water to fuel their higher metabolism rates, decreasing energy for growth and reproduction. Also, because less oxygen dissolves in warmer water, fish that normally live in cooler environments have a harder time breathing as water temperature rises.

For all of these reasons, global warming is likely to have a devastating impact on the availability of fish for human consumption. Research on Lake Tanganyika (O'Reilly et al. 2003), a deep-water lake filling the rift valley bordering the Democratic Republic of Congo, Tanzania, Zambia, and Burundi in East Africa, for example, indicates diminishing fish catches tied to warming lake waters. Fish from the lake, approximately

200,000 tons per year, supply between 25 and 40 percent of the animal protein consumed by communities in the surrounding region. It is estimated that as many as ten million local inhabitants depend upon the lake, the second largest source in Africa for freshwater water and food. The study suggests that as water temperatures increase, the fish population will further decline. According to Andrew Cohen of the University of Arizona, who participated in the study, "Our research provides the strongest link to date between long-term changes in lake warming in the tropics, recorded by instruments, and declining productivity of the lake's ecosystem, as seen in sediment cores . . . . This work provides a clear indication of the regional effects of global climate change, and especially global warming, on tropical lake ecosystems" (quoted in National Science Foundation 2003).

Already these effects are being felt by local residents. In the waterside village of Kalalangabo in the impoverished Kigoma region of Tanzania, people fish the lake for dagaa, a tiny nocturnal sardine. Piles of the fish are sold in local markets and are consumed by everyone, even the poorest households. Fisherman from the village paddle their small wooden boats out during the night in search of good fishing spots. They hang kerosene lamps over the sides of the boats, seeking to lure zooplankton, the primary diet of the dagaa. If the zooplankton come to the light, the dagaa follow and are swept up in the fishermen's nets. Each night, thousands of fishermen take to the lake hoping for a good catch. But local fishermen have begun reporting that dagaa catches are dropping. Retired dagaa fisherman Myonge Seph, age 46, who now fixes the cracks in his sons' fishing boats by carefully filling them with small pieces of cotton dipped in bright yellow palm oil, explained to *Living on Earth* reporter Jori Lewis (2006) that it is not as easy as it used to be to catch the prized fish: "Oh, it was so good. When we used to fish with our fathers, it was really good. There were so many dagaa. People could fish five thousand tons. In tons! Back in those days there was so much dagaa . . . . We fish because we have no other job. Our grandfathers fished here. Our fathers fished here." The viability of dagaa fishing for future generations, however, is one more in the long line of risks to human subsistence of global warming.

4

A Disturbed Planet

Heat Stress, Pollutants, and Environmental Diseases

On July 25, 1991, Juan de la Cruz (pseudonym), a 25-year-old Latino farmworker, fell ill suddenly during a day spent picking cantaloupes on a corporate-owned agribusiness farm in the San Joaquin Valley of California (NASD 2002). Cantaloupe harvesting is known to be one of the most arduous agricultural jobs. Usually, the melons are hand-harvested at "full-slip" (when the fruit breaks easily from the vine). Workers begin picking the mature fruit early in the morning once there is sufficient light. They work stooped over, pulling the cantaloupes from vines growing on the ground, and place them in a bag draped over their shoulders. Workers keep picking until their bags are full, at which point they weigh about 50 pounds (23 kg). They then carry their heavy load to a collecting truck that slowly drives through the field alongside each crew of workers. Cantaloupe workers are paid on a per-piece basis, with a day's wages being determined by how many trucks a crew of 10 to 15 workers loads in a day. After the picking crews begin working, they continue without breaks until midday. When the trucks reach the end of a melon row, it takes several minutes for them to turn around, during which workers drink water and rest their increasingly weary backs. The day is long, the work is taxing, and the rewards are limited. Among the most economically disadvantaged groups of workers in the United States, farmworkers have elevated rates of work-related injuries, suffer from pesticide exposure, and are burdened with numerous infectious and degenerative diseases. Environmental health problems are frequent among farmworkers. On the morning of July 25, the day that Juan fell ill, the ambient temperature was 70°F (20°C) with a relative humidity of 70 to 80 percent. By noon, the temperature had climbed to 95°F (35°C). Ultimately, it reached a high of 101°F (38°C) with a relative humidity of about 25 percent. These conditions created significant risk for heat-related illness.

At approximately 9:00 a.m., Juan told his foreman that he was suffering from a headache and generally was not feeling well. He was perspiring heavily and requested an aspirin. Afterward, however, he went back to work for another hour before completing the harvesting in the field he was in and walking to the bus with his fellow crew mates so that they could be taken to a new field to resume working. On the bus, Juan became severely ill. His symptoms included anxiousness, nausea, and shortness of breath. The workers on the bus became alarmed. The driver stopped when he spotted a county road-maintenance crew, and one of the road-workers called a local emergency medical service. The caller was told to put Juan in the shade of a tree and to wait for the arrival of an ambulance, which took about 20 minutes. When they arrived, the paramedics found that Juan was disoriented, hyperventilating, and vomiting. He was hoisted into the ambulance and taken to an emergency room, arriving almost one and a half hours after the call was placed to the EMS. Seeing his obvious distress, hospital staff quickly admitted Juan and found that he had a body temperature of 105.6°F. Additionally, he was suffering from metabolic encephalopathy (abnormality of brain function) and seizure disorder. He was placed on a ventilator but developed renal failure and pneumonia. He died about 35 hours later. The cause of death was listed by the coroner as complications of hyperthermia (heat stroke) with acute bronchopneumonia. Juan's brother, who had been working with him that day in the cantaloupe field, took Juan's body home to Mexico for burial. With little protection or political power, Juan's case joined those of many other farmworkers who are injured or die on the job as a result of workplace exposure to hazardous conditions. Juan's specific problem, hyperthermia triggered by body exertion at heightened temperature, in addition to being a specific risk for farm labor, has become a dangerous and increasingly frequent disease of global warming. This and related health threats of extreme weather are the focus of this chapter.

Living in a Warming Environment: Heat Exhaustion and Stroke

Despite significant cultural ability to adapt to diverse climatic conditions, human health and well-being are significantly linked to air temperature. When the body's core temperature goes above its comfort zone (around 98.6°F), veins and capillaries expand, the heart begins to beat faster, and blood flows to the outer layers of skin, releasing heat to the cooler external environment. If this method does not adequately cool the body, the brain signals glands in the skin to release sweat. Evaporation of the sweat pulls additional heat from the body core. At high temperatures, especially when the body is working hard, these body-cooling mechanisms may be inadequate, as was the case with Juan. During the 2007 Chicago Marathon, for example, on a day when temperatures soared to 88°F (31°C) with high humidity, 300 runners required medical attention, one of whom died, and organizers were forced to shut down the second half of the race four hours after it began. The heat spell that engulfed Chicago struck the eastern half of the U.S., setting new records in more than 30 cities (O'Driscoll 2007).

Studies show that heat-related mortality rates are generally lowest at a mean daily temperature of 66°F (19°C), although the exact rates vary by region. As the temperature either rises above or falls below that mark, the rate of mortality increases. As Keatinge and Donaldson (2004) point out, the number of excess deaths annually beyond those expected at 66°F per year provides a useful measure of both heat-related and cold-related mortality rates.

There is a continuum of health problems caused by exposure to excessive heat, ranging from benign disorders like heat cramps involving muscular spasms due to salt deficiency, often brought on by exercising; to heat syncope, which involves fainting caused by peripheral vasodilatation; to more debilitating conditions like heat exhaustion involving dehydration, weakness, and possibly nausea and vomiting, although the core body temperature may not be elevated and tissue damage does not occur; to a severely life-threatening condition called heat stroke. The latter is characterized by raised core body temperature above 104°F (40°C) and neurological dysfunction (Grogan and Hopkins 2002). Even with medical intervention to lower body temperature, more than 50 percent of heat stroke victims die within a short period after onset.

Heat stroke is not new to medicine, as there are historical records documenting the condition that go back several centuries (Contenau 1954). During the time of the Roman Empire, the disease was described among soldiers and there was even a recommended treatment, namely drinking olive oil mixed with wine while rubbing these liquids on the body surface. During the Middle Ages, physicians recommended stimulating friction on the skin and bloodletting as effective methods for releasing heat from the body during heat-related health events. In the 18th century, heat stroke was thought to be caused by drinking cold water, and public water pumps often bore signs warning drinkers about the risk of sudden death from drinking cold water on a hot day (Casa et al. 2007). The systematic scientific record on heat stroke dates to 1743, when over 10,000 people in China died in a single month during a hot-weather spell (Sharma 2005).

With global warming, the health risks of hyperthermia and heat-related health problems have begun to mount and to attract worldwide medical attention (Sharma 2005). In 1995, for example, Chicago experienced a summer heat wave—one of the deadliest in U.S. history—that killed at least 700 people, more than twice the number that perished in the famous Chicago Fire of 1871. City streets buckled under the punishing heat, records for greatest volume of electrical use on a single day were shattered, and power grids in the city failed, cutting residents off from the electricity used to power their fans and air conditioners (Whitman et al. 1997).

Misery caused by the Chicago heat wave was not equally distributed, however. Some neighborhoods suffered far greater loss of life than did others. Klinenberg (2002) used fieldwork, structured interviews, and archival research to develop a "social autopsy" of the Chicago heat wave. Based on this research, he argues that several social breakdowns, including the communal and physical isolation of seniors, the institutional desertion of poor neighborhoods, and the reduction of clients being served by public assistance programs, all directly contributed to the high fatality rate and to the specific pattern of death across the city.

In 2006, a heat wave spread across North America, resulting in the deaths of over 200 people. In parts of Canada, especially in provinces along the U.S. border like Saskatchewan, Manitoba, Ontario, and Quebec, persistent heat developed as the month of July progressed into August. Withering heat and drought had hit this region during the summers of 2002, 2003, and 2005, although large, frequent storms dropped above-normal quantities of rain on parts of Ontario and Quebec during these weather events. By mid-July 2006, temperatures soared to 107.8°F (42.1°C) in some places. Winnipeg, Manitoba, for example, experienced the highest average maximum temperature of any July on record. In Val Marie, Saskatchewan, the average daily maximum July temperature was 90.2°F (32.3°C), about 9°F (5°C) higher than average. Similarly, on August 1, the nighttime minimum temperature in Toronto was the highest ever recorded. Record levels of power consumption occurred in Ontario during this period as people attempted to battle the exhausting heat with air-conditioning. Power consumption reached 26,854 megawatts by midday, beating the previous record by an amount sufficient to light up a city the size of London. To limit heat-related health problems, the City of Toronto was forced to open a number of public cooling stations, although only after first resisting this measure (Crowe 2006). But community activists, some of whom referred to the heat wave as "our silent Katrina," complained that not enough was being done to aid the poor. Tom Cooper, a community development coordinator at McQueston Legal and Community Services in Hamilton, reported:

> We've seen rooming houses where windows don't open, where the air doesn't circulate. A lot of these places become very hot during the day and cool down very slowly. We've heard about homeless people who get escorted out of local (air-conditioned) malls by security guards who think they're loitering. This affects people who are elderly, living in poor housing or have mental health problems. [Quoted in Dunphy 2006:1]

Broader research that reflects on Cooper's concerns was conducted on four urban areas in southern Ontario over a 17-year period from 1980 to 1996. The study recorded between 8,000 and 10,000 deaths due to heat-related causes at times when the air temperatures climbed above 90°F (32°C) (Smoyer et al. 2000). Researchers examined the association of demographic, socioeconomic, and housing factors with heat-related mortality. Among the elderly, for example, mortality was found to be significantly higher on heat-stress days compared to non-heat-stress days (i.e., below 90°F/32°C) in all but one of the cities in the study (also see MacKenbach et al. 1997).

As the 2006 heat wave continued, the weather became more varied. On July 17 and July 30, respectively, major thunderstorms hit Ontario and Quebec. Over 450,000 people lost power in Quebec during the storm. On August 2, a vicious storm caused heavy damage across central and eastern Ontario. Eight tornadoes were confirmed in the region, the largest single-day tornado outbreak in Ontario since 1985. This series of storms killed at least four people and injured many others while causing extensive property damage and destroying forested areas. After August, however, temperatures across most of the region returned to normal. Responding to the impact of the heat wave, Dan Lashoff, science director at the Natural Resources Defense Council's Climate Center observed, "This is exactly the kind of event we expect to see more frequently due to global warming" (quoted in Ocampo 2006).

In all, during the summer of 2006, 780 Canadians, mostly elderly individuals but infants as well, died from direct heat causes. In addition, there were approximately 400 indirect casualties, such as several people who drowned trying to escape the oppressive heat. The greatest number of heat deaths, nearly 600 people, was in Ontario (Weather Almanac 2006).

In response to changing weather conditions, in the year 2000, Environment Canada's Meteorological Service launched the Canadian Natural Hazards Assessment Project in collaboration with the Office of Critical Infrastructure Protection and Emergency Preparedness, the Institute for Catastrophic Loss Reduction, several private insurance companies, teams of emergency responders, and a number of scholars and engineers. The project collected and analyzed historic and contemporary weather data and began issuing technical reports for policy makers and the general public. One of the conclusions of the project concerns the growing frequency of weather-related disasters:

> Over the past decade, Canada has experienced many of its largest natural disasters, and experts believe that even bigger and more devastating ones are inevitable. While geophysical disasters, such as earthquakes, have remained relatively constant in this country over the past 50 years, weather-related disasters have skyrocketed. Climate change is projected to exacerbate this

situation in the future, as it is expected to increase the frequency and severity of some extreme weather events. [Environment Canada 2003]

Looking to the future effects of global warming, Environment Canada (2004) further reported that barring very successful mitigation efforts to lower greenhouse gas production: "Due to the increasing impacts of climate change, heat-related deaths in Canada [will] increase dramatically in the 21st century. By the 2050s, . . . heat-related deaths [will] more than double and by the 2080s, the deaths [will] triple in South Central Canada."

Even more dramatic than the impact of changing weather on Canada during the year 2006 were events in Europe three years earlier. During the summer of 2003, much of Europe was hit by a massive heat wave that drove temperatures as much as 50°F (10°C) above average for a blistering ten-day period. In France, temperatures climbed to about 104°F (40°C), resulting in approximately 15,000 deaths nationally, 1,000 of them in Paris alone (Kalkstein et al. 2007). In the United Kingdom, an air-temperature record (a record that for central England dates to 1659) was set on August 10, as the 100°F (37.5°C) mark was breached for the first time, and at Brogdale in Kent temperatures reached 101.3°F (38.5°C).

Many people were caught offguard, especially the sick and elderly, including people who were hospitalized for other conditions. Throughout Europe, it is estimated that the deaths of at least 35,000 people during the heat wave were associated not only with sustained high temperatures during the daylight hours but also by that fact that nighttime low temperatures rose nearly twice as fast as daytime temperatures. The lingering nighttime warmth deprived people of normal relief from blistering daytime heat and the opportunity to recuperate from heat-related physical stress. It has been estimated that by the year 2020, the number of deaths related to heat waves will double beyond current levels because of global warming (Epstein 2002b).

These events in Europe were not a one-time occurrence. Extreme heat struck the continent again in 2006 with near-record temperatures on some days, reviving the spectre of the 2003 heat wave. In the U.K., temperatures on buses in the hottest parts of the country were record at 126°F (52°C), and temperatures in the London subway system reached 117°F (47°C) in some places. Overall for the month of July, a new record was set in the south of London when temperatures hit 97.34°F (36.3°C), surpassing an earlier high set in 1911. According to Peter Stott of the U.K. Met Office's Hadley Centre for Climate Prediction and Research:

We think by 2040, a summer like 2003 will be a regular event; the chances of it happening will increase from one in 250 all the way to one in two. . . . We have an increasing amount of confidence that we are observing rising temperatures caused by human-induced rising greenhouse-gas concentrations. Unless the world changes what it is doing, we are going to see these extreme temperatures very much more. [Quoted in McCarthy 2006]

There is growing concern among health experts that rising temperatures present a perilous threat to people with heart problems, especially the elderly or those with certain heart diseases. According to Dr. Gordon Tomasilli, chief of cardiology at Johns Hopkins University, the primary risk is atherosclerosis, or hardening of the arteries. Notes Tomascilli, "Rust develops much more quickly at warm temperatures and so does atherosclerosis" (quoted in Environmental News Network 2007). To release heat from the body through the skin, the heart must beat at a faster rate while blood pressure drops, a dangerous combination for people with fragile cardiovascular systems. Pollution, another product of global warming, increases the risk for people with cardiovascular difficulties. Additionally, escalating the flow of blood to the body's surface reduces the amount of oxygen received by the brain, the muscles, and other body organs. This loss creates a sense of fatigue while diminishing mental alertness. Sweating also contributes to fatigue because it increases blood viscosity, making it harder for the heart to pump efficiently. Finally, because sweating for a period of time depletes electrolytes that are needed by the body for muscle functioning, it contributes to muscle cramping. While there remain many uncertainties in the connection between global warming and heart disease, the age patterns of people already succumbing to current prolonged heat waves, such as during 2003 in Europe, affirms the concerns of physicians like Tomasilli.

A full assessment of the role of global warming on the frequency and intensity of heat waves has been encumbered by disagreements among scientists about the precise nature of this climatic event. A starting definition of a heat wave is an unusually prolonged period of particularly high climate-related heat stress that both leads to temporary modifications in human activity and produces adverse health effects for the local population. As Robinson (2001) points out, however, assessment of the impact of global warming on the frequency of heat waves has been hindered by a lack of a clear, rigorous definition of this climatic episode that does not make reference to human impact and response. Additionally, until recently, there was no simple meteorological index of the complex interactions that take place between the human body and the thermal environment.

Human thermoregulation is designed to maintain a constant core body temperature. This necessitates the elimination of internal heat generated by metabolism, a process that primarily involves the transfer of heat from the body to the surrounding atmosphere through the skin, as well as, but to a much lesser degree, by the lungs. If the temperature level of the atmosphere is high enough to hinder the loss of excess body heat, the core temperature rises, producing various health problems and eventually death, although at what atmospheric temperature these events occur varies depending on individual vulnerability.

It is evident that urban environments, with their large populations and often significantly concentrated impoverished sectors, and pre-existing high rates of pollution and other threats to health, are at particular risk for the heat effects of global warming (Kalkstein and Scott 2007). This is true for another reason as well. Extreme heat, and its resulting adverse health outcomes, are exacerbated by what has been called the "urban heat island effect." This term refers to the climatic effects of urbanization, namely that cities tend to be warmer than the surrounding less densely urbanized areas, especially at night (Comrie 2007). Compared to their hinterlands, cities have "fewer winter frosts, an earlier thermal springtime, and higher overnight minimum temperatures in summer. Depending on the city and humidity levels, the latter can reduce the relief from daytime high temperatures and increase weather stress" (Comrie 2007:331).

Applied climate meteorologists Laurence Kalkstein and J. Scott Greene (2007) have calculated current and projected (for the years 2020 and 2050) heat-wave deaths in the larger cities of the U.S. Midwest based on analysis of three established climate models: the United Kingdom Meteorological Model, the Global Fluid Dynamics Laboratory Model, and the Max Planck Institute for Meteorology Model. While they concluded that the number of lives spared because of warmer winters would be negligible, the number of lives lost due to hotter summers would be significant in a number of cities as reported in Table 5 below.

Table 5. Heat-Wave Deaths in U.S. Midwestern Cities Related to Global Warming

City	Current Deaths in Present Climate	Year 2020 Climate Average Deaths	Year 2050 Climate Average Deaths
Buffalo, NY	33	34.3	55.3
Chicago, IL	191	400.7	497.3
Cleveland, OH	29	39	52.3
Detroit, MI	110	162.7	219
Indianapolis, IN	36	55.7	70
Kansas City, MO	49	115	127.3
Minneapolis, MN	59	129.3	174.7
Pittsburgh, PA	39	54	79.7
St. Louis, MO	79	160	185.3

As noted, at greatest risk are those already suffering from cardiovascular and respiratory disease, but also the very young, the elderly and frail, the poor (because they are more likely to lack the resources to escape the effects of rising temperature through air-conditioning or other costly strategies), and narcotic drug addicts (because drugs that block the activity of parasympathetic nerves impair sweating and other anatomical coping responses to heat exposure). Heat stress, in other words, constitutes a "last straw" of additional pressure on vulnerable groups with other significant health problems (Comrie 2007).

Living conditions are also critical to the impact of rising temperature. An example of particularly harsh conditions is seen in the community of Cité Soleil on the northern edge of Port-au-Prince, the capital of Haiti. Approximately three square miles (5 km2) in size, this community was estimated to house as many as 400,000 people in the mid-1990s, although reliable population estimates are hard to make because of frequent migration in and out of the area. As Maternowska (2006:3) observes, "No one really wants to live in Cité Soleil. It is noisy, dirty, politically turbulent, and violent, but it offers cheap housing, the cheapest in all of the capital." While there are large houses on the central avenue, off the main road the dirt streets are "crowded by thousands of tiny shacks situated near dumping areas, open sewers, and putrid-smelling canals." In addition, it is very hot: "During the dry season, the sun beats down so hard that the earth cracks." Almost all roofs are made of tin, which traps the heat "and makes the homes feel like ovens." Under such conditions, morbidity and mortality rates are already sky high. As the residents say in Creole: "*Ah . . . n ap peri*" ("Ah, we're perishing"). With the advance of global warming, producing increasing heat and more intense storms, conditions are likely to only get worse, much worse. Already barely habitable, Cité Soleil may well cross the line beyond which even the narrowest basis for survival is lost. Even in a poor country like Haiti, the wealthy are likely to feel only limited effects of global warming. In a pinch, it is always possible for the wealthy of Port-au-Prince to fly to Paris, Miami, or New York to escape rising summer heat. The poor, by contrast, literally are imprisoned and, if the heat goes up, condemned to sicken and die. In short, it is the poor who will feel the heat of global warming to a far greater degree than the wealthy, although it is the latter who have contributed far more to its development.

Storms

It is evident that storms linked to global warming can cause an array of diseases. Identifying the range of health problems associated with acute storms is critical because United Nations analysts predict that by the year 2010, as many as 50 million people will be displaced by storms and environmental disasters, many of them tied to global warming. In fact, it is possible that "despite the catastrophic destruction wreaked by Hurricane Katrina and subsequent Hurricane Rita, these effects may be minor compared to the devastation caused by future hurricanes" (Petterson et al. 2006). Exemplary of the future of storm-related health problems is Hurricane Ivan, an incredibly powerful storm that directly or indirectly killed at least 70 people in the Caribbean and another 50 in the southern United States in 2004 during its 12-day rampage.

Ivan developed began as a large tropical wave that moved off the west coast of Africa on August 3, 2004. At its height, the stormed reached Category 5 status on the Saffir-Simpson Hurricane Scale, a rating tool used to assess and rank the power of hurricanes on a grid between 1 and 5. Wind speed is the determining factor in the scale. Category 5 hurricanes, which are termed "Catastrophic," achieve a sustained wind speed above 155 miles (250 km) an hour. The top speed for Ivan's winds was 200 miles (320 km) an hour, winning it the title of the worst storm of the season and the sixth most powerful hurricane on record in the Atlantic Basin, and ninth in terms of its drop in central pressure (see Table 6), although its place was overtaken by Hurricane Dean in 2007. At its peak while still in the Gulf of Mexico, Ivan was as big as the state of Texas. Upon landfall in Gulf Shores, Alabama. it spawned 117 tornadoes in nine states. Three of the most devastating of these hit the towns of Blountstown, Marianna, and Panama City Beach in Florida.

Some of the worst destruction caused by Ivan occurred on the Caribbean island of Grenada, which, in the words of a Caribbean disaster official, suffered "total devastation." Heavy rainfall exceeding ten inches caused extensive freshwater flooding; roads were blocked by fallen utility poles

Table 6. The Ten Most Intense Atlantic Basin Hurricanes (Based on Drop in Central Pressure) 1851–2005

	Hurricane	Year	Minimum Pressure
1	Hurricane Wilma	2005	882 mb
2	Hurricane Gilbert	1988	888 mb
3	The Labor Day Hurricane	1935	892 mb
4	Hurricane Rita	2005	895 mb
5	Hurricane Allen	1980	899 mb
6	Hurricane Katrina	2005	902 mb
7	Hurricane Camille	1969	905 mb
8	Hurricane Mitch	1998	905 mb
9	Hurricane Ivan	2004	910 mb
10	Hurricane Janet	1955	914 mb

Source: U.S. Department of Commerce 2006.

and trees. Thirty-nine people were killed on the island and the capital city of St. George's was severely damaged. At least 80,000 island residents were left without power and more than 14,000 homes were damaged or destroyed. Several key buildings were ruined, including the residence of the prime minister. An eye-witness in St. George's reported

The weather was fair with some rain and mild to moderate gusts until about 1400, then Ivan arrived with a fury I hope never to see again. As the wind intensified the boats would swing in 180-degree arcs, and several began dragging anchor. Two people were seen fending off each others' boats and trying to reset their anchors as the full brunt of the storm hit. The front-side wind came directly down the lagoon, and visibility was reduced to 50 feet at most. All that could be seen were part of houses and roofs flying by. As the eye passed over, visibility improved and we could see that very few boats were left at anchor. [Caribbean Compass 2004]

Most government ministries and public services were paralyzed for several days immediately following the hurricane, furthering local suffering. Food shortages were still being reported weeks after Ivan had passed. Extensive looting occurred in the aftermath of the storm, contributing further to the scope of economic losses. The agricultural sector was devastated. Of gravest concern was the destruction of cash crops (e.g., nutmeg production, which accounts for 80 percent of agricultural exports). Prior to Ivan, the poverty rate in Grenada was estimated at 32 percent, with approximately 13 percent of the population living in extreme poverty. Before the storm hit, Grenada's economy had been projected to grow by 4.7 percent; instead it contracted by nearly 3 percent in 2004. The storm left behind devastating scenes of destruction and despair, with half of island residents left homeless, most jobless, and the economy in shambles.

Another important impact of global warming, as seen in several of the examples presented earlier, is parching due to inadequate rainfall. The threat of parching is not only loss of habitable and cultivatable land but also its impact on prevailing weather patterns. As Epstein (2000) observes, "Parching enlarges the pressure gradients that cause winds to develop, leading to turbulent winds, tornadoes and other powerful storms."

Troubled Air: Global Warming and Respiratory Problems

Ozone

The natural layer of ozone in the upper atmosphere, what is sometimes referred to as the "ozone shield," is considered to have been a critical force in allowing the evolution of life on earth because it blocks harmful ultraviolet radiation from reaching the surface of the planet and the species that dwell there, including humans. One effect of global climate change, however, is an increase in ozone (O3) concentration at lower atmospheric levels. This occurs because the chemical reactions that create ozone from its precursor substances—emitted especially by cars, power plants, industrial boilers, refineries, and chemical factories—proceed at a quicker pace at higher temperatures and in the presence of sunlight. This development has the opposite effect on planetary life than upper atmosphere ozone; at ground level, ozone is a harmful pollutant. It damages lung tissue (especially the cells that line air spaces in the lung), causes air passage inflammation, increases sensitivity to allergens, reduces the volume of air taken in during a full breath, and slows the speed of exhale, creating a mounting threat to people already suffering from asthma or other lung diseases such as emphysema and bronchitis. Among otherwise healthy individuals, even modest exposure to ozone can cause chest pains, nausea, and pulmonary congestion. Children are particularly sensitive to the damaging effects of ozone because they commonly spend more time outdoors than adults, take in more air than adults proportionate to their body weight, and are more likely to have asthma. Similarly, research has shown that ozone exposures are associated with poorly controlled asthma among the elderly (Meng et al. 2007). Additionally, there is growing evidence that living in communities with comparatively lower income increases the vulnerability of residents to air pollution (Cakmak et al. 2006).

Beyond damage to the lungs, ozone exposure weakens the immune system—especially those components involved in antibacterial host defense, such as effective phagocyte elimination of microbial pathogens—diminishing the body's natural capacity to fight infections (Hollingsworth et al. 2007), a significant loss in a time of increased pathogenic exposure. Research in 12 French cities during the 2003 heat wave on the dual effects on mortality of high daily temperature and peak ozone found that elevated minimum and maximum temperature and ozone all increased mortality, with a considerable degree interaction effects between temperature and ozone (Dear et al. 2005). These results suggest that ozone will be an important contributor to adverse health outcomes as global warming causes longer, more intense, and more widespread high-ozone periods each year (Firor and Jacobson 2002, Knowlton et al. 2004).

Dust

In the summer of 1936, the U.S. and Canada were hit by a major drought. Three-quarters of both countries were in great need of rain. In some parts of the U.S., such as the central Great Plains, the drought was particularly harsh. In Oklahoma, for example, the precipitation level for August was only seven percent of normal. As a result of the drought, the prairie soil dried out and turned to dust, which was blown away in large black clouds by eastward winds. At times the dust storms blackened the sky. There were 68 such storms recorded in 1936 and 72 the following year (Weather Almanac 2006). This climatic and environmental disaster forced an exodus of people, especially poor and working people from Texas, Arkansas, Oklahoma, and the surrounding Great Plains area, as over half a million people were left homeless (Egan 2006).

The events of 1936 are noteworthy because the potential impact of global warming on dust pollution has not been well explored. In areas without an increase in rainfall, the dryer conditions and soil desiccation produced by global warming will increase the concentration of dust blown into the lower atmosphere. For people living on the islands of the Caribbean, for example, clouds of dust that have their origin in the expanding deserts of Africa, and are blown by trade winds across the ocean, have become a respiratory irritant. Particulate pollution has been linked by the American Lung Association (2007) to a range of health threats, including asthma, chronic bronchitis, decreased lung function, and premature death.

Allergens

Another effect of a warming climate is that pollen production is going up, triggered by higher levels of carbon dioxide in the air. Tests on ragweed (Ambrosia artemisiifolia), a potent producer of pollen allergens and the main trigger for hay fever, indicate heightened levels of carbon dioxide produce taller plants, greater biomass, and more pollen. For example, in 2001 Lewis Ziska, a plant physiologist at the U.S. Department of Agriculture, planted ragweed at three sites in Maryland. These "ragweed farms" all had the same soil, were planted with the same batch of seeds, and were watered using common schedules and quantities (Ziska et al. 2003). The sites differed, however, by location; one was an urban site, a second was located in a suburban area, and the final site was rural. Ziska and co-workers found that the city plants were larger, flowered earlier, and produced five times as much pollen as those planted at the rural site. Moreover, they had a higher level of toxicity. They concluded that two factors accounted for these differences: the city plants experienced warmer temperatures and were exposed to 20 percent more carbon dioxide. Studies like this confirm that carbon dioxide turbocharges the growth of plants whose pollen triggers allergies, while warmer weather prolongs the period of pollen production. Other research shows that ragweed plants normally produce one billion pollen grains per season. When exposed in the laboratory to double the normal level of carbon dioxide, they produce 61 percent more pollen (Wayne et al. 2002).

At the same time, global warming already is contributing to early bud bursts in the spring and to the spread of pollen-producing weeds. Over the past three decades, allergy-causing trees have been releasing pollen one to two weeks earlier than in the past. Further, in recent years plants like ragweed have been showing up in new places. While uncommon in Europe in the past, since the turn of the 21st century it has been seen in Eastern Europe, particularly Hungary, but also in Italy and France and further north in Scandinavia. More generally, the conditions of global warming, especially increases in carbon dioxide levels, have been found to support the expansion of various invasive and opportunistic weedy species of plants, including Canada thistle (Cirsium arvense), field bind-weed (Convolvulus arvensis), leafy spurge (Euphorbia esula), perennial sowthistle (Sonchus arvensis), spotted knapweed (Centaurea maculosa), and yellow star thistle (Centaurea solstitialis) (Ziska 2003). Overall, an emergent pattern is that global warming favors quick-growing plants like weeds and is a threat to slower-growing species. Species with longer life cycles have fewer generations and take longer to evolve, making them less adaptive to rapidly changing conditions. In short, with global warming, weeds win and people suffer the consequences.

Asthma on the Rise

As a result of the floral changes described above, another significant health consequence of global warming is an escalation in rates of allergies and asthma. Currently, allergic diseases constitute the sixth leading cause of chronic illness in the United States, affecting the lives of 17 percent of the population. Asthma, characterized by episodic inflammation and narrowing of small airway passages in the lungs, affects about eight percent of the U.S. population, but the rate of affected individuals has been steadily climbing in recent years, especially in low-income, ethnic minority neighborhoods in cities. Thus, in 1980 asthma was found to affect only about three percent of the U.S. population according to the U.S. Centers for Disease Control and Prevention (Akinbami 2006). Asthma among children has been increasing at an even faster pace than among adults, with the percentage of children with asthma going up from 3.6 percent in 1980 to 9 percent in 2005. Among Puerto Ricans, for example, the rate of asthma is 125 percent higher than for non-Hispanic white people and 80 percent higher than non-Hispanic black people. The asthma prevalence among American Indians, Alaska Natives, and African Americans is 25 percent higher than white people

(Akinbami 2006). As is so often the case with health, including health conditions directly affected by global warming, the poor and marginalized suffer the gravest consequences.

A number of developed countries have levels of asthma that are even greater than those in the U.S., such as Australia in which 13 percent of the population are affected, and New Zealand, which has the highest incidence at 20 percent. Asthma is far less common in developing countries, as would be expected given the role of industrial pollutants in triggering this condition, with rates in sub-Saharan Africa and the Indian subcontinent at approximately three percent, mostly in urban populations. In Kenya, for example, asthma is virtually unknown in rural areas, but it is increasing among city-dwellers.

The people of the Tokelau Islands (formerly the Union Islands) in the South Pacific constitute an important case study of changing patterns of asthma in developing countries in light of global warming. Tokelau is a colonial territory of New Zealand consisting of three coral atolls, Fakaofo, Nukunonu, and Atafu, arrayed in a line running southeast to northwest midway between Hawaii and New Zealand. Together they comprise a land area of less than five square miles (8 km2). The population of Tokelau is poor, with an average annual purchasing power per capita of approximately $1,000 (Parker 2006). Tokelau lacks cars and industrial production, although it does have electricity and land-line telephones. On Fakaofo, there is so little liveable space that its small domestic pig population lives on a low-lying coral shelf that falls largely underwater at high tide. Asthma was unknown in Tokelau before March 2005 (Wessen 1992), when Cyclone Percy slammed into the atolls. Stronger than it was expected to be and of longer duration, the cyclone submerged villages on Fakaofo and Nukunonu under three feet of seawater, causing significant erosion, damaging roads, disrupting power, and washing away banana, coconut, and pandanus crops. Much of the population was forced to evacuate to New Zealand. In the aftermath of the move, asthma began to show up among Tokelauan children living in Wellington. Movement of Tokelauans to New Zealand has continued, and they now constitute the sixth largest Pacific ethnic group in the country and account for three percent of New Zealand's Pacific population, suggesting they may constitute a growing population at risk for the development of climate-related asthma (Statistics New Zealand 2007).

Increases in rates of asthma around the world have occurred despite improvements in air quality produced by the passage and enforcement of clean air legislation, such as the Clean Air Acts of 1963 and 1990 in the United States. In other words, existing legislation and regulation have not kept pace with changing climatic conditions and their health consequences. Compounding the problem of air quality is the fact that airborne pollens have been found to attach themselves to diesel particles from truck or other vehicular exhaust floating in the air, resulting in heightened rates of asthma in areas where busy roads bisect densely populated areas, most notably in poorer inner-city areas. Research by the American Cancer Society (Abrahamowicz et al. 2003) found that a six percent increase in cardiopulmonary deaths occurs for every elevation of 10 µg/m3 in particulate matter concentration in the air. Exhaust from the burning of diesel fuel is a complex mixture of vapors, gases, and fine particles, including over 40 known pollutants like nitrogen oxide and known or suspected carcinogenic substances such as benzene, arsenic, and formaldehyde. Exposure to diesel exhaust irritates the eyes, nose, throat, and lungs, causing coughs, headaches, lightheadedness, and nausea, and also causing people with allergies to be more susceptible to allergy triggers like dust or pollen. Many particles in disease fuel are so tiny they are able to penetrate deep into the lungs when inhaled. Importantly, diesel fuel particles appear to have even greater immunologic effects in the presence of environmental allergens than they do alone (Diaz-Sanchez et al. 1997). As Pandya et al. (2002) indicate, "This immunologic evidence may help explain the epidemiologic studies indicating that children living along major trucking thoroughfares are at increased risk for asthmatic and allergic symptoms and are more likely to have objective evidence of respiratory dysfunction."

Importantly, the damaging effects of diesel fuel pollution appear to go beyond playing a synergistic role in the development of asthma. Recent research suggests that exposure to a combination of microscopic diesel fuel particles among people with high blood cholesterol (i.e., low-density lipoprotein, LDL, or "bad cholesterol") increases the risk for both heart attack and stroke significantly above levels found among those exposed to only one of these health risks (Gong et al. 2007). According to André Nel, chief of nanomedicine at the David Geffen School of Medicine at UCLA, who led the study of duel exposure, "When you add one plus one, it normally totals two. . . . But we found that adding diesel particles to cholesterol fats equals three. Their combination creates a dangerous synergy that wreaks cardiovascular havoc far beyond what's caused by the diesel or cholesterol alone" (Environment News Service 2007). The synergy begins when free radical molecules that are attached to diesel exhaust particles enter the body through the lungs and pass into the circulatory system. Another source is the fatty acids that comprise LDL cholesterol, which produce free radicals during cell metabolism. Free radical molecules are highly unstable because they have an odd number of electrons in their outer ring. As a result, they react quickly with other compounds in order to "steal" an electron and gain stability. When the "victimized" molecule loses its electron, it in turn becomes a free radical, and a chain reaction called oxidation is produced that is known to be damaging to living cells and tissues. Of interest to the Los Angeles research team was the consequences of both sources of free radical production coming into contact. Experiments revealed that the two mechanisms worked in tandem to stimulate genes that promote cell inflammation, a primary risk for hardening and blockage of blood vessels (atherosclerosis) and, as narrowed arteries collect cholesterol deposits and trigger blood clots, for heart attacks and strokes as well. Atherosclerotic cardiovascular disease is the leading cause of death in developed countries.

Another exacerbating effect of global warming on air quality is the growing frequency (fourfold since the 1980s), and size (sixfold since the 1980s) of wildfires. Smoke from wildfires is composed of a mixture of various gases and fine particles from burning trees and other plants. It is known to irritate the respiratory system and worsen chronic heart and lung diseases including asthma, with potentially significant effects on population morbidity and mortality. Research in Indonesia, for example, on the effects of wildfires that blanketed the country in 1997 found that a fire-induced increase in air pollution was associated with a one percent drop in child survival over a five-month period of high exposure. Notes Jayachandran (2006:1), "This implies 16,400 infant and fetal deaths are attributable to the fires. Indonesia's under-2 mortality rate during this period was 6 percent; assuming the effect of pollution was mainly on infant deaths (rather than fetal deaths), this represents a 17 percent increase in under-2 mortality."

Studies have shown that modern wildfires are larger and harder to contain than in the past because hotter summer and fall weather accelerates evaporation. In 2006, the number of fires exceeded existing records in both the number of reported fires as well as acres burned. Almost 100,000 fires were reported to fire-control authorities and just under ten million acres burned; this is a 125 percent increase above average rates for the prior ten years. To assess changing wildfire patterns, Westerling and co-workers (2006) compiled a comprehensive database of large fires in forests in the western United States since 1970 and compared it with available hydroclimatic (e.g., snowfall) and land-use data. They found that large wildfire activity increased suddenly and significantly during the mid-1980s, marked by more frequent and longer-lasting fires and longer wildfire seasons (notably an increase of 78 days). The greatest increases were found in the mid-elevation Northern Rockies forests, in areas that had not been greatly altered by human activities that might have contributed to fire risk. Rather, more frequent fires were strongly associated with increased spring and summer temperatures and an earlier spring snowmelt. This new era of wildfires was inaugurated in 1988 in Yellowstone National Park. Fires in the park that year lasted over three months and burned 600,000 acres of forest despite significant and costly fire-control efforts (involving 25,000 firefighters and a price tag of $120 million) were only brought under control by the fall of snow in the middle of September (Running 2006). Many climate scientists expect that the size of the acreage burned by wildfires will double across a number of western states in the period between 2070 and 2100. Hardest-hit states will be Montana, Wyoming, Utah, and New Mexico, with likely effects on the quality of breathable air in these areas during fire seasons (Glick 2006).

Mold

Increased moisture produced by global warming has been found to facilitate the growth of mold and resulting respiratory and other health complaints caused by mold exposure. Molds are curious types of living organisms that have been on earth for millions of years. They are neither plant nor animal, but rather are a kind of fungus, one of the five kingdoms of life. There are thousands of different types of fungi, perhaps as many as 100,000 in all, although only about 0.5 percent, such as Stachybotrys and Chaetomium, have been identified as human pathogens (Brandt and Warnock 2003).

Molds are not composed of organs or functional components like animals and plants. Unlike animals, molds have cell walls. While plants also have cell walls, those found in molds are composed mostly of chitin (the hard, semitransparent material that forms the exoskeletons of crabs and lobsters) and glucan (a complex sugar molecule). Also unlike plants, molds cannot produce their own nutrients using photosynthesis. Rather, they secrete enzymes that digest the medium in which they are embedded (e.g., the trunk of a fallen tree or the wall of a home) and absorb the liquefied nutrients produced through chemical reaction (Brandt et al. 2006).

The word mold is derived from the Norse world mowlde, which means fuzzy. Molds, which come in many different colors and can be furry, slimy, or powdery, are ubiquitous, growing almost anywhere both indoors and outdoors, although they require the presence of moisture and nutrients to survive. Possible sources of nutrients vary, but the ability of molds to thrive on diverse building materials and household items (including wood, fabric, leather, gypsum, fiberboard, drywall, stucco, paints, wallpaper, carpet, fabric, upholstery, and many insulation materials, as well as human oils, skin cells, and other organic substances) allows them to live inside homes, offices, and other buildings. There is variability in the preferred environment of mold types, with some being cryophytes (adapted to living in low temperatures), some being thermo-tolerant (can live in a wide range of temperatures), and some being thermophiles adapted to living in high temperatures). Similarly, the quantity of moisture required varies among mold types. Some are xerophillic (can live in quite dry environments), some are xero-tolerant (can live in environments with a wide range of moisture levels), and some are hydrophilic (require high moisture levels) (Lillard 2007). As a group, molds are distinguished from other multicelluar fungi because they are composed of branching filamentous structures called mycelium.

Molds can be the source of highly beneficial chemicals, such as penicillin, a drug that has saved numerous lives. Yeast, a type of fungus related to molds, is important in the production of bread, beer, and other foods. Molds, however, also can be sources of illness, and, with global warming, mold-related health problems are become progressively more common, although some people are much more sensitive to molds than others. Most molds thrive in the kinds of warm, wet environments produced by heavy rains. In recent years, an increasing incidence of mold-related human diseases has been linked to exposure in water-damaged buildings associated with flooding, such as occurred in Louisiana in the wake of Hurricanes Katrina and Rita (Ratard et al. 2006).

Molds cause human disease in several ways. The first stems from their means of reproduction. Molds reproduce and spread by making small, lightweight, and long-lived spores that are capable of traveling through the air to diverse destinations, while resisting dryness and other adverse environmental conditions. Mold spores are a primary source of negative health reactions to this group of organisms. Ventilation and air-conditioning can help to move spores throughout indoor environments, although the dynamics of spore transport are not yet fully understood. Exposure also can occur in a dusty environment, if the components of dust include spores or mold fragments. The majority of mold spores have aerodynamic diameters of 2–10 µm, putting them in a size range that allows penetration of the upper and lower respiratory tract (Brandt and Warnock 2003). As is the case with pollen, diesel fuel particles attach themselves to mold spores creating yet another hybrid delivery system for harmful substances to areas deep within human lungs (Epstein 2002a). Additionally, although the mycelium of molds are usually well anchored to the surface on which they are growing, parts break off and people are exposed to fragments that can prove irritating to body tissues. Some molds produce mycotoxins, such as aflatoxin, zearalenone, trichothecenes, and moniliformin, and it is these noxious chemicals—found in both spores and mold fragments—that are particularly harmful to humans. Aflotoxin B1 (one of four varieties), for example, is known to be carcinogenic. People can be exposed to mycotoxins through skin contact, inhalation, or ingestion. Symptoms and diseases caused by exposure include allergies (the most common types of diseases associated with exposure to mold), coughing or wheezing, eye irritation, chronic bronchitis, hypersensitivity pneumonitis (an immune-mediated disease), learning disabilities, mental deficiencies, heart problems, cancer, multiple sclerosis, chronic fatigue, lupus, fibromyalgia, rheumatoid arthritis, multiple chemical sensitivity, bleeding lungs, memory and hearing loss, and dizziness. Mycotoxins can also cause suppression of immune system function, putting sufferers at risk for a wide range of other health conditions common in individuals with compromised immune systems (Brandt et al. 2006).

One of the specific health problems associated with mold exposure is aspergillosis, a condition caused by molds from the genus Aspergillus that requires hospitalization for effective treatment. Aspergillus molds are quite common in the soil, on decaying vegetation, and indoors. The genus Aspergillus includes over 185 different species, approximately 20 of which have so far been identified as causative agents of opportunistic disease (with Aspergillus fumigatus being the most common). The medical term Aspergillosis labels a broad spectrum of specific diseases, including allergic bronchopulmonary aspergillosis, pulmonary aspergilloma, and invasive aspergillosis (Stevens et al. 2000). All organs and organ systems in the human body are subject to infection (Denning 1998). How sick any particular individual becomes with any of these conditions depends on his or her prior immune state. Exposure can lead to episodes of acute asthma that develop into end-stage lung disease. Individuals with an encumbered immune system are less resistant to the effects of exposure and are more likely to develop more extreme symptoms. Aspergillus is known to colonize lung cavities previously caused by diseases like tuberculosis, and hence are of concern to syndemic researchers (see Chapter 6). The invasive forms of aspergillosis commonly are associated with high levels of both morbidity and mortality (Denning and Stevens 1990). The reaction of human tissue to aspergillosis is quite acute and includes inflammation and necrosis (tissue death). As the mold proliferates inside the body, it continues to form new branches at a 45 degree angle. Watching this process at high magnification has led observers to say that growth of the mold has "the overall appearance of an army on the march" (Mycoses Study Group 2007). Invasion of blood vessels, thrombosis, and infarction are quite common. The mortality rate for invasive aspergillosis is 50 to 100 percent.

Overall, the risks of mold exposure are especially high among infants and children, the elderly, pregnant women, and people with pre-existing immune-compromising health conditions (e.g., being malnourished, cocaine addiction, HIV infection) or immune damage caused by prior mold exposure. With increased exposure due to global warming, greatest health impact from molds is likely to among these highly vulnerable populations.

Conclusions

As seen in this chapter, global warming is likely to have quite diverse weather-related health impacts, with various configurations of warming-related health problems becoming manifest in different places and over time. Indeed, it may be this variability that is particularly challenging for human capacity to respond effectively. Local adaptation to parched conditions will ill prepare a community for heavy rains and flooding. At the same time, communities are likely to be hit by multiple weather-related health problems at any point in time, such as heavy rains, polluted drinking water, damaged food production capacity, and mold-related respiratory and other health problems. Global warming, in short, is of great health importance for current and future generations because of its potential to severely tax our ability to respond effectively. The result is likely to be considerable loss of life, mounting disease burden, and further decline in overall well-being. While some colder climes may prosper from warmer weather, the global disruptive effects of climate change are likely to touch everyone, with greatest harm being visited upon subordinate and marginalized populations.

5

Agents of Suffering

The Spread of Waterborne and Vector-Borne Infections

On the Eve of Calamity

According to David Byrne (2004:4), the European Union Commissioner for Health and Consumer Protection, from the standpoint of the spread of infectious disease, the world may be "on the eve of a 21st-century calamity." While health forecasts are fraught with uncertainty, one gauge of the seriousness of the potential human impact of global warming on health can be seen through a consideration of the worldwide influenza pandemics of the 20th century. Influenza is a zoonotic disease, with birds and pigs being the primary animal hosts. There were three influenza pandemics during the century, each causing widespread illness, mortality, social disruption, and significant economic loss. These occurred in 1918, 1957, and 1968. In each case, mortality rates were determined primarily by five factors: the number of people who became infected, the virulence of the virus causing the pandemic, the speed of global spread, the underlying features and vulnerabilities of the most affected populations, and the effectiveness and timeliness of the prevention and treatment measures that were implemented (World Health Organization 2004). These factors unite a range of biosocial causal forces, including production, communication, and transportation technologies; the medical and public health infrastructures; the specific pathogens involved and the nature of their current and past interactions with human hosts; and the pre-existing health status of affected individuals and populations. All of these, in turn, are shaped, to greater or somewhat lesser degree, by overarching political economic structures globally and locally. The emergence, course, and impact of epidemics, in short, are sculpted by the configuration of human social relationships including prevailing patterns of social inequality (Baer, Singer, and Susser 2003, Singer and Baer 2008).

The 1957 pandemic was caused by the Asian influenza virus (known as the H2N2 strain, a designation derived from two viral surface glycoproteins: hemagglutinin [H] and neuraminidase [N]), a novel pathogen for which humans had not yet developed immunities. The death toll of the 1957 pandemic is estimated to have been around two million globally.

A little over a decade later, the comparatively mild Hong Kong influenza pandemic erupted in the wake of the spread of a virus strain (H3N2) that genetically was related to the more deadly form seen in 1957. The pandemic was responsible for about one million deaths around the world (United Kingdom Department of Health 2004). In both of these pandemics, death was caused not only by the primary viral infection but also was propelled by secondary bacterial infections among influenza patients. In other words, what was significant about both of these deadly epidemics is that many of the people who suffered the worst consequences did not suffer from a single disease but the adverse effects of two interacting diseases. As noted, this phenomenon of syndemic interaction among co-morbid diseases under specific configuring social conditions is discussed further in Chapter 6 with reference to the spread of multiple, interrelated diseases as a result of global warming.

The worst 20th-century influenza pandemic was the 1918 outbreak, which epidemiologists estimate was responsible for the deaths of between 40 and 100 million people worldwide, making it one of the most deadly events in human history. More people died of the so-called "Spanish flu" pandemic (which did not actually originate in Spain) in the single year of 1918 than during all four years of the Black Death (bubonic plague), a scourge that lasted from 1347 to 1351. It is estimated that 20 to 40 percent of the world's population fell ill during the 1918 pandemic, which was caused by the H1N1 viral strain. About 2.5 percent of infected individuals died, significantly more than in other influenza pandemics (Taubenberger and Morens 2006).

The pandemic had devastating effects as the disease spread along trade and shipping routes and other corridors of human movement until it had circled the globe. In India, the mortality rate reached 50 per 1,000 population (Crosby 2003, Taubenberger et al. 1997). Arriving during the closing phase of World War I—and no doubt aided by the disruptions caused by the war—the pandemic had a great impact on mobilized national armies. Half of U.S. soldiers who died in the Great War were victims of influenza, not enemy bombs and bullets. It is estimated that almost half a million Americans died during the pandemic. Noted one alarmed scientific observer: "[If the pandemic continues] civilization could easily disappear from the face of the earth within a matter of a few more weeks" (quoted in Barry 2004:C1).

The death toll was caused in part by viral pneumonia characterized by extensive bleeding in the lungs resulting in suffocation. Many victims died within 48 hours of the appearance of the first symptom. In fact, it was not uncommon for people who appeared to be quite healthy in the morning to have died by sunset. Among those who survived the first several days of viral infection, many subsequently died of secondary bacterial pneumonia. Moreover, it has been argued that countless numbers of those who expired quickly were also infected with tuberculosis, which would explain the notable plummet in TB cases after 1918 (because so many carriers perished of influenza) (Noymer 2006). Again, as seen with the other two 20th-century global influenza outbreaks, disease interaction appears to have been critical, underlining the importance of syndemics in the production of major public health crises.

Significantly, despite advances in biomedical treatments, vaccines, and public health surveillance—and contrary to earlier public health assumptions that infectious diseases were on their way to becoming less significant determinants of health globally—as affirmed by the SARS (Severe Acute Respiratory Syndrome, H5N1 avian flu) outbreak of 2003, fast-moving infectious disease pandemics are not a thing of the past. In fact, most leading virologists and epidemiologists now expect that the 21st century will see major pandemics with significant loss of life. It is noteworthy that, unlike in cooler climes, in tropical areas influenza knows no seasons; it is a year-round event. With increased global warming, wider areas will be subject to continual influenza infections, including sickness caused by new mutant strains. Consequently, global warming is likely to play a growing role in the course of future influenza outbreaks.

Infections with two different modes of transport and transmission are of primary (but not sole) concern in this chapter. First, there are diseases that live in and are spread by water, which the storms caused by global warming are moving to new environments. Second, there are diseases caused by pathogens that are carried and transmitted by insects or other vectors, which are able to expand their zone of activity because of global warming.

Waterborne Pathogens

Many lives are put at risk by infections caused by waterborne pathogens, a group of highly infectious agents that are numerous and spreading. Waterborne diseases currently are the source of 90 percent of deaths from infectious disease in developing countries, and with further global warming, their impact is likely to grow in developed nations as well. Disease-causing organisms that live in water, or in water-dwelling host species, include giardia, cholera, cryptosporidium, rotaviruses, enteroviruses, Coxsackie viruses, cyclospora, and both the hepatitis A and E viruses. Various kinds of health risks are caused by these microbes. Some infect wounds, others cause diarrhea and dehydration, still others can cause infections that lead to organ failure (Comire 2007, Rose et al. 2001), as illustrated below.

Vilnuficus

The effect of global warming on waterborne diseases is seen in the case of shellfish poisoning caused by the bacterium *Vibrio vulnificus*, a member of the same family of bacteria responsible for cholera. *V. vulnificu*, a not yet very well-known organism found in oysters, clams, and crabs, was only discovered to be a source of human disease in 1979. The cause of a growing number of sea food–related deaths, it also can infect wounds (e.g., puncture wounds from the spines of fish like tilapia), as well as trigger gastroenteritis and septicemia, producing a mortality rate of between 20 and 50 percent, depending on the nature of the infection and the prior health status of the sufferer. In two of the cases that occurred in Florida in 1998, for example, one involved a man who was infected when a blue crab scratched his hand while another sufferer had a cut on his foot that was exposed to seawater (Doyle 1998). Most deaths from *V. vulnificus*, which occur within 48 hours of infection, are preceded by fever, chills, lowered blood pressure, and blistering of the skin. At greatest risk are people with co-morbid health problems, such as liver disease or diseases like HIV, diabetes, and cancer that result in a compromised immune system.

At home in warm seawater, *V. vulnificus* is now found in the Gulf of Mexico, along the Atlantic Coast as far north as Cape Cod, and the entire length of the U.S. West Coast (Oliver and Kaper 2001). Infections peak during summer months. As the fall arrives and seawater cools, the pathogen's impact diminishes (Rose et al. 2001). As global warming advances, and seawater grows ever warmer, however, and greater variability in rainfall and water runoff occur, rates of morbidity and mortality caused by this pathogen are projected to rise considerably. Because infection levels go up following flooding events, coastal storms present a particular risk for *V. vulnificus* infection.

In Taiwan, for example, *V. vulnificus* began showing up in 1985, especially in southern Taiwan where the surface temperature of seawater is usually about 64°F (18°C), except during the summer when the temperature goes up to 79–84°F (26–29°C). Cases of the infection have tended to occur during the summer months. A survey of the distribution of the organism in seawater drawn from five major harbors in Taiwan found that *V. vulnificus* is a local species throughout the coast waters and aquatic habitats of the island nation. Clinical information on 84 patients from five hospitals with *V. vulnificus* infection from 1995 to 2000 collected by Po-Ren Hsueh and co-workers (2004) found that over 80 percent suffered from underlying medical conditions, especially liver disease (e.g., hepatitis B and C), diabetes, and illicit steroid use. As a result of *V. vulnificus* infection, 60 percent of the patients had skin infections and half were suffering from deep skin infection with necrotizing faciitis, or, as it is commonly known, "flesh-eating bacteria." As this example suggests, the further spread of *V. vulnificus* is a significant health threat, especially for particularly vulnerable populations.

Cholera

As noted, related to *V. vulnificus* is *Vibrio cholerae*, the pathogen that causes cholera, which is also a waterborne intestinal disease of global significance. Cholera has held a central role in public health since John Snow mapped cases of infection in London in the mid-19th century and found a significant concentration of cases around a public water pump on Broad Street. Changes in ocean temperature, pH, and salinity are linked to increases in cholera infections, as is a rise in the frequency of violent climatic events (Colwell 1996). The 1992–1993 cholera epidemic in Dhaka and adjoining areas of Bangladesh, for example, followed heavy monsoon rains. Between December 1992 and March of the following year, over 100,000 cases were diagnosed and almost 1,500 deaths were recorded. The epidemic was caused by a strain of the pathogen (known as *V. cholerae* 0139) that produces large amounts of enterotoxin that causes severe watery diarrhea and dehydration, making it especially harmful to people who had no built-up immune defenses for the 0139 strain.

During the same period as the Bangladesh outbreak, a cholera epidemic struck Latin America. Almost a million cases of infection were diagnosed and deaths numbered in the thousands. The epidemic spread rapidly, and within three years (1991–1993) was causing illness and death in most countries in the region. In Peru, for example, the earliest cases were identified in 1991, marking the first time cholera had been seen there during the 20th century. The disease spread quickly through coastal cities and along waterways (Monastersky 1996). Case-control studies in Peru found a strong association between drinking water and risk of infection. Cholera also was associated with the consumption of unwashed produce, the eating of food sold on the street by informal sector vendors, and some stocks of crabmeat (Guthmann 1995).

Important determinants of the effects of weather-related waterborne infection are the prevailing local pattern of hygiene and the structure of public health, including available human resources. The ethnically diverse people of the south-central African nation of the Republic of Zambia, for example, are known to suffer from several major chronic health problems, including malaria, schistosomiasis, and malnutrition, as well as acute diseases such as measles, typhoid, and dysentery. In addition, the country experienced major cholera epidemics in 1991,

1992, and 1993 and several since then as well. A decaying infrastructure fostered the spread of the disease; in the city of Kitwe, for example, broken equipment in sewage treatment and water plants and a lack of chlorine were critical factors. Like its cousin *V. vulnificus*, *V. cholerae* is expected to produce ever more frequent epidemics in the era of global warming. As Paul Epstein (2000) stresses, algae blooms caused by warming seas may play a significant role in coming cholera epidemics, as floods flush fertilizer and sewage into the sea. A specialist in tropical public health, Epstein is well aware of the devastating impact of cholera, having come down with the disease himself after a meal of shellfish during the late 1970s while working in Mozambique. He notes:

> Fertilizer and sewage can each combine with warmed water to trigger expansive blooms of harmful algae. Some of these blooms are directly toxic to humans who inhale their vapors; others contaminate fish and shellfish, which, when eaten, sicken the consumers. Recent discoveries have revealed that algal blooms can threaten human health in yet another way. As they grow bigger, they support the proliferation of various pathogens, among them *Vibrio cholerae*. [Epstein 2000]

Further, it is likely that *V. cholerae* will spread because of the flooding caused by the rising sea levels, especially in low-lying coastal areas in tropical regions, including many resource- and nutrient-poor nations.

Cryptosporidium

Another pathogen that can be spread by storms is *Cryptosporidium parvum*, as seen in the 1993 outbreak in Milwaukee caused by flooding of the Mississippi River that set off the largest waterborne-disease outbreak in U.S. history (Epstein 2005). During a two-week period, one-fourth of Milwaukee's 1.6 million residents came down with cryptosporidiosis, the disease that is caused by this protozoan parasite. Reservoirs for *Cryptosporidium* exist in domestic animals, especially cattle and dairy cows, as well as in wildlife such as deer. Rain-driven runoff from farming areas can introduce *Cryptosporidium* into drinking water supplies. *Cryptosporidium* belongs to a family of pathogens called Apicomplexans that, in addition to causing cryptosporidiosis, are responsible for malaria and toxoplasmosis in humans as well as a wide range of livestock diseases.

Humans infected with *Cryptosporidium* suffer from painful stomach cramps, severe diarrhea, high fever, and dehydration. Over 100 people died during the Milwaukee epidemic, primarily those with other health challenges, including advanced age and HIV infection. Indeed, cryptosporidiosis, which was first recognized in 1976, has become a life-threatening complication in AIDS patients, and it is also contributing to rising rates of morbidity in children, especially when it is combined with pediatric malnutrition. A study in Onitsha, an urban area in Nigeria, for example, involving an examination of stool samples for *Cryptosporidium* among 144 children under the age of ten brought for hospital treatment, found that 64 (44 percent) were infected with one or more parasites. *Cryptosporidium* was detected in the stools of 12 patients (eight percent), mainly in diarrheal stools (Ekejindu and Ochuba 2004). Research in Brazil has found that over 15 percent of cases of childhood diarrhea are associated with *Cryptosporidium* infection (Gennari-Cardoso et al. 1996, Loureiro et al. 1990). A study of poor children in Brazil, residents of a favela (urban shantytown), found that low birth weight and location were risk factors for symptomatic infection with *Cryptosporidium* (Newman et al. 1999).

In short, *Cryptosporidium* is a parasitic agent among children that is probably responsible for many cases of acute diarrheal disease, a primary threat to the health and survival of small children internationally. Spread of this disease as a result of global warming is a significant concern for public health efforts. As agricultural economist Patricia Kocagil of Pennsylvania State University observed, "Cryptosporidiosis is one of many waterborne diseases whose prevalence could increase with increased precipitation and flooding triggered by climate change" (quoted in Pennsylvania State University Press Release 1998). Support for this conclusion is found in an examination by Curriero and co-workers (2001) of the 548 gastrointestinal disease outbreaks that occurred in the United States between 1948 and 1994 documented in the Environmental Protection Agency waterborne disease database, which determined that 68 percent were preceded by very heavy rainfall.

Concern is enhanced by the transmission patterns of *Cryptosporidium*. Oocysts (a thick-walled casing that serves to transfer the protozoa to new hosts) are transmitted by drinking contaminated water or eating contaminated food, through fecal transmission from infected animals, and person-to-person. Water treatment plants often cannot insure the removal of all *Cryptosporidium* oocysts because they are very tiny (only four to five micrometers in diameter) and are protected by their thick covering from chlorine and other chemical disinfectants.

Research by Boris Striepen and co-workers (2004) has found that *Cryptosporidium*'s survival depends on what have been called "salvage enzymes" that are used to steal nutrients away from its host. This finding was tied to the discovery that *Cryptosporidium* has lost its ability to synthesize two groups of organic compounds called pyrimidines and purines, which are fundamental building blocks of DNA and reproduction. The loss of the capacity to synthesis these substances was particularly surprising for researchers because recent genetic analysis of a related parasite, *Toxoplasma gondii*—which causes encephalitis—showed that the ability to make pyrimidine is critical for development and virulence. Striepen and co-workers demonstrated that the parasite overcomes this deficit by stealing pyrimidines and purines from the cells of its host. Further study showed that the parasite not only salvages the building blocks for making DNA, it also harvests some of the genes involved in pyrimidine and purine production. These findings underline why microbes—complex and varied in their infection strategies—can present such enormous challenges to medicine and public health, and why prevention of conditions that foster their spread is critical. While the ability to acquire genes from other organisms has been described in bacteria through a process known as "gene transfer" (see Chapter 6), this was the first time it has been seen in a protozoa. Researchers, in fact, found that the enzymes used by *Cryptosporidium* constitutes an "evolutionary patchwork" composed of components of protozoan, bacterial, and possibly algal origin (Striepen et al. 2002).

Naegleria

A lesser-known pathogen, and one less frequently a cause of illness in humans, is a heat-loving and free-living amoeba known as *Naegleria fowleri*. First discovered over 250 years ago, amoebas are one-celled protozoa that move about using a temporary projection called a pseudopod. While infection with this waterborne microbe currently is rare, it is almost always fatal, and the cause of death is particularly frightening: damage done to tissue as the amoeba enters the body through the nose (often during water-centered activities like swimming and diving that can push water up the nose), makes its way up the olfactory nerve and into the brain, where it feeds on brain cells. Infection triggers the development of primary amebic meningoencephalitis, a brain inflammation. The first symptoms of infection are alterations in sense of taste and smell, sudden-onset headache, and stiffness of the neck. As the disease progresses, victims appear confused and disinterested in the people around them, lose their balance, have seizures, and begin hallucinating. The disease has a rapid progression, almost always leading to death within a few weeks at most (Cogo et al. 2004).

Found widely dispersed around the globe, *Naegleria* prefers warm lakes and rivers (above 80°F/27°C), hot springs, the areas around warm-water discharge pipes of industrial plants, poorly maintained swimming pools, and even in warm soil. The amoeba has not been found in nor does it appear able to tolerate seawater. In arid climates, cases of *Naegleria* infection have been reported following inhalation of the microbe's cysts floating in the air (Gibbs and Johnson 2006). Infection with *Naegleria* tends to occur during dryer summer months, when air temperature is hot and water temperature is warm. Notably, in light of the effects of global warming, the number of infections increases during heat waves. Between 1995 and 2004, 23 people in the U.S. died of *Naegleria* infection. In the first nine months of 2007, it was responsible for six known deaths. Although more than half of *Naegleria* cases have occurred in the U.S., infections have been diagnosed on every continent. In Europe, cases have been reported in the Czech Republic, Belgium, and the United Kingdom. In total, outside of the U.S. aapproximately 200 cases of primary amebic meningoencephalitis have been reported worldwide (Gibbs and Johnson 2006). Co-infection with AIDS has been found in at least one patient, suggesting a potential for syndemic interaction (De Jonckheere and Brown 1997). As noted by Michael Beach, a specialist in waterborne illness at the CDC, "This is a heat-loving amoeba. As water temperatures go up, it does better . . . . In future decades, as temperatures rise, we'd expect to see more cases" (quoted in Kahn 2007:6).

The Spread of Vectorborne Infectious Diseases

Currently, infectious diseases cause approximately 37 percent of all deaths in the world, a percentage that is expected to go up as a result of global warming. Epstein (2000), for example, points out that a temperature rise of only 3.6°F (2°C) would more than double the metabolism rate of mosquitoes, including species that spread deadly human diseases such as malaria. Warming at this level could also expand malaria's domain of active infection from 42 percent to 60 percent of the planet. The same is true of a host of other mosquito-borne diseases. The significance of this shift, he notes, is that "infectious illness is a genie that can be very hard to put back into its bottle. It may kill fewer people in one fell swoop than a raging flood or an extended drought, but once it takes root in a community, it often defies eradication and can invade other areas" (Epstein 2000:1).

Microbes evolved at least three billion years before animals and plants (suggesting a pre-pathogenic history), and new and altered versions continue to appear. While only a small percent are pathogenic for humans, those that are have significant capacity to move into new niches as opportunities arise with significant consequence for human health. That diseases move is not a new phenomenon, and humans have long played an active if unintentional role in this process. As people travel, either within a particular region or as they dispersed historically across the planet's landmasses, they always carry their endemic diseases with them. The extinction of other hominid species, such as the Neanderthals of Europe following the movement of Homo sapiens northward from Africa, and the great loss of life suffered by various contemporary human populations, such as the native peoples of the new world or Tasmania following European colonial expansion, were promoted by the spread of diseases to new areas as a consequence of population migration. (Other political and economic factors—such as intentional extermination, forced removal, disruption of indigenous subsistence patterns—were at play as well, however.) Domesticated animals also have been storehouses of diseases, carried along by migrating human populations. Moreover, throughout their family and species-specific evolutions, pathogens have found ways to diffuse by diverse means. Global warming, by disrupting natural ecosystems, has contributed to a very rapid movement of a growing number of disease-causing viruses, bacteria, fungi, and other pathogenic organisms. This migration of microbes is occurring at a time when the planet's human population is not only enormous but is increasingly concentrated in megalopolises, placing an unprecedented number of people in rapid harm's way for a host of old, new, and renewed diseases. Of special importance is the fact that various pathogenic species that previously were restricted in their distribution by seasonal temperatures have begun invading new areas in response to climate changes. As Richard Ostfeld, an environmental researcher at the Institute of Ecosystem Studies, notes, "We're alarmed because in reviewing the research on a variety of different organisms we are seeing strikingly similar patterns of increases in disease spread or incidence with climate warming" (quoted in CBS News 2002).

Vector-borne ailments that are being spread by global warming include dengue, malaria, West Nile fever, Rift Valley fever, hanta virus, plague, encephalitis, yellow fever, and Lyme disease (Epstein 2007, Harvell et al. 2002). Each of these threats is discussed below.

Dengue

The impact of global warming on the contemporary and future reach of disease vectors is well illustrated by the case of dengue, a malady for which no vaccine or specific pharmaceutical treatment exists. Dengue has been called "breakbone fever" because of the agonizing pain it produces in the joints of infected individuals. Other symptoms include stomach pain, headaches, nausea and vomiting, pain behind the eyes, and body flushes. There are four viral strains, and co-infection with more than one strain can produce a significantly more severe and increasingly more common condition known as dengue hemorrhagic fever (DHF). The incidence of DHF has increased dramatically in recent decades (Centers for Disease Control and Prevention 2006a). For example, endemic in India for over two centuries as a relatively benign and self-limited disease, in recent years dengue infection has been more dramatic while the prevalence of DHF has gone up. Delhi, in northern India, for example, has experienced seven dengue outbreaks since 1967 (Gupta et al. 2006).

Worldwide, dengue afflicts 50 to 100 million people in tropical and subtropical areas, especially in cities and their surrounding regions. Malaysia has been particularly hard hit, with thousands of individuals falling victim each year to this debilitating and sometimes fatal disease. In 2006, for example, 4,600 patients were admitted to hospitals in Karachi, Pakistan, a city of at least 14 million people. Of these patients, 35 percent were found to be suffering from dengue. There were at least 52 dengue-related deaths in 2006 in the Sindh province of Pakistan, almost all of them in Karachi. The actual death toll is believed to be higher as many deaths in remote villages and towns go unreported (Jamil et al. 2007).

Dengue has been spreading rapidly in recent years. In Thailand, the prevalence of dengue has increased from a recorded annual rate of 9 per 100,000 population in 1958 to 189 per 100,000 40 years later (Thailand Ministry of Public Health 1999). In Latin America, it has moved southward, reaching Buenos Aires by the end of the 1990s, and northward as well. As a result, during the first nine months of 2007, over 625,000 cases of dengue were reported in Latin American countries, especially Brazil, Venezuela, and Colombia, including over 12,000 cases of DHF, and 183 fatalities. Mexico, in particular, has seen an alarming increase in the number of cases of DHF, which now accounts for approximately one in four dengue cases in the country. The Mexican government reported that the number of cases of DHF may be double what was seen in 2006. Overall, the number of cases of dengue in Latin America is expected during 2007 to surpass the 1,015,000 cases reported in the record-setting year of 2002 (Melia 2007).

Dengue is slowly moving into North America as well. As Shope reports, the mosquito *Aedes albopictus*, a vector for dengue, was introduced into the Americas in the 1980s

> and now represents a potential risk for transmission of dengue in the United States. The mosquito that established itself in the United States is the diapausing form [i.e. having a dormancy phase], and it appears to have adapted well to the more northern states. Now in both Asia and North America, there is the potential with global climate change for the vectors of dengue to move further north, perhaps much further north than today. [Shope 1992:365]

Additionally, dengue has spread to northern Australia, making its scope a global affair.

In the past, dengue was not found above 3,300 feet above sea level because climates beyond that altitude were inhospitable to the *Aedes aegypti* mosquito, the insect vector that most commonly carries the disease to human populations. Like other members of its insect family, *A. aegypti* mosquitoes acquire disease-causing pathogens when they consume a blood meal from infected animals or people. The pathogen reproduces inside the mosquito's body and the offspring travel, by way of bodily fluids, to the mosquito's mouth parts, through which they enter a new victim when the mosquito feeds. *A. aegypti* mosquitoes can live and transmit viruses only where temperatures infrequently fall below 50°F (10°). Today, because of warming, dengue is found at 7,200 feet in the Andes in Colombia and is beginning to be identified at ever higher elevations (Martens et al. 1995, Natural Resources Defense Council 2006). In the United States *A. aegypti* mosquitoes have moved as far north as Chicago. McAllen, Texas, suffered an outbreak of dengue fever in 1995 (Patz et al. 1998). Another outbreak occurred in Hawaii in 2001.

A. aegypti breeds in old tires and other small water-holding containers, a trait that allows them to multiply in urban settings away from large bodies of water and close to concentrated human populations. They thrive in urban slums that contain multiple breeding sites and little in the way of government- or privately sponsored mosquito control efforts. The mosquito is well adapted to human residences and frequently enters buildings to feed and to rest. As Hayden et al. (2007:1) found in their study along the U.S.-Mexico border, "*Ae. aegypti* has adapted readily to urban settings, particularly in the tropics and sub-tropics in areas where crowded conditions, population movement and lack of infrastructure such as piped water and adequate solid waste disposal contribute to the transmission of dengue fever." In other (wealthier) settings, such as enclosed spaces with air-conditioning, the mosquito may be limited in its capacity to spread dengue (Reiter et al. 2003). Similarly, in their cross-sectional study along the U.S.-Mexico border area, Brunkard and colleagues (2007) found recent dengue infection in two percent of Brownsville (U.S.) and seven percent of Matamoros (Mexico) residents. The study also found past infection rates of 40 percent in Brownsville and 78 percent in Matamoros. Significantly, "low income across both cities was the dominant risk factor for both recent and past dengue infection" (Brunkard et al. 2007), but not having air-conditioning and good street drainage (which resulted in flooding and blocked garbage collection trucks from entering neighborhoods after a storm) were also important.

In other words, like other diseases that discussed above, the climate-related spread of dengue will affect poorer individuals and populations far more than wealthier ones.

Malaria

Also of grave concern is the widening geographic domain of malaria, a disease for which no vaccine currently exists, although treatments are available. Even for survivors, the consequences can be harsh. Finkel (2007) details the case of Methyline Kumafumbo, an undernourished three-year-old girl from North-Western Province, Zambia, a forested region sandwiched between the borders of Angola and the Democratic Republic of the Congo. For every 1,000 children under the age of five in the province, there are 1,353 cases of malaria annually, a statistic clarified by the fact that some children are infected more than once each year. Methyline was taken to the hospital, a ten-mile hike, by her grandmother when the child began to exhibit symptoms of malarial infection. As with all cases of the disease, Methyline's infection began when she was bitten by a female mosquito seeking protein-rich blood to nourish her eggs. As part of the process of sucking a tiny amount of blood from the victim, the mosquito injected the wound she had inflicted with saliva, which serves as an anticoagulant easing the flow of blood. Malaria-causing parasites gather in the mosquito's salivary glands and travel into the bodies of human victims with the mosquito's saliva. Once in a new human victim, like Methyline, the wormlike parasites migrated quickly to the girl's liver and embedded themselves in liver cells, where they fed and multiplied. Within a week, each parasite had consumed a liver cell and replicated as many as 40,000 times. At this point, infected cells exploded and the parasites re-entered Methyline's bloodstream. This time their target was red blood cells, in which they continued to feed and replicate. By now, the few parasites that first entered Methyline's body had grown to hundreds of thousands of invaders, each targeting a red blood cell, which it consumed. Before long, Methyline began to show the outward symptoms of the destruction going on inside her frail body, including headaches, muscle pain, fever, soaking sweats, and seizures. Some of the parasites made their way to Methyline's brain, where they latched on, causing swelling of the affected brain tissues. Once in the hospital, Methyline fell into and lay in a coma for a week, on the verge of death, her small back firmly arched, her thin arms made rigid by the disease. Treated with doses of quinine, she eventually began to respond. Her eyes opened. She began drinking water and eating porridge. She seemed on the road to recovery. But she never came all the way back from her painful journey into the world of the sick. As is the case with many young victims, malaria had inscribed its telltale mark on Methyline's young body; she suffered permanent neurological damage.

Known to be a very ancient disease, malaria has long been identified with the tropics because the Anopheles mosquito that transmits malaria parasites (such as *Plasmodium falciparum*) only thrives where temperatures regularly exceed 60°F (20°C). Thus, as Epstein (2000) reports,

> In the 19th century, European colonists in Africa settled in the cooler mountains to escape the dangerous swamp air ("mal aria") that [was believed to foster] disease in the lowlands. Today many of those havens are compromised. Insects and insect-borne infections are being reported at high elevations in South and Central America, Asia, and east and central Africa.

For example, in Kenya malaria traditionally was only found in three districts of the country. Today it has spread to 13 districts. In 2005, South Africa's environment minister warned that the country could face a quadrupling of malaria cases by 2020 (Struck 2006). Richards Bay, South Africa, for example, which was once malaria-free, had 22,000 cases in 1999. Today it is estimated that there are 300 to 500 million cases of malaria each year in Africa alone, resulting in between 1.5 and 2.7 million deaths, more than 90 percent occurring among children under five years of age. Malaria is the reason "nearly 20 percent of all Zambian babies do not live to see their fifth birthday" (Finkel 2007:41). Notably, as many as 100 million extra cases of malaria occurred worldwide by the close of the 20th century than would have occurred without global warming (Pennington 1995). Malaria now is showing up in places it was never seen before, or not seen for many decades. In the U.S., Houston experienced a malaria outbreak in recent years, and cases have been diagnosed as far north as New Jersey, New York, and Michigan. Jamaica, which had been malaria-free since the 1960s, was hit by an epidemic in 2007, with hundreds of people in the capital city of Kingston being diagnosed. Malaria also is spreading in the Korean peninsula, in southern Europe, and in the countries that comprised the former Soviet Union. It is, in short, because of global warming, rapidly becoming a planet-wide threat.

The *P. falciparum* parasite develops in about four weeks in temperatures below 77°F (25°C). At temperatures above that mark, however, the parasite reaches maturation in just two weeks. Anopheles mosquitoes normally only live for a few weeks. As a result, global warming has begun to play a role in increasing the likelihood that the parasites will mature inside the mosquito in time for the infection of a new wave of victims that are bitten by the mosquito. Further, global warming has a direct effect on the metabolism of pathogenic organisms, producing increased rates of growth and cell division (Platt 1995). Epstein (2000) has calculated that an increase in temperature of only 4°F (2°C) will more than double the metabolism of mosquitoes, leading to more frequent feedings and, as a result, expanded opportunities for the transmission of infection. Flooding helps to create conditions that allow mosquito breeding, including the creation of stagnant puddles of water that are appealing sites for mosquitoes to lay eggs, a further contribution of global warming to the spread of malaria.

In 1996, Socrates Litsios (1996), a senior scientist with the WHO Division of Control of Tropical Diseases, wrote a small book entitled *The Tomorrow of Malaria* in which he described the disease's long history as well as attempted public health eradication efforts. In the closing pages of the book he expressed hope for the tomorrow of malaria as a result of global prevention and treatment initiatives. In light of the impact of global warming, however, it is not at all clear that such optimism is warranted for what, in ancient India, was aptly called the "King of Diseases."

West Nile Fever

Named after the district of Uganda where it was first identified in 1937, West Nile is closely related to St. Louis encephalitis virus, which is found in the United States, and to Kunjin virus, which is found in Australia, some western Pacific islands, and parts of Southeast Asia. West Nile first appeared, rather unexpectedly, in North America in 1999 (Hayden et al. 2005). While identified rather recently, the disease may be ancient; a credible case, for example, has been made by John Marr of the Virginia Department of Health and infectious-disease expert Charles Calisher of Colorado State University for the possibility that Alexander the Great died of West Nile (Pearson 2003). In recent years, as it has spread across North America, it has infected over 20,000 people in the United States and Canada and killed over 800 people. In 2006, almost 4,269 cases of West Nile infection and 177 West Nile–related deaths were reported in the United States, a 14 percent increase from 2005 and the greatest number of new cases reported since 2003. The North American outbreak disclosed novel routes of transmission, including through blood transfusion, organ transplant, intrauterine exposure, and breast feeding (Hayes et al. 2005).

In the past, West Nile virus had been described in Africa, Europe, the Middle East, west and central Asia, and parts of Oceania. By 2006, the occurrence of West Nile infection among humans or animals had expanded to 52 new counties that previously had not reported the disease (Centers for Disease Control and Prevention 2007). While many West Nile infections are not life-threatening, it can lead to encephalitis (inflammation of the brain). Recent outbreaks of West Nile encephalitis have developed in Algeria (1994), Romania (1996–1997), the Czech Republic (1997),

Congo (1998), Russia (1999), the United States (1999–2003), Canada (1999–2003), and Israel (2000). In Israel, for example, there were 417 confirmed cases of West Nile infection, with 326 hospitalizations, 58 percent of which developed into encephalitis (Chowers et al. 2001). In the earlier Romanian outbreak, 500 cases were reported, with a fatality rate just below ten percent. One of the recent victims of West Nile was an elderly West Haven, Connecticut, resident who was admitted to the hospital after she began experiencing a high fever, headache, and mental confusion. Blood and spinal fluid tests showed that she been infected with West Nile. X-rays showed that the woman's brain was inflamed, suggesting West Nile encephalitis. Similar symptoms have shown up across the U.S., especially among seniors. The Colorado Department of Public Health and Environment (2004), for example, has reported multiple cases across the state with similar dire outcomes among the elderly.

The primary cause of West Nile's increasing presence is the spread of the *Cluex pipiens* mosquito, which thrives in arid weather. An urban mosquito, *C. pipiens* generally lays its eggs in the damp basements of human dwellings, as well as in house gutters, sewers, and polluted puddles of water. West Nile infection has had a major impact on bird populations, infecting over 135 species (as well as almost 100 other animal species) and leading to significant population drops in heavily infested species like crows. West Nile also has spread rapidly across the island nations of the Caribbean, after first being detected in 2001 (in the Cayman Islands), although the total number of cases has been limited thus far (Komar and Clark 2006).

Rift Valley Fever

In the final days of 2006, a number of sudden deaths occurred in the Garissa District in Kenya's North Eastern Province. Soon 11 fatalities had been reported, sparking anxiety at the Kenya Ministry of Health (Nguku et al. 2007). Blood tests showed that those who died had been struck by a disease called Rift Valley fever, a mosquito-borne phlebovirus most commonly found in livestock. The epidemic soon spread to neighboring provinces, leading to 404 reported cases and 118 deaths by the end of January 2007. Nine years earlier in North Eastern Province, a human outbreak of Rift Valley fever led to infection among approximately 90,000 people, and 478 deaths. In 1977–1978, almost 20,000 people were infected in Egypt. Outbreaks have been reported as well in Saudi Arabia and Yemen.

Patients in the 2006–2007 Kenyan epidemic initially suffered from influenza-like illness with eight percent of patients subsequently developed hemorrhagic syndrome, encephalitis, or retinitis. Inflammation of the retina is one of the most common complications of Rift Valley infection, with one to ten percent of patients suffering some degree of permanent vision loss.

Rift Valley fever was first identified as a sheep disease early in the 20th century, with the virus that causes the disease first being isolated in humans in Kenya in 1930 (Meegan and Bailey 1989). In livestock, the disease causes abortion and death. An outbreak in Kenya in 1950–1951, for example, killed over 100,000 sheep. In humans, the first epidemic was associated with the Senegal River Project, which resulted in the flooding of the lower Senegal River area. In the 2006–2007 outbreak, infection followed unusually heavy rains, with three times the average precipitation during the previous eight years and 13 times that of the previous year (Nguku et al. 2007). It is this association with heavy rains and flooding that has caused concern that Rift Valley fever may become another infection spread by the effects of global climate change.

Hanta

Also of growing concern is the climate-based spread of disease-bearing rodents, like those responsible for the outbreak of hanta virus and of hantavirus pulmonary syndrome, a highly lethal infection of the lungs, in the U.S. Southwest in 1993. Hanta virus can move from animals to humans when people inhale viral particles found in the urine and feces of disease-bearing rodents like mice (Yanagihara 1990). In the mid-1990s outbreak, a six-year drought (which appears to have eliminated many predators), followed by intense downpours (which produced bountiful crops of piñon nuts and grasshoppers), allowed a significant jump in the white-footed mouse population and contributed to increased human exposure to rodent droppings in and around people's homes. There are now around 500 cases a year of hanta virus infection occurring across the U.S. but concentrated in the Four Corners states of the Southwest (Centers for Disease Control and Prevention 2006b), an area character-ized by wetter winters and consequential increases in the types of vegeta-tion eaten by rodents. In that many bird species that have been hard hit by West Nile feed on mice that carry the hanta virus, the later disease may be benefiting from its syndemic linkage to the former disease.

Plague
Heavy rains and flooding also are linked with other diseases as well. One of the best known and feared is the plague. The term *plague* has a dual use in English, labeling both a specific disease as well as particularly harsh and memorable epidemics of historic note. The word *plague* tends to produce considerable public response, including fear and possible

stigmatization, and hence it has found its way into literature and other expressions of popular culture.

The natural reservoirs of plague are usually what are called sylvatic (literally "forest-dwelling" but implying species that do not live in or near human settlements) rodent species. However, because of interaction, peridomestic rodents (species that have adapted to life among human populations) may act as important liaison hosts that transmit infection between the sylvatic reservoir and humans. In 1994, for example, a long monsoon in northern India, followed by 90 consecutive days at 100°F (38°C), drove countless wild-dwelling rats into cities. In August of that year, a large rat die-off occurred in Mamala, a village near the city of Beed in the state of Maharashtra. The following two months saw cases of pneumonic plague in Beed. Shortly afterwards, cases began to be diagnosed in the industrialized coastal city of Surat, 190 miles (300 km) further to the west. People in Surat complained that the source of the disease was the rubbish and carcasses of animals drowned by the flood that had not been cleaned up but rather had been left in heaps rotting in the street. Fleeing the floods themselves, rats were attracted by the piled trash (Nandan 1994).

Reviews of clinical records and results of epidemiologic studies in Surat confirmed reports of an outbreak of acute respiratory illness presented as fever, cough that produced blood, and a high fatality rate, especially in the early stage of the epidemic (Campbell and Hughes 1995). As word of the disease spread through the city, hundreds of thousands of people fled in mortal panic. At the same time, an epidemic of bubonic plague came to light in a section of Maharashtra state that had been devastated by an earthquake the previous year.

Both bubonic and pneumonic plague are caused by the pathogen *Yersinia pestis*, a gram-negative bacillus carried by rodents and their fleas. Most outbreaks of plague are the bubonic form, and usually are caused by flea bites that transmit the bacillus. When a flea is infected, the bacteria multiply within the flea until their sheer density blocks the organism's stomach. The flea reacts by biting voraciously to quell its mounting hunger. Unable to digest the blood, the flea vomits it up, along with bacteria, into the bite wound, thereby infecting the rat, other animal, or human on which the flea is attempting to feed. Within a few days of exposure, acute fevers and chills set in, and sufferers exhibit malaise, muscle pain, nausea, and prostration. In the bubonic form, infected individuals endure painfully swollen lymph nodes. The pneumonic form of plague infects the lungs, allowing person-to-person transmission through respiratory droplets. In this form, there is productive bloody cough and air pockets in the lung fill with fluid. Without treatment, plague can be fatal, with mortality in untreated cases reaching 50 to 90 percent (Hoffman 1980).

The 1994 plague took a heavy toll of lives and ultimately cost India $2 billion. In part, this cost was the consequence of other nations' reactions to the outbreak. A number of countries closed their borders to travelers from India, restrictions on imports from India were imposed, several airlines canceled their flights to the beleaguered country, and at least one nation stopped all postal traffic from the subcontinent.

A recent outbreak of plague in Kazakhstan was traced to the onset of warmer spring weather combined with wetter summer weather, resulting in expanded great gerbil (*Rhombomys opimus*) populations. Fleas that infested the gerbils carried the *Y. pestis* bacteria that causes plague. Analyses showed that a temperature increase of 1.8°F (1°C) produced a 50 percent increase in the prevalence of *Y. pestis*. According to Stenseth et al. (2006:13112):

> Warmer spring conditions lead to an elevated vector-host ratio, which leads to a higher prevalence level in the gerbil host population. Moreover, these climatic conditions that favor increased prevalence among gerbils . . . also favor increased gerbil abundance, which means that the threshold density condition for plague will be reached more often, thus increasing the frequency with which plague can occur.

Encephalitis

Global warming is contributing to the dissemination of various disease-causing ticks and mosquitoes that transmit encephalitis, as seen in the case of West Nile virus (BBC News 1999, Cross and Hyams 1996). Warmer climates have led to notable jumps in encephalitis rates in various countries as far north as Sweden. In the U.S., since 1987, major outbreaks of encephalitis have been recorded in Florida, Mississippi, Louisiana, Texas, Arizona, California, and Colorado. An encephalitis outbreak claimed three lives in New York City, for example, in the summer of 1999 (Union of Concerned Scientists 2005).

Encephalitis epidemics often are triggered by climate change. Extraordinarily heavy rainfall in 1962 in Venezuela, for example, produced a total annual precipitation level that was double that seen on average during the preceding five years. The resulting water-soaked environment created ideal breeding conditions for mosquitoes while forcing the keepers of livestock to crowd their animals into unflooded areas. Under these conditions, a serious outbreak of Venezuelan equine encephalitis (VEE) in people occurred from the far northwest of the country to the far northeast. During the epidemic, VEE virus was isolated in various mosquito species, most frequently in *Aedes taeniorhynchus*, but also in *Aedes serratus*, *Anopheles aquasalis*, *Psorophora confinnis*, and, for the first time, *Aedes scapularis* (Sellers et al. 1965). A prolonged rainy season in 1995 led to another VEE outbreak that began in northwestern Venezuela and spread westward into Colombia, resulting in at least 13,000 encephalitis cases in humans and an uncertain number of equine deaths. VEE virus is transmitted rapidly by mosquitoes among horses and from horses to humans. Horses are known to be the principal amplifying hosts of VEE epidemics because they develop and sustain high levels of virus in their blood systems and attract large numbers of biting mosquitoes. About four percent of humans who are infected with VEE develop neurological symptoms, a disease course that is seen primarily in children and the elderly (Daza et al. 1995). VEE infection during pregnancy can cause fetal infection and birth defects. VEE epidemics can have significant social impact, disrupting everyday social life, damaging economic activities, and debilitating health care operations.

In the period between September 1998 and April 1999, a significant outbreak of encephalitis and respiratory illness occurred in Malaysia. Epidemiologic investigation identified the cause as a previously unknown virus. The new pathogen was given the name Nipah virus after the area in Malyasia in which it was first discovered (Chua et al. 1999). During the initial wave, 265 people were diagnosed as infected; of these, 40 percent died. Nipah virus also was found to cause relapse encephalitis. One Malaysian patient relapsed with encephalitis more than four years after his initial infection. He, like almost all of the victims, was directly involved in the raising or butchering of pigs. Control of the infection required the massive slaughter of pigs and considerable economic loss. Subsequently, a small epidemic occurred in Singapore in which 11 individuals who handled pigs imported from Malaysia fell ill, one of whom died. Outbreaks also have occurred in Bangladesh and neighboring parts of India. Ultimately, it was determined that the Nipah virus was related to another pathogen that had caused several outbreaks in Australia, where it was at first called the equine morbillivirus and later labeled the Hendra virus after the town where it first appeared. Among the victims of this virus was a prominent horse trainer named Vic Rail (Murray et al. 1995). In this case, those who fell ill to Hendra infection all had close contact with horses, which also became sick and later died. Both the Nipah and Hendra virus were determined to be members of the *Paramyxoviridae* family of viruses. Further, it is believed that certain species of "flying foxes" (pteropid fruit bats) are the natural hosts of both the Nipah and Hendra viruses. These bats are found across a wide area encompassing parts of Australia, Indonesia, Malaysia, the Philippines, and some of the Pacific islands. It is not yet understood how the virus is transmitted from bats to animals or from animals to human. Research by Chua, Chua, and Wang (2002) found that reductions in the availability of flowering and fruiting forest trees used for foraging by fruit bats led to the encroachment of the bats into cultivated fruit orchards. Environmental and climatic changes that facilitate changes in subsistence patterns can trigger the movement of emergent and often quite fatal diseases like Nipah and Hendra to new areas. As Chua, Chua, and Wang (2002:265) observe, "Evidence suggested that climatic and anthropogenic driven ecological changes coupled with the location of piggeries in orchards allowed the spill-over of this novel paramyxovirus from its reservoir host into the domestic pigs and ultimately to humans and other animals."

Yellow Fever

Yellow fever is an old disease (with accounts dating to the 17th century) being spread anew by global warming. Named for the yellow pallor of its victims (caused by jaundice), it has played an important role in various historic events, including the defeat of French control of Haiti (by devastating the French colonial army and thereby assisting in the liberation of the world's first black nation). Infection with the yellow fever virus (a member of the *flavivirus* family) causes a wide range of symptoms, some comparatively mild (muscle pain, backache, headache, tremors, loss of appetite, nausea, and vomiting), some severe (bleeding from the mouth, nose, eyes, and stomach; loss of kidney function). Unlike many of the diseases discussed in this chapter, a vaccine for yellow fever has been available for many years. Unvaccinated populations, however, continue to be infected in Africa, Central America, and South America, resulting in over 30,000 fatalities a year. In 2001, the World Health Organization (2001) estimated that yellow fever causes 200,000 infections a year. Spread among humans is quickest in what has been called "urban yellow fever," characterized by the introduction of the virus to domesticated mosquitoes (like *A. aegypti*) that are adapted to living in large cities. A recent outbreak of yellow fever that set off fears of a potential urban epidemic occurred in Colombia, Peru, Brazil, and Bolivia in 2004; although controlled, the outbreak caused 40 deaths. In the assessment of virologist Robert Shope (1991), "If I had to guess which vector-borne diseases would pose the greatest threat in case of global warming in North America, I would say those transmitted by Aedes aegypti mosquitoes—yellow fever and dengue." This conclusion is based on the observed rapid northward migration of the mosquito, an ancient descendant of the common fruit fly.

Lyme Disease

Named in 1977 for the picturesque town of Lyme on the coast of Connecticut, after cases of arthritis were observed in a group of children, Lyme disease is caused by the bacterium *Borrelia burgdorferi*. This microbe is carried by a deer tick called *Ixodes scapularis*, which lives in the fur of both deer and mice. As populations of these animals have increased (because of the elimination of predators and resource competitors) and as human populations (and their peculiar land-use patterns, from housing developments to golf courses) have spread and affected more areas, the number of people being bitten by deer ticks has jumped significantly. A study conducted by researchers at the Center for Health and the Global Environment at Harvard Medical School concluded that Lyme disease is increasing in North America as warmer winters allow ticks to proliferate (Britt 2005).

Lyme disease, which is characterized initially by an expanding rash called an erythema chronicum migrans at the site of tick attachment and flu-like symptoms that, if left untreated, can develop into irregular heart rhythm, facial paralysis (Bell's palsy), swelling and pain in the joints, arthritis, and various other significant health problems, is now prevalent in many parts of North America, Europe, and Asia. There are over 16,000 Lyme disease cases reported in the United States each year, making it the most common vector-borne disease in the country. An illustrative case, as reported by the Centers for Disease Control and Prevention (2003), involves

> an east-coast family [that] has moved out of the city [to a] new home in the suburbs, complete with woods for hiking and deer in the surrounding area. The kids love to play outdoors. One day, Joey, the family's 10-year old son, notices a red, bull's eye shaped rash on his arm. He feels tired, has a headache and achy muscles. His mother isn't sure if this could just be summer flu, but she's alarmed enough to take Joey to the doctor's office—over his objections. In the waiting room, she notices a brochure about Lyme disease, and realizes that Joey has a classic infection. The doctor is able to treat this early infection with a course of antibiotics, and Joey recovers completely.

Despite this happy ending, spread of the disease has set off intensive debates about appropriate treatment, as some health care providers and researchers advocate prolonged antibiotic treatment and others discount the health benefits of this approach. Those in the former camp maintain that short-course antibiotic intervention does not necessarily kill the pathogen resulting in long-term, increasingly debilitating symptoms. Global warming promises to expand the range of suitable habitats for the parasite's hosts and hence the number of people being infected, while further intensifying the debate (Brownstein et al. 2005).

Accelerating Dissemination

The spread of many vector-borne infections is gaining speed. As Paul Epstein notes, "Things we projected to occur in 2080 are happening in

2006. . . . Our mistake was underestimation" (quoted in Struck 2006: A16). Further, increased heat and upper-atmosphere ozone depletion resulting from global warming and other sociogenic causes raise UV-B radiation exposure for all species. Because microorganisms reproduce quickly, they are capable of very rapid genetic change, allowing for ever faster development of pathogen resistance to the chemical arsenal of biomedicine and pest control, as well as, sometimes, enhanced virulence. Additionally, the same factors that cause global warming, environmental pollution, and the buildup of chlorinated hydrocarbons suppress the effectiveness of the human immune system. In other words, there are synergistic interactions triggered by global warming that can have significant impact on human health. Similarly, malnutrition, which, as we have seen, rising climates will cause in many parts of the world, also adversely impacts the immune system, increasing human vulnerability to spreading diseases, including strains of fast-mutating pathogens for which people lack immune system preparation through prior exposure. It has been established that the absolute virulence of many pathogens is kept in check by the body's natural defense systems. If these are compromised by a deteriorating environment and worsening diet, previously harmless pathogenic strains can become lethal. This pattern is seen in AIDS, which involves viral attack on key components of the immune system, which, once sufficiently compromised, allows a host of opportunistic infections from a wide variety of pathogens that had previously been constrained by immune system activity.

Global Public Health and the Environment

In their chapter on environmental health, McMichael, Kjellström, and Smith (2001:379) stress the importance of developing an "integrated 'ecological' understanding of the interplay between human populations and the natural environment, and the consequence for human health of contaminating, depleting, or overloading that environment." Achieving this goal, they argue, is hindered by several factors. In the developed world, the growth of ever-greater technological capacity to measure specific exposures that are culturally associated with lifestyle (such as smoking), however much they reflect significant structural forces rather than individual lifestyle choices (e.g., the advertising and promotional work of the tobacco and food industries) have limited focus on "more diffuse lower-concentrations exposures in the external environment, result[ing] in that latter topic attracting less attention and having lower credibility" (McMichael et al. 2001:433). In the developing world, the emergence of specific health systems interventions (e.g., pesticides, vaccination) for "the age-old scourges of diarrheal disease, acute respirator infections, tuberculosis, and vector-borne infections" similarly have led to the wider ecological dimensions of these health problems being somewhat neglected. As detailed above, overlooking the broader ecological factors in the spread of vector-borne and other infections is a serious misstep fraught with risks for current and future health. As argued in the next chapter, in fact, in the time of global warming a comprehensive ecological approach is needed, one that examines the biosocial character of multiple disease and social structural interactions.

6

Ecosyndemics

The Interaction of Changing Environment and Disease

Parasites and disease will do well on a warming earth. They are, by defin-
ition, organisms that colonize and exploit. Those species of parasite that
are already common will be able to spread and perhaps colonize new sus-
ceptible hosts that may have no prior genetic resistance to them.

Andrew Dobson and Robin Carper, parasitologists

What is Disease?

Although various diseases were examined in the previous three
chapters, the concept of disease was not specifically defined. In that
a goal of this chapter is the presentation of a broadened understanding
of disease in light of the effects of global warming, the starting point is
a consideration of the conventional way disease is conceived. Within
biomedicine, disease is thought of as any deviation from or disruption
of the normal structure or function of a body part or system, including
the mind, that is characterized by a configuration of signs (detectable
by physicians) and symptoms (experienced and reported by sufferers).
While some diseases are recognized that have no distinct symptoms (e.g.,
hypertensive disease), physicians are hesitant to validate a disease known
experientially to victims but undetectable to medical specialists (e.g., various folk illnesses). Critical to this model is the understanding that diseases, as distinct, bounded entities in nature, are part of an immutable
physical reality and therefore have an existence independent from the
social and cultural contexts in which they are found. It is for this reason
that they are subject to objective description by a trained diagnostician.

Cancer, for example, is a meta label that refers to a large number of
specific diseases or kinds of cancer, all of which are characterized by the
development of (observable) abnormal cells (caused by a genetic muta-
tion) that divide uncontrollably and have the capacity to both infiltrate
and destroy normal body tissue. From the perspective of biomedicine,
cancer is neither a cultural construction nor is it peculiar to any individual sufferer or specific group. Rather, cancer is accepted as a bona
fide component of material reality, even though it is recognized that it
often is not easy to diagnose (especially in its earliest stages)—although

133

this problem is seen as a shortcoming of available medical technology or practitioner ability, and not a question of cancer's physical existence. Diagnosis sometimes is based on the fine-grained, microscopic examination of biopsied tissue by a well-trained eye skilled at spotting abnormal cell structures. The difference between normal and cancerous cells, however, is not always evident and requires, in the end, a human decision.

Michel Foucault (1975:129) referred to this capacity of medicine to "see disease" as the clinical gaze, noting that its historic development offered biomedicine "an objective, real, and at last unquestioned foundation for the description [and classification] of diseases." The clinical gaze, the capacity of the trained eye to see beneath surface appearances into underlying realities, did not, however, eliminate ambiguity or human judgment in the diagnostic process. In the specific case of breast cancer, for example, according to the National Cancer Institute (2002), several alternative diagnostic approaches are available, with high-quality mammography being recognized as "the most effective technology presently available . . . . Efforts to improve mammography focus on refining the technology and improving how it is administered and X-ray films are interpreted." Despite advanced technology, in other words—what might be called a cyber clinical gaze—human interpretation is needed because the difference between normal cells and diseased ones is blurry at the edges. At all turns nature resists reduction into the neat categories humans and their physicians (as well as patients) desire.

An Emergent Alternative Syndemic Perspective

Isolating individual diseases, giving them unique labels (e.g., breast cancer, AIDS, malaria, tuberculosis), and spotlighting their specific nature, array of signs and symptoms, and immediate causes has allowed the development of modern pharmaceutical, surgical, and other biomedical treatments. Many of these have proven to be quite effective, if not always in curing at least in containing disease and extending life. Nonetheless, it has become increasingly clear that diseases, as well as other health conditions that are not always labeled as disease per se (e.g., malnutrition, drug abuse, violence victimization), do not exist in nature in isolation as distinct entities. They often are found in tandem, multiple diseases anatomically, chemically, psychologically, and behaviorally intertwined in the same individuals and same populations. An example is the contemporary interconnection of AIDS and famine in many of the nations of southern Africa. As de Waal and Whiteside comment:

> HIV/AIDS has created a new category of highly vulnerable households— namely, those with ill adults or those whose adults have died. The general

burden of care in both AIDS-affected and non-AIDS-affected households has reduced the viability of farming livelihoods. The sensitivity of rural communities to external shocks such as drought has increased, and their resilience has declined. The prospects for a sharp decline into severe famine are increased, and possibilities for recovery reduced. [de Waal and Whiteside 2003:1237]

Moreover, diseases do not simply coexist with other diseases in overlapped space within the same population, the bodies of their individual members, or the organs of individual sufferers. Rather, diseases interact synergistically in substantial ways that impact the health of the individuals and populations they infect. The lines between individual diseases and between diseases and other health conditions, in short, are blurry as well.

Consequently, an alternative understanding of disease has developed in recent years, known as the syndemic perspective. Emerging first within medical anthropology in response to grappling with health disparities and the heavy burden of multiple diseases found in impoverished, subordinated populations like U.S. ethnic minorities and colonized populations (Marshall 2005, Singer 1994, 1996), the syndemic perspective has diffused into public health (Freudenberg et al. 2006, Gielen et al. 2007, Milstein 2004, 2008) and beyond (Ventura and Mehra 2004). This perspective is characterized by three components. First, rather than focusing on individual diseases, it is concerned with the manifold and often complex interconnections found among co-morbid diseases and other health conditions in a population, especially the specific biological and other linkages between maladies that unfold over time and have consequence for human life. As a result, the syndemic approach allows a new way of thinking about disease in relational rather than categorical terms (Singer and Clair 2003), including drawing attention to how diseases and other health conditions promote and reinforce each other and thereby increase the overall burden on sufferers. As Chadwick (2003:119), an environmental biologist, explains with reference to new ways of looking at the concept of species: if you look at them one way "you see individual things; look the other way, you see processes, relationships—things together. This is the new level in understanding biology."

Second, the syndemics perspective points to the fundamental importance of the interacting social and environmental conditions that promote the emergence and transmission of disease, including the severity of the health impact of sickness at the individual and group levels. Of special concern is the development of concentrations or clusters of disease (i.e., the co-coexistence within populations of at least two but often multiple co-morbid diseases and other health conditions that create the opportunity for disease interaction). Syndemics are of importance because when diseases interact their health effects sometimes are not merely additive, they are multiplicative.

Finally, stemming from its focus on connections and permeable boundaries, the syndemics perspective assesses disease within its encompassing biocultural environment. Unlike traditional environmental health models, however, the physical environment, or nature, is not thought of as a reserve of things not-human nor as being separate from and independent of human action. Rather, there is a strong concern with the historic ways the "natural" environment no less than the built environment of hamlets, villages, towns, cities, and megacities has been shaped and influenced by human action, both intentional and otherwise. Of special concern are the ways in which all affected environments, both those deemed natural and those that are undeniably of human origin, reflect social inequalities within and between societies. The latter is of critical significance because: 1) syndemics commonly emerge among socially marginalized groups—precisely because of their subordinated social status; 2) human impact on the surrounding world reflects the exercise of power in society; and 3) effective public health responses to syndemics require attention to their underlying causes while selected responses commonly reflect structures of inequality. As Krieger (2001:674) emphasizes, it is important to think "critically and systematically about intimate and integral connections between our social and biological existence—and, especially in the case of social production of disease and ecosocial theory, to name explicitly who benefits from and is accountable for social inequalities in health."

All three of these arenas are important in understanding the role of global warming in the emergence of new syndemics, as well as how we should respond to them to protect human health.

Types of Syndemic Interactions

Concern about syndemics has been driven by growing awareness of the regularity of interactions among diseases; by recognition that these connections shape disease course, expression, and transmission; and by realization that morbidity and mortality are significantly enhanced by the effects diseases and other health conditions have upon each other. Disease interactions are of several different kinds. First, in some syndemic exchanges—such as interactions between diabetes and SARS—changes in biochemistry or damage to organ systems caused by one disease, such as a flagging immune system (as seen in the diabetes-related decline in the number of Natural Killer cells), promotes the progression of another disease (SARS) (Rickerts et al. 2006). This is the relationship that exists also between HIV infection and a multitude of "opportunistic" bacterial (e.g., Listeria), mycobacterial (e.g., tuberculosis), fungal (e.g., candidiasis), protozoal (e.g., toxoplasmosis), and viral (e.g., human papilloma virus) pathogens and possibly viral-caused malignancies (e.g., Kaposi's sarcoma). HIV and tuberculosis (TB), for example, the aptly termed "cursed duet" (Chretien 1990:25), form a globally significant and spreading syndemic. Co-infection with *Mycobacterium tuberculosis*, the pathogen that causes TB, and HIV leads to accelerated replication of HIV and more rapid disease progression (Goldfeld and Ellner 2007, Zang et al. 1995). Approximately 30 percent of AIDS-related deaths are most immediately due to tuberculosis. Similarly, individuals with TB who are not co-infected with HIV have a ten percent chance over the course of their life time of developing overt tuberculosis, while those who are co-infected have a 50 percent chance (Grange 1997, Grange and Zumla 2002). The annual risk of a TB-infected individual developing an active (i.e., worsening) case of the disease is eight to ten percent among those co-infected with HIV; this is about 40 percent higher than among TB patients who are not co-infected with HIV (Antonucci et al. 1995, Dolin et al. 1994). In other words, co-infected individuals have roughly the same chance of developing an active case of TB in a single year as individuals who only suffer from TB do for their whole life. Consequently, over the last decade HIV has played a significant role in expanding the number of people who develop overt TB by millions of cases. Moreover, in HIV-infected TB patients, there is increased incidence of adverse reactions to available drugs for treating the disease and poorer patient compliance with therapy. Because of the far-reaching impact of HIV on TB, including changes in the natural course of the disease, researchers have adopted the term "the new tuberculosis" (De Cock 1994) to differentiate the current TB pandemic from the ancient TB scourge. Although during the 1990s the burden of HIV/TB co-infection fell disproportionately on sub-Saharan Africa, rapid and extensive spread to Asia and beyond has become an equally disturbing feature of this expanding global syndemic.

Second, one disease can assist the physical transmission of another. Syphilis infection, which causes genital-tract ulceration (chancres), for example, appears to facilitate the sexual transmission of HIV (McClelland et al. 2005, Reynolds et al. 2006, Singer et al. 2006). Breaks in the skin or mucous membranes caused by syphilis bleed easily during sexual contact, creating openings for HIV transmission during intercourse with an infected partner. Chesson and co-workers (2003) used this knowledge to develop a mathematical model to assess the role of syphilis infection in new HIV cases among African Americans. They concluded that for the year 2000, approximately 545 new cases of HIV (three to five percent of all new cases) among African Americans were a consequence of the facilitative effects of infectious syphilis on HIV transmission. Additionally, syphilis infection is associated with the perinatal transmission of HIV from infected mothers to their infants (Lee et al. 1998).

A third type of syndemic relationship involves one disease contributing to the virulence of another. A syndemic interaction between HIV-1 (the predominant strain of HIV found in the U.S.) and herpes simplex viruses has now been demonstrated in a series of epidemiological and clinical studies (Lusso et al. 2007). This research shows that HIV-1 infection alters the natural history of herpes simplex virus type 2 (HSV-2) in co-infected individuals by exacerbating the clinical impact and frequency of HSV-2 flareups (i.e., the development of lesions). Additionally, HSV-2 infection exacerbates the risk of HIV acquisition. A study of men at high behavioral risk for HIV infection, for example, found that 68 percent with a pre-existing case of HSV-2 infection subsequently became infected with HIV, while only 46 percent of those without HSV-2 infection contracted HIV infection (Holmberg et al. 1988). Similar results were found in a study of patients at a clinic for sexually transmitted diseases (Stamm et al. 1988). Moreover, there is evidence that HSV-2 infection contributes to HIV disease progression (Lingappa and Celum 2007). Individuals who are co-infected with HIV-1 and HSV-2 have higher viral loads than HIV-1 patients not infected with HSV-2 (Reynolds and Quinn 2007). As Schacker (2001:46) notes, there is growing evidence that "significant biological interaction between these two viruses [results] in more efficient sexual transmission of HIV-1 and an increased rate of HIV replication during both clinical and subclinical HSV reactivation."

Fourth, it is possible for gene mixing to occur among different types of pathogenic agents. This has been described in most detail thus far in several plant and animal species, such as occurs between avian leukosis virus and Markek's disease virus (MDV) in domestic fowl. Both of these cancer-causing viruses are known to infect the same cells of birds within the same flock. In co-infected cells, the retroviral DNA of the avian leukosis virus can move into the MDV genome, producing altered biological properties compared to those of the parental MDV (Davidson et al. 2002). Similarly, consequential gene exchange has been described for different strains of the same pathogen. As Escrui et al (2007:e8) point out, "Genetic exchange by recombination, or reassortment of genomic segments, has been shown to be an important process in RNA virus evolution, resulting often in important phenotypic changes affecting host range and virulence."

The frequency of gene reassortment among human pathogens is less clear than is the case among plant or some animal species but of significant potential concern as animal diseases adapt to and infect human hosts—something they have been doing at an increasingly rapid pace—and as new diseases come into contact with each other. A known case of gene recombination in human diseases involves the movement of genes among the seven different strains of HIV-1 in co-infected individuals, a pattern that has had a dramatic impact on the evolutionary history of this virus, including its capacity for drug resistance and overall virulence (Abecasis et al. 2007, Steain et al. 2004). Co-infection with more than one strain of HIV in what is known as a "superinfection" makes it possible for gene mixing to occur. Recombination of the genomes of different HIV strains means that resistance mutations to specific treatments that have developed in distinct viral populations can be joined, contributing to the development of viruses with the capacity for multi-drug resistance (Nora et al. 2007).

Also of note in this regard are the 1957 and 1968 influenza pandemic viruses that appear to have evolved through gene reassortment of Eurasian wild waterfowl influenza strains with the previously circulating human H1N1 strain that caused the 1918 human influenza pandemic (Taubenberger and Morens 2006). Gene mixing among pathogens adapted to animal species with related strains adapted to infecting humans may, in fact, be an important source of new human epidemics because they allow the presentation of novel forms of an older disease that are unfamiliar to the human immune system (Bean et al. 1992). As Belshie observes,

> In 1957, dual infection of an individual animal—probably a human, but possibly another species, such as a pig—with an avian H2N2 influenza and a human H1N1 influenza resulted in the emergence of a new influenza virus containing the hemagglutinin, the neuraminidase, and the gene for one of the polymerase proteins (PB1) from the avian virus, along with the remaining five genetic segments from the human H1N1 influenza virus. [Belshie 2005:2209]

This gene exchange allowed another deadly flu pandemic to sweep through human populations. Notably, reassorted influenza viruses of the form that caused the 1957 human pandemic continue to circulate among turkeys on farms and in live bird markets in New York City and elsewhere (Schäfer et al. 1993), and these birds may serve as reservoirs for future human outbreaks of novel influenza viral strains.

Fifth, in some cases, co-infection with two diseases may open up multiple syndemic pathways. A lethal synergism has been identified, for example, between influenza virus and pneumococcus that is the source of excess mortality from secondary bacterial pneumonia during influenza epidemics. According to McCullers and Rehg (2006), there is mounting evidence that the influenza virus alters the lungs in ways that contribute to infection with pneumococcus. Other consequential changes, such as alteration of the immune response which weakens the body's ability to clear pneumococcus (or, alternately, by amplifying the inflammatory cascade), have also been described in the literature as well.

Additionally, there are a set of apparent syndemic interactions for which the pathways of disease interaction have not yet been established. A recently identified case is the likely syndemic relationship between kidney disease and heart disease. It is now apparent that kidney disease is capable of accelerating the development of heart disease even before it has significantly damaged the kidneys. At the same time, heart disease speeds up kidney damage among people with kidney disease. Both diseases have common risk factors: high blood pressure and diabetes, but as yet, the precise corridors of this two-way syndemic interaction are not clear. One suspected link is in the bone marrow. Both the heart and kidneys are known to send electrical signals to the bone marrow to produce a type of stem cell that helps keep body organs in good condition. In cases of both kidney and heart disease these signals diminish, with the damaging result being a decline in the body's built-in organ repair capacity. Needless to say, the morbidity and mortality consequences of this decline can be severe.

Popular awareness of kidney function and chronic kidney disease are limited. Consequently, it has been called a "quiet epidemic," although in the U.S. alone there are almost 20 million sufferers. The disease is characterized by a loss of kidney activity, resulting in the body being less and less able to clear the blood system of poisonous waste products. Until kidney damage is fairly advanced, patients often do not have any identifiable symptoms. Of mounting concern is the fact that end-stage renal failure is becoming more common and the case load of people requiring dialysis or kidney transplant has doubled in each of the last two decades. Notably, however, most people with chronic kidney disease die of heart disease before kidney function is lost.

Heart disease causes a narrowing of the arteries throughout the body, including in the kidneys. In a study of 37,000 people screened in the National Kidney Foundation's Kidney Early Evaluation Program, McCullough and co-workers (2007) found that participants who suffered from both chronic kidney disease and known heart disease had a threefold increased risk of death (at 16 months) compared to those who did not suffer from these two diseases. In another recent study of kidney disease (Tsui et al. 2007), a large national cohort examination of adult veterans, patients under the age of 70 who were infected with hepatitis C (HCV) were found to be at significantly heightened risk for developing end-stage renal disease. Again, the pathways linking these two diseases are not yet known. What is clear, however, is that interaction between heart disease and HCV with kidney disease is a very dangerous syndemic, and more broadly, that disease interaction plays a central role in patterns of morbidity and mortality in all human groups.

Social Origins of Syndemics

Conceptualizing risks to health in syndemic terms points to the importance of moving beyond a narrow focus on biology to an inclusion of a close examination of social conditions and the structure of social relations in the development of disease concentrations, the frequency of disease co-morbidity, and the health outcomes of synergistic disease interactions. In syndemics, interface among diseases or other health-related problems reflects in no small measure the impact of a configuration of adverse social factors including poverty, stigmatization, oppressive social relationships, and health care disparities. These conditions put disadvantaged, socially devalued and subjugated individuals and groups at heightened risk for disease exposure while limiting their access to timely and effective prevention and health care intervention. Additionally, as a result of the physical effects of suffering discrimination, rejection, stigmatization, internalization of oppression, status inconsistency, low cultural consonance, and related stressors, as well as exposures to noxious living and working conditions, subordinated populations commonly encounter new disease threats in a heightened state of vulnerability (i.e., in a less than optimal state of health and with already compromised immune and other body systems) (Baer, Singer, and Susser 2003, Dressler and Bindon 2000, Easton 2004).

The morbidity and mortality statistics for African Americans, for example, a group that has suffered health disparities since their first (forced) arrival in colonial America, exemplify this pattern. In 2002, African Americans comprised just under 13 percent of the population of the United States (U.S. Bureau of the Census 2005). Despite declines in recent years, the rate of infant mortality among African Americans has remained at double the rate of white Americans for decades. African Americans have higher morbidity and mortality rates from heart disease, cancer, asthma, diabetes, HIV/AIDS, and many other diseases (Umar 2003).

The nature of these health disparities are illustrated by the case of hypertension. African Americans have one of the highest prevalences of hypertension in the world. Compared with whites, hypertension among African Americans develops at an earlier stage of life, and at all ages average blood pressure is significantly higher. In particular, African Americans have higher rates of what is called "stage 3 hypertension," the level at which health complications associated with high blood pressure are most evident. Earlier onset, higher prevalence, and a higher rate of stage 3 hypertension results in an 80 percent higher stroke mortality rate, a 50 percent higher heart disease mortality rate, and a 320 percent greater rate of hypertension-related end-stage renal disease among African Americans compared with the general U.S. population (BlackHealthCare.com 1999). As Krieger (2006:471) emphasizes,

Conditions such as economic deprivation and racial discrimination can increase the risk of hypertension via pathways involving lead exposure, damaged kidneys, excessive body mass index, unmanaged hypertension due to lack of access to adequate health care, and increased allostatic load . . . with the last of these defined as "the wear and tear of the body and brain resulting from chronic overactivity or inactivity of physiological systems that are normally involved in adaptation to environmental change."

At present, while the life expectancy for white males in the United States is 76.7 years, for their African American counterparts it is only 67.8 years. Among white females, the average life expectancy is 79.9 years compared to 74.7 years for African American females. African Americans have been found to be at significantly greater risk of death, including premature death, than whites. Most existing studies show a 30 percent higher age-adjusted risk of mortality among African Americans. Much of the difference, which reflects a greater disease burden, is explained by disparities in the socioeconomic status (SES) of African Americans compared to whites. In an analysis of several national studies, for example, Franks and his colleagues found that

African-Americans experience about 67,000 more deaths than they would have had their mortality rates been similar to whites. This translates into 2.2 million more YLL [annual years of life lost]. After adjusting for SES, these numbers drop to about 38,000 lives and 1.1 million YLL. Thus, roughly 29,000 of the lives lost and 1.1 million years lost annually may be attributable to differences in income and education between the groups. [Franks et al. 2006:2472]

The additional mortality burden among African Americans after statistical adjustment for socioeconomic status is believed to be a consequence of the health damage caused by being subjected to racism and related forms discriminatory treatment that result in various adverse chemical changes in the bodies of stressed populations, changes that cause health damage. More than 100 studies—most of which were published since 2000—document the significant adverse health effects of being subjected to racial discrimination. Some studies link blood pressure to recollected encounters with prejudice. Others record the cardiovascular reactions of volunteers subjected to racist imagery during laboratory experiments (Drexler 2007). Cumulatively, they affirm that exposure to bigotry is a source of physical disease. Further, African Americans who perceive they are being subjected to racism—and thus have a conscious experience of mistreatment—have been found to have higher blood pressure than those who do not share this perception (Krieger and Sidney 1996).

Moreover, lower socioeconomic status and being the object of racism have been found to interact, increasing the damaging health effects of each condition. While poverty appears to be a critical factor in health disparities, household income is not the only issue involved. Whereas health disparities generally are strongly influenced by poverty, disparity is greatest among poor people who live in areas with a high percentage of other poor people in the local population. Thus, poor people in cities with smaller impoverished populations are at lower risk of dying than those in cities with large impoverished populations. In other words, the density of poverty in an area appears to be a crucial determinant of the health status of the poor (Budrys 2003). Consequently, the level of concentration of the poor is an important metric for determining the rigidity of the structure of inequality.

Studies of differences by location among the poor show that the sociophysical environment in which people live—that is, their conscious experience of their surrounding community including issues of danger, stress, comfort, and appeal—is also an important determinant of their health. Feelings of hopelessness and powerlessness in a community have been found to be good predictors of health risk and health status. There is, in short, a biology of poverty and social injustice that puts subjugated populations at a heightened level of vulnerability to disease (Leatherman and Goodman 1998).

A recent example of this vulnerability is seen in the case of antimicrobial drug–resistant *Staphylococcus aureus*. This staph strain, which can cause skin infections that are usually mild but with the capacity of developing into pneumonia or bloodstream diseases, was initially seen in hospitals and nursing homes (Maree et al. 2007). It was, in fact, the first bacterium in which resistance to penicillin was discovered, just four years after the drug entered into mass production. Currently, almost 100,000 Americans suffer potentially dangerous infections caused by *S. aureus*, and deaths tied to these infections may exceed those caused by AIDS (Klevens et al. 2007). A new study by Hota and co-workers (2007) at Rush University Medical Center and John H. Stroger, Jr. Hospital in Chicago found that the greatest risk factors for infection with this emergent disease strain were prior experience with incarceration, being African American, and having residence in public housing. Being poor and a member of a marginalized ethnic minority, in conjunction with the living conditions and experiences this entails—from overcrowding to lack of sanitary conditions to high rates of arrest and incarceration—has become a risk factor for what began as a disease of clinical settings. Of note, analysis of the genetic makeup of an untreatable case of

S. aureus infection in a Michigan patient in 2002 found various genes for antibiotic resistance, most importantly a vanA gene that is responsible for resistance to the drug vancomycin (the primary medicine used to treat methicillin-resistant staph infection). This gene had jumped into the *S. aureus* from another organism, carrying with it the potential to make *S. aureus* resistant. According to infectious diseases expert Peter Collignon of the Canberra Hospital in Australia, "This well done scientific study has shown that, in people, the vanA gene can jump from a relatively non-aggressive germ like enterococcus into a very aggressive germ like *Staphylococcus aureus*" (quoted in Sallah 2003).

A similar pattern of a disease becoming concentrated among the poor is seen in the case of HIV, which was first observed among gay men but is not disproportionately found among the poor and ethnic minorities in the United States. Freudenberg and colleagues (2006), for example, have described a syndemic comprised of HIV, TB, and street violence among the inner-city poor in New York that began in the mid-1970s. This syndemic was produced by oppressive social conditions exacerbated by budget and policy decisions involving cuts to health and social programs that were intended, ostensibly, to save money for the city. Instead, these decisions contributed to deteriorating living conditions, a 20 percent rise in the numbers of poor people in the city despite an overall population decrease of 10 percent, and a rise in the health burden of the poor:

> First, city, state, and federal budget cuts diminished the public health, public safety, medical, and social service infrastructures that respond to health emergencies, compromising their ability to respond effectively to emerging threats such as HIV infection and crack addiction. Second, the cuts led to reductions in services such as drug treatment, preventive clinical services, health education, and policing and thus contributed to increases in TB, HIV infection, and homicide. Third, these policy decisions amplified other trends that were pushing vulnerable populations such as the homeless, drug users, the incarcerated, single mothers, and the unemployed into living situations that put them squarely in the path of TB, HIV infection, and violence. [Freudenberg et al. 2006:431]

In the aftermath of these changes, TB rates began to rise following a century of declining infection (Paolo and Nosanchuk 2004). At the same time, AIDS cases also became more frequent, particularly among drug users (Centers for Disease Control and Prevention 2005). Homicide rates began going up and continued to climb through 1990 (Freudenberg et al. 2006). A similar pattern has been described for inner-city Hartford, Connecticut (Singer 1996), involving intertwined substance abuse, street and domestic violence, and AIDS and a second syndemic involving HIV, chlamydia, and gonorrhea (Singer et al. 2006). Likewise, Stall and co-workers (Stall et al. 2003, Stall and Mills 2006) have described a syndemic involving HIV, drug use, and partner violence among men who have sex with men in San Francisco.

As these three examples from three different U.S. cities suggest, at the population level an emergent disease like HIV can, under conditions of social discrimination and marginalization, come to be closely and consequentially intertwined with several different diseases and other threats to health, forming various distributional clusters. In time, these independent syndemics may merge to form a "supersyndemic," a dynamic that syndemic theory predicts is most likely to occur in populations that suffer multiple structural disadvantages and the resulting interconnected breakdown of social infrastructures and safety nets, interpersonal social relationships, households, and immune defenses. The contemporary health of African Americans, for example, which, as noted, is characterized by multiple overlapping, intertwined, and mutually reinforcing diseases (e.g., hypertension, heart disease, diabetes, HIV/AIDS) might well best be described as reflecting a supersyndemic within an oppressed and marginalized population.

Modern epidemiology, with its heavy focus on inter-individual variations in risk, often fails to assess the underlying social causes of disease clustering because, as McMichael (1995:634) observes, it is "oriented to explaining and quantifying the bobbing of corks on the surface waters, while largely disregarding the stronger undercurrents that determine where, on average, the cluster of corks ends up along the shoreline of risk." Some epidemiologists, as well as their colleagues across health-related disciplines, however, do focus squarely on the undercurrents. Like Peter Townsend (1986), they recognize that the poor or other socially marginalized groups do not exist in isolation; rather, their exacting life situations are the product of structural barriers from which the privileged directly benefit. In other words, as Townsend argues, the rich exist because there are poor and vice versa. Adds Krieger (2007:662), a corollary of this proposition "is that unfair relations between groups shape the characteristics of the groups themselves, including their health status." In syndemic terms: social inequality and injustice + sociogenetic impacts on the environment + resulting disease interactions = syndemics.

While a variety of syndemics have already been described in the literature (Cubillos-Garzon et al. 2004, Helfand et al. 2005, Herring and Sattenspiel 2007, Hotez 2003, Johnson and Martin 2005, Marshall 2005, Singer et al. 2006, Young 2004), the pace of syndemic development is likely to be significantly accelerated by global environment change. A specific impact of a warming planet on syndemic formation will involve the array of diseases that come together from various regions of the planet, co-infect populations and individuals, and interact to the detriment of sufferers, issues that are discussed below.

The Emergent Model of Ecosyndemics

From a syndemic perspective, what is critical is not that diseases move, but rather where, and why they move, and what happens to them in their new environments. Critical questions include: To what degree will they cluster with other diseases in new host populations? Which other diseases will they encounter there? How will they interact with these newly encountered disease counterparts? What consequence will these interactions have for human health? The term *ecosyndemic* was developed (Singer 2007) to label the specific facilitative roles of global warming on environmental change, disease movement, disease clustering, and biological interaction among diseases and other health conditions, and the impact of these exchanges on disease burdens and global health trends. As David Byrne, the European Union Health Commissioner, has stressed,

> it is one thing to speak of how to address an outbreak of a particular zoonoses, however big. It is quite another matter to address a pandemic brought about by the convergence of human and animal influenzas, for example. Here, we could be talking of the most devastating consequences. . . . While we have witnessed the deaths of millions of animals in Europe over the past couple of years, are we prepared for the deaths of 10 or 20 million of our fellow citizens arising from the mutation of a human and animal virus that we cannot control? I do not want to be seen as a prophet of doom. But I am obliged to ring the alarm bell as the European Commissioner for Health. [Byrne 2004:4]

As with the original term *syndemic*, it is understood that human action, as it is structured through unequal social relationships, including disparities of power and oppressive exploitation, discrimination, and consequent social suffering, are critical to the production of global warming and the development of ecosyndemics. Consequently, ecosyndemics, it is argued here, are likely to concentrate among the poor and other marginalized groups, who are least able to obtain adequate diets, sanitary and protective living conditions, low-stress life experiences, and access to prevention and care.

The potential for an ecosyndemic is seen by events in the Horn of Africa in 1997–1998 when drenching rains, which were 60 to 100 times heavier than normal, and constituted the heaviest downpours recorded in the area since 1961, set off an epidemic of cholera as well as two mosquito-borne epidemics: malaria and Rift Valley fever (Epstein 2000), creating the opportunity for inter-disease contact and adverse synergistic interaction. According to the World Health Organization (2003):

> Africa reported 211,748 [cholera] cases in 1998, the highest number of cases ever reported and accounted for 72 percent of the global total. There had

been a sudden increase of cholera at the end of 1997 in the Horn of Africa, and this continued throughout 1998 and spread to many other countries. . . . This recrudescence is most probably related to the continuing effects of major disasters caused by El Nino. . .

At the same time, malaria struck, producing over 30 percent of all illness in the Horn of Africa during this period. The rains also caused Rift Valley fever–infected mosquito eggs to hatch in abundance. First hit by newly hatched adult mosquitoes were livestock, followed by humans. Almost 90,000 people in northeastern Kenya and southern Somalia were infected and over 200 people died of Rift Valley fever. Combining infections among both animals and human, it is believed that the Horn of Africa epidemic was the worst Rift Valley fever epidemic in the world to date (World Health Organization 1998).

Ecosyndemic Trends

A starting point for thinking about the ecosyndemics ushered in by global warming is the examination of what have been called the "neglected tropical diseases" in that these may begin to spread to virgin terrain as the conditions that facilitate their diffusion are produced by global warming. As Hotez et al. (2007) observe, since the turn of the 21st century the powerful nations that comprise the Group of Eight (G8) forum (Canada, France, Germany, Italy, Japan, Russia, the United Kingdom, and the United States), which collectively control 65 percent of the wealth in the world, have devoted considerable attention to the issue of health. Primarily the focus of this attention has been on three global pandemics: HIV/AIDS, tuberculosis, and malaria. These so-called "big three diseases" cause almost six million deaths and the loss over 165 million disability-adjusted life years annually across the globe. Of these three diseases, malaria is most directly affected by global warming because it is spread by climate-sensitive vectors, while HIV/AIDS and TB are transmitted through direct human contact (i.e., the sharing of body fluids and airborne droplets, respectively). However, all three of these diseases are of concern in the age of global warming because of their capacity for syndemic interaction with other diseases. Still, as Hortez emphasizes, however important global public health efforts focused on the big three are,

Conspicuously absent from these activities. . . has been commensurate advocacy for a group of diseases that exclusively affect the poor and the powerless in rural and impoverished urban areas of developing countries. An increasing body of evidence indicates that this group of "neglected tropical diseases" may not only threaten the health of the poor as much as HIV/AIDS, tuberculosis, or malaria, but even more importantly, may have effective treatment and prevention strategies that can be delivered for less than US$1 per capita per year. [Hotez et al. 2007]

Additionally, neglected tropical diseases are of importance because of their potential to spread beyond the tropics and to become components of regional or global ecosyndemics as a result of global warming, especially among the poorest populations who often have woefully inadequate water supply, sanitation, and housing.

Even within sub-Saharan Africa and parts of Asia and the Americas, where they are endemic, the neglected tropical diseases do not tend to occur in isolation nor are they are likely to spread outside of the regions where they currently are found as isolated conditions. Populations in affected areas are polyparasitized, (i.e., suffering from multiple parasites at once), including being subject to disease vectors that can transmit several different pathogens at once; they are also at high risk for infection with the big three diseases; and they are extremely poor, creating a catastrophic burden of disease and setting up the conditions for significant syndemic formation and diffusion.

Most notable among the neglected tropical diseases, Hotez et al. (2007) point to three vector-borne protozoan infections: leishmaniasis, human African trypanosomiasis (sleeping sickness), and Chagas disease (a South American form of trypanosomiasis); three bacterial infections: trachoma, leprosy, and Buruli ulcer; seven helminth infections: hookworm, ascariasis, trichuriasis, lymphatic filariasis, onchocerciasis, guinea worm (drancunculiasis), and schistosomiasis; and cysticercosis (an infection caused by the pork tapeworm), several parasitic infections, and food-borne trematodiases (intestinal flukes).

Intestinal fluke disease, for example, is persistent in various rural areas, especially among school-age children, women of child-bearing age, and the poor. As Fried et al. (2004:159) indicate, "Intestinal fluke diseases are aggravated by socio-economic factors such as poverty, malnutrition, an explosively growing free-food market, a lack of sufficient food inspection and sanitation, other helminthiases, and declining economic conditions." Overall, neglected tropical diseases cause over half a million deaths annually and represent the fourth most significant set of global communicable diseases, following lower respiratory infections, HIV/AIDS, and diarrheal diseases. As a group, these diseases are characterized by their negative impact on childhood development, their tendency to produce adverse pregnancy outcomes, their physically disfiguring effects (which often elicit stigmatization), and their impairment of working capacity among sufferers (increasing risk for household failure and lowering overall productivity).

While all neglected tropical diseases are not likely to spread beyond their current endemic populations (because their mobility is determined by more than climatic factors, such as requiring a number of different intermediate host species as part of their life cycle of developmental phases or because their threshold for establishment in a new area is greater than the number of hosts available), others may be components of future regional or even global ecosyndemics. The latter are adapted to "capitalize on improved opportunities for transmission and to establish [themselves in new places] whenever opportunities arise" (Dobson and Carper 1992).

At the regional level, current diffusion is seen in the case of one strain of sleeping sickness (*Trypanosoma brucei gambiense*). Transmitted by tsetse flies (*Glossina spp.*), sleeping sickness is found in 36 African countries and has long been endemic in central Africa, where it is one of the major diseases of humans and their domestic animals. While the *T. b. rhodesiense* (or the Rhodesian strain as it is called) has been relatively quiescent in recent decades, the Gambian strain has been surging in central Africa. Infection with the Gambian strain is characterized by a long asymptomatic period followed by subacute fevers ending in late-stage chronic meningoencephalitis, a condition that resembles both meningitis, an inflammation of membranes of the central nervous system, and encephalitis, inflammation of the brain. Over 27,000 cases of Gambian sleeping sickness were reported in the Congo in 1998, and current epidemics in Angola, southern Sudan, and Uganda are producing 100,000 new infections each year (Murry et al. 2000). Analysis by Rogers (1979) of the bioclimatic tolerances of tsetse flies provides data for predicting how patterns of climate change in tropical Africa might affect the future distribution of sleeping sickness. Examination of these data by Dobson and Carper (1992) shows that the mean monthly density-independent mortality rate for tsetse flies is most closely related to mean monthly saturation deficit (which is an index of humidity) and, to a lesser extent, to average monthly temperature. Based on data for 91 sites throughout tropical Africa in terms of these climatological conditions, 94 percent of the sites within the present known distribution of Gambian sleeping sickness are within the predicted bioclimatic limits. With a two-degree increase in temperature for sub-Saharan Africa produced by global warming, Dobson and Carper predict further spread of sleeping sickness into southern and eastern Africa.

Because, as noted in Chapter 4, increases in environmental temperature are likely to speed up development stages in the life cycle of many parasites, long-term increases in temperature are likely to lead to global increases in the ranges of those neglected tropical diseases transmitted by insects, such as lymphatic filariasis. Known as elephantiasis because it causes significant enlargement of the leg (as well as arms, the genitals, and breasts, because of thickening of the skin and underlying tissues), this filarial disease is already found in over 80 countries, where it puts more than a billion people at risk of infection. According to the World Health Organization (2000), over 120 million people have already been infected, one-third of them developing seriously incapacitating and disfiguring symptoms that often become sources of social rejection. Individuals who do not develop visual expression of the disease suffer internal damage to the lymphatic system and kidneys. Currently, lymphatic filariasis is especially common in Africa and India, but is also well established in South Asia, the western Pacific, and parts of the Caribbean and South America, and the prevalence of infection is increasing. In Tanzania, for example, more than ten million people live in areas endemic for filariasis, and of these almost 12 percent are infected (Makunde et al. 2003). Rapid growth of urban populations in shantytowns and other slum areas of poor megacities has contributed to the spread of this disease as it creates multiple potential breeding sites for mosquito vectors. In that filariasis sufferers can be physically incapacitated, the disease contributes to household failure and further impoverishment; in other words, it is a disease of the poor that causes further impoverishment.

Damage from the disease is caused by infestation by threadlike, parasitic filarial worms (*Wuchereria bancrofti* and *Brugia malayi*) that, upon entering the body during a mosquito bite (by crawling from the mosquito's mouthparts into the puncture wound), circulate in the blood and lodge in the lymphatic system, an essential component of the immune system that is responsible for maintaining a delicate fluid balance between body tissues and blood. Often acquired during childhood, the disease may not be expressed symptomatically for many years. Immune response is critical in that both chronic and acute manifestations of filariasis are more common in refugees or other newcomer populations (e.g., soldiers) than in local populations continually exposed to infection (beginning in utero). Manifestations in newcomer populations not seen in lifelong residents of endemic areas include hives, rashes, asthma symptoms, and other allergic reactions. These symptoms suggest possible manifestations of the disease as it diffuses to new areas and infests populations with naïve immune systems.

Only in recent years has it become clear that many of the symptoms of elephantiasis are not directly caused by the lymphatic filariasis per se but rather are the result of secondary bacterial skin infections. Elephantiasis, in fact, appears to be a product of a syndemic interaction between a parasitic worm and a species of bacteria known as Wolbachia, which, it is beginning to be realized, may be the most common infectious bacterium on earth. The worms responsible for elephantiasis are infested by these quasi-symbiotic bacteria (e.g., death of the bacteria results in death or sterility of the worm), as are many species of insects and nematodes.

Not only are disease-causing filarial infected with Wolbachia, but these bacteria appear to play a critical role in human disease production. To a significant degree, in fact, the pathogenicity of nematodes is a consequence of the intense response of the human immune system to Wolbachia exposure, which suggests why newcomers to an endemic area have atypical reactions to filarial infestation (Hoerauf et al. 2003).

Recent research on possible syndemic interaction between HIV and filarial worms (*Wuchereria bancrofti*) in co-infected adults shows slightly higher HIV load and lower levels of CD4 immune cells (which are targeted by HIV) compared with the HIV-only group, but differences did not prove to be statistically significant (Neilsen et al. 2007). However, research in Kenya (Gallagher et al. 2005) with HIV-infected women (n = 83) found they are two times more likely to have peripheral blood and/or placental malaria and two times more likely to have lymphatic filariasis infection compared to matched HIV-negative women. Women with HIV and malaria tended to show an increased risk for mother-to-child HIV transmission, although this difference was not statistically significant. Mother-to-child transmission of HIV, however, was found to be significantly higher in women who were co-infected with one or more worm species (48 percent) versus women without helminth infections.

There also is strong interest in examining interactions between filarial worms and malaria, as both are found in the same populations and both can be transmitted by the same mosquito vector, *Anopheles gambiae*. Also, helminth co-infection is known to affect how well the immune system manages malaria. In animal research, co-infected mice have been found to develop more severe disease, in terms of both level of anemia and loss of body mass, than did mice infected with malaria only (Graham et al. 2005). Human research by Chadee and co-workers (2003) in Georgetown, Guyana, in South America, where filarial worms and malaria are quite well established, found that of 769 people tested for filariasis during a one-year period, 13 percent were positive for nematode infection; of these, three percent were co-infected with malaria. Similarly, of 509 people tested for malaria, four percent were positive for the disease; of those with malaria, three percent were also infected with filarial worms. Similar results are reported for a study in Orissa, India (Ravindran et al. 1998). Although rates of co-infection in these settings were limited, the National Institute of Allergy and Infectious Diseases (NIAID) is sponsoring a new study of the potential interaction between these two parasites, findings of which are not yet available. Interaction between the two pathogenic species inside a common vector or host could have important implications for the health of co-infected individuals and for the spread of these two diseases as an outcome of global warming.

Climate change is likely to have significant impact as well on the global movement of leishmaniasis, a disease (called *kala azar*, "black fever," in India) that is spread by sand flies (biting insects that resemble mosquitoes). The most common symptoms of leishmaniasis are skin sores (which can leave permanent scarring) that erupt weeks to months after infection. In mucocutaneous forms of the disease, lesions can lead to partial or even total destruction of the mucous membranes of the nose, mouth, and throat cavities and surrounding tissues, resulting in disabling disfigurement. Other significant symptoms, including damage to the spleen and liver, may not develop for several months or even years after infection.

Currently, most cases of visceral leishmaniasis (VL), the most severe expression of this disease, are found in India, Bangladesh, Nepal, Sudan, and Brazil. There are half a million new cases of the disease in these countries each year, of which 5,000 prove fatal. The disease is also found in Iraq and has been reported among U.S. troops stationed there in both recent U.S.-Iraq wars. In Europe, it is endemic in the Mediterranean region. Existing evidence indicates that the strain known as *Leishmania infantum* is prevalent only within narrow isotherms, in January (5 to 50°F/-15 to 10°C) and July (65–80°F/20–30°C). This suggests that temperature is a significant barrier to the spread of this disease into northern Europe. Killick-Kendrick (1996) has argued that while there are no sand flies in Britain at present, in about 20 years the country may have a climate that is warm enough to sustain sand fly populations and leishmaniasis. *Phlebotomus perniciosus* sand flies already have been found as far north as Paris. Current models of global warming in Europe predict "a dramatic increase" in visceral leishmaniasis in northern Europe (Kuhn 1999:2).

The epidemiology of visceral leishmaniasis is undergoing important changes as a result of increasing levels of co-infection with HIV. HIV/VL co-infection is reported in over 30 countries in Africa, Asia, Europe, and South America. The World Health Organization reports that over 70 percent of HIV cases in southern Europe are co-infected with VL (Molina et al. 2003). In particular, Spain, Italy, and southern France are seeing a growing incidence of co-infection among youth, including those engaged in injection drug use (which may serve as a vector-free route of VL transmission). While traditionally a rural disease, leishmaniasis is now showing up in urban areas, particularly among HIV-infected individuals. People with HIV who are co-infected with leishmaniasis have a lowered level of immune capacity to contain the infection and keep it from progressing to VL. VL, in turn, has been found to stimulate the replication of HIV. VL/HIV, in short, represents a growing ecosyndemic with potential to spread to many parts of the world as a result of global warming.

Hurricane Katrina: A Case Study in Potential
Ecosyndemic Social Ecology

The potential of global warming to trigger ecosyndemics is illustrated by Hurricane Katrina. The official death toll for Hurricane Katrina, the "great deluge" that hit New Orleans and the Mississippi Gulf Coast in 2005, was 1,723 as of August 2006, although almost 1,000 people were still missing at that time. More than one million others were displaced by the uncompromising storm (Petterson et al. 2006). The Category 5 hurricane, one of the three strongest to ever make landfall in the United States, devastated 150 miles of the gulf coastline and plunged half a million homes into rising polluted floodwater. A sister storm, Hurricane Rita, battered the area two weeks later. Writing about poorer neighborhoods in the aftermath of Hurricanes Katrina and Rita (a time period that in New Orleans has come to be called "post-K"), Hartman observes:

> The city . . . staggers the imagination: mile after mile of partially and totally destroyed housing, stores and other small businesses, with precious little sign of any rebuilding effort or human activity of any sort. Fallen trees and abandoned vehicles are everywhere. Whole sections of the city still have no electricity, water, sewer service, telephone service, traffic lights, daily mail service. Massive, massive heaps of debris—garbage, furniture, carpets, refrigerators, and other appliances are everywhere. [Harman 2005:3]

To borrow the words of President Alexander Hamilton, made in reference to a massive squall he endured in the Caribbean as a teenager, for many people of New Orleans and surrounding areas, the storm and subsequent events made it seem "as if a total dissolution of nature was taking place" (quoted in Chernov 2004:37).

Hurricanes can be so destructive because their swirling winds literally pull energy out of warm tropical waters and push it into the atmosphere. Consequently, warmer ocean water produces stronger storms. During the days leading up to Katrina's transformation into a Category 5 storm, the water in the Gulf of Mexico was 5°F above normal for late August, turning the gulf into "a veritable hurricane refueling station" (Kluger 2005). Hurricanes build up strength over the sea; when they make landfall, they unleash their accumulated water and energy in a great gushing wave. It is this powerful surge of water that makes hurricanes so destructive, although Katrina's sustained winds of up to 150 miles (240 km) per hour added to its impact.

In the view of many observers, global warming is the reason gulf waters have been so heated in recent years, and it is also the reason some weather forecasters felt that the 2005 hurricane season was going to be memorable. For example, William Gray of the Tropical Meteorology

Project at Colorado State University, a well-respected weather scientist, and his colleagues (Klotzbach and Gray 2006) projected twice the usual number of tropical storms would occur in 2005 based on an analysis of an array of climatic and oceanic data (although Gray remains hesitant to interpret warming gulf waters as a product of global warming). In fact, Gray underestimated the number of storms that would occur, as there were almost three times as many as usual. During 2004, tropical storms caused a disquieting $50 billion in damages; notably, the following year the level of destruction doubled. In fact, the 2005 hurricane season in the Atlantic Basin broke many weather records. A total of 27 named tropical storms and one unnamed subtropical storm developed during the year, shattering the previous record of 21 storms set in 1933. Similarly, the 15 hurricanes that occurred in 2005 exceeded the old record of 12 hurricanes that had been set 36 years earlier (Klotzbach and Gray 2006).

As a result of massive flooding, extensive infrastructure destruction, and considerable social disruption caused by Hurricane Katrina in New Orleans and beyond, the potential for diseases and injuries of various kinds was enormous. Concern about contamination in the dark, filmy sediment left behind by Katrina's floodwaters was especially high. Tests by the Environmental Protection Agency in the first weeks after the hurricane found high levels of *E.coli* bacteria (ten times the federal safety limit), as well as lead, arsenic, and other noxious substances (Appel 2005a). As Brinkley (2006:297) reports, "The overwhelming concern of health officials during the flooding was stopping the spread of disease. Reports of rashes, dizziness, dehydration, headaches, chemical burns, along with hundreds of other maladies [became] frequent." Thus, Robbie Ethridge, an anthropologist at the University of Mississippi who participated in relief efforts in Mississippi, found that many of the survivors at a makeshift shelter "had scrapes and cuts on their legs and feet, arms and hands. With neither clean water nor medicines, even the most minor abrasion had become infected. Hence, many people could not walk" (Ethridge 2006:807).

Susan Briggs, the physician appointed to oversee the Federal Emergency Management Agency's (FEMA) disaster-response medical teams in Louisiana and Alabama, began a program to inoculate residents for tetanus and hepatitis A and B. Hepatitis is a significant danger among people exposed to untreated sewage in floodwaters as well as through contaminated or unrefrigerated food. Noted Briggs, many of the people in the affected areas "have no electricity, no clean water, no air conditioning . . . . There are collapsed structures and stray animals. There are huge amounts of stray dogs, and people have been bitten" (quoted in Appel 2005a). Briggs and other doctors had to treat numerous cases of diarrhea, rashes, and upper-respiratory illnesses.

Some skin problems were caused by exposure to crude oil spilled into the floodwaters by refineries like the one operated by Murphy Oil USA. It is estimated that over 25,000 barrels of crude oil, which can burn the skin upon contact, were dumped from the Murphy refinery into the Chalmette and Meraux neighborhoods of the city. Another oil spill of over 75,000 gallons occurred at the Bass Enterprise storage depot near Venice, downstream from New Orleans (Appel 2005b). People exposed to the crude developed rashes and severe staph infections. In the words of one observer, "People are walking around getting sick and dizzy and throwing up and diarrhea. That's just not normal. We all got sore throats every couple of days. I'm sure we're going to get sick" (quoted in Brinkley 2005:355).

The spread of various vector-borne infections was also of grave concern among public health officials. Prior to the storm, Louisiana was a major site of West Nile virus infection, with over 175 cases reported for the state out of a total of 2,744 cases reported nationally in 2005. Eight of the pre-Katrina cases resulted in the death of the infected individual. Standing pools of stagnant water left behind by the hurricane appeared to be an ideal breeding ground for mosquitoes. Although within the first several months after Katrina, there were three new cases of West Nile virus reported in Jefferson Parish and two in Orleans Parish, as well as 21 cases elsewhere in the state, it does not appear that the storm produced a significant jump in West Nile virus cases in the state (Louisiana Department of Health and Hospitals 2005). Brinkley (2006:299) suggests that mosquitoes were kept in check after the storm by the appearance of a massive swarm of dragonflies that "blanketed New Orleans, hovering just inches above the smelly floodwater, eating every mosquito in sight." Others have suggest that hurricanes do not initially cause new cases of West Nile virus because intense downpours temporarily flush out the small pools of water in which vector mosquitoes lay their eggs. In subsequent months, however, swarms of flies, roaches, and mosquitoes occupied areas of the city, according to Jayme Necaise, an entomologist with the Audubon Nature Institute Insectarium (Foster 2006). Studies have shown that a single abandoned swimming pool can produce thousands of mosquitoes within a short period. Steve Sackett, an entomologist affiliated with the New Orleans Mosquito and Termite Control Board, said:

> We have thousands of pools. We know a bunch of them are breeding mosquitoes, and there's the potential for West Nile virus. . . . We're concerned with pest problems, but we're really concerned with disease transmission. . . . One of the things that we've seen is a change in the mosquito species that were living in the pools. Where they came from I don't know, but we had quite a few of these larvae swimming in some pools. [Quoted in Guillot 2006]

Included among the mosquitoes identified by Sackett are those that serve as vectors for West Nile virus. To control mosquito breeding, the city launched an aggressive program of releasing western mosquito fish (*Gambusia affinis*) in aerially identified pools of standing water. Each fish consumes large numbers of mosquito larvae while giving birth to young who continue the feast over time.

The same pattern is seen with another disease vector, the rat. Thousands of rats drowned in Hurricane Katrina, their dead bodies showing up amid and adding to the debris in the toxic floodwaters. Being resourceful and well dispersed, many rats survived the storm, however, and were subsequently seen in large packs, particularly along the wharf front of the city or even nibbling at the bodies of the storm's victims. Piles of rotting garbage and rubble, as well as the shelter afforded by abandoned homes and uncut weeds, created a welcoming environment for the surviving rats. According to Erick Kinchke, owner of a pest control service in New Orleans, "They have more to eat than before the storm. Just look at all the piles of garbage, the stuff lying around, the empty buildings. This is a rat's paradise" (quoted in Foster 2006). Illustratively, Becky Zaheri, a volunteer in the New Orleans post-storm cleanup effort, distainfully reported "today we saw a few mice [and] 13 huge rats coming out of one pile" (quoted in Mott 2006). Given their short gestational period and average litter size, a mated pair of rats is capable of producing over 350 million descendents within three years. Thus Leonard Douglen (2005), executive director of the New Jersey Pest Management Association, with reference to New Orleans noted:

> The current population of rats in the affected areas can reproduce at a rate of an entire new generation within three months. The gestation period is a scant twenty-two days and a female rat will give birth to an average litter of eight. In their brief lifespan of nine months, each will produce an average of twenty new rats.

An unchecked and growing rat population is an enormous risk to health. Almost 20 years before Katrina, a study found that 20 of 94 (21 percent) Norwegian rats trapped in New Orleans were infected with *Angiostrongylus cantonensis* (Campbell and Little 1988), a roundworm that transmits eosinophilic meningitis, a potentially fatal infection of the membranes covering the brain and spinal cord. Although usually found in Southeast Asia and the Pacific Basin, in 2002 an outbreak of eosinophilic meningitis was reported in the United States among travelers returning from a Caribbean trip. Of greater concern was the potential for the spread of bubonic plague. The disease is not unknown to New Orleans, an outbreak having occurred there in 1914. Plague control efforts were implemented for several years following the outbreak, after which the city was declared plague-free. Subsequently, however, the U.S. Public Health Service identified bubonic plague among rats that were captured in New Orleans in 1919–1920 (New Orleans Department of Public Property 1947). Absence of the disease in the years prior to Katrina, however, appears to have spared the city of yet one more devastation.

The hurricane did lead to the spread of norovirus infection. This virus causes at least half of all gastroenteritis cases globally, a disease marked by stomach pain, diarrhea, lethargy, weakness, muscle aches, headache, and vomiting. Named after the city of Norwalk, Ohio, which witnessed an intense outbreak of acute gastroenteritis among elementary school children in 1968, the norovirus has been radiating globally with a significant increase in infections in 2006. While it can be spread through various means, including hand-to-hand contact, touching infected surfaces, and by contaminated food, it also is transmitted by water, including municipal waterlines, wells, lakes, swimming pools, and even ice machines. Some of the crowded shelters set up in the wake of Katrina became transmission zones for norovirus.

Also seen in the aftermath of the storm was at least one potential case of Chagas disease (some times called American trypanosomiasis) transmission in a 74-year-old woman living in a rural area near New Orleans (Dorn et al. 2007). Previously, only a handful of autochthonous infections with this disease had been reported in the U.S., although the disease is endemic in Latin America (and found among travelers to and from Latin American countries). If untreated, Chagas is known to lead to heart problems, malformation of the intestines, and potential death.

In the Louisiana case, the sufferer had over 50 triatomine (kissing bug) bites on her body and the corpses of 20 triatomine, the vector known to transmit the protozoan parasite *Trypanosoma cruzi* that causes the disease (in part by secreting a protean called T c52 that has immunosuppressive effects), were found in her house by a fumigator. The woman reported never seeing the blood-sucking bugs in her home until after the hurricane. Research by Guzman-Tapia et al. (2005) has described the role hurricanes can play in the spread of triatomine and Chagas disease. *T. cruzi* is known to infect wild opossums and raccoons in the U.S., and public health officials speculated that the significant increase in the armadillo population in the months after Hurricane Katrina contributed to the emergence of an expanded kissing bug population that began to search out other bloodmeal sources as the armadillo population dropped back to pre-Katrina levels (Dorn et al. 2007).

Beyond vector-borne diseases, mold blooms developed in many of the flooded homes of New Orleans and the surrounding inundated areas of Louisiana and Mississippi. Richard Paat, the head of a temporary clinic established in East Biloxi, Mississippi, reported in the immediate aftermath of Katrina: "We're seeing a lot of asthma from inhaling the mold. . . and mouth sores from the bad water" (quoted in Appel 2005a). Also reported in the flood zone were many cases of *V. vulnificus* infection. According to CDC spokesperson Von Roebuck, "People had open wounds and walked through floodwater with sewage in it. . . . And these folks were having these wounds infected with *Vibrio*" (quoted in Appel 2005a). Between August 29 and September 11, 2005, public health surveillance identified 22 newly diagnosed cases of *Vibrio* illness among Katrina victims, five of whom subsequently died of the infection (Engelthaler et al. 2005).

Complicating the health impact of Katrina was the damage done by the storm to area hospitals. Prior to Katrina, New Orleans boasted nine major hospitals. One of them, Charity Hospital, was a nonprofit facility created to provide care to the poor. As a result of flooding, the hospitals lost most of their primary electrical power, while backup generators tended to be located in basement areas that quickly filled with water. New patients could not be seen and existing patients could not be adequately cared for and had to be evacuated. But assistance in moving patients to safe settings did not arrive. At Charity Hospital, staff operated ventilators by hand for two days so that gravely ill patients could breath. The inattention given to hospitals by government rescue organizers typified the post-K experience. A now well-known part of the story of Katrina was the way the storm exposed the failure of government to respond effectively to the devastation. As summarized by Oscar Zavala, a patient at a New Orleans hospital suffering from a bacterial infection: "What hurts in my soul is that we waited for the government response and it never came. My government is the first one there whenever something happens in a foreign country . . . and here they failed from the very beginning" (quoted in Diaz 2005:1).

From an ecosyndemic perspective, what is significant about Hurricane Katrina is that it occurred in one of the wealthiest, resource-rich nations in the world, and while the emergence of a devastating syndemic fortunately was averted—as much by luck as by public health response—the grave potential was evident as was the specter of what such a disease event might spell in a resource-poor setting.

Conclusions

It is evident that there is much to learn about the potential for one or more significant 21st-century syndemics to emerge from the interaction among mobile neglected tropical diseases, or between them and the so-called big three infections (HIV, TB, and malaria), or in interaction with any of the array of diseases endemic to endpoints of tropical disease migration. Needless to say, global warming opens up the possibility for various kinds of novel interactions among diseases, some of which could develop into ecosyndemics of historic proportion. Certainly, syndemic interaction among migrating diseases and endemic diseases raises one more important flag regarding the seriousness of global warming and the threats it presents to human health and well-being, especially among highly vulnerable populations, including the poor. While the administrator of the National Aeronautics and Space Administration (NASA) in the Bush administration, Michael Griffin, has questioned whether it is appropriate to take action to mitigate the effects of global warming, those in harm's way of ecosyndemics, in particular those at the bottom of the global socioeconomic pyramid, have already demonstrated they are far less reluctant to call for change.

Concern with advancing scientific understanding of the nature of syndemics under conditions of global warming suggests several lines of future inquiry. First, there is a need for research that investigates the precise physical and social processes by which syndemics emerge, including the social conditions that foster the clustering of multiple epidemics in particular populations. Second, there is a need to better understand processes and pathways of interaction between various kinds of diseases as well as between diseases and other adverse health-related factors like malnutrition, structural violence, discrimination, stigmatization, and toxic environmental exposure that reflect unequal and unjust social relationships. Third, there is a need for improved understanding of factors that determine which diseases are most likely to spread, and spread rapidly, and which are much less likely to do so. Fourth, there is a need for research on how syndemics function to produce specific kinds of health outcomes, in light of the wide array of climatic, social, behavioral, and attitudinal factors that may affect syndemic development. Fifth, there is a need for closer examination of how global warming enables the spread of diseases and otherwise impacts on human health, particularly among subordinate populations. Finally, there is a need for a better understanding of how the public health and medical systems, as well as communities and national and international organizations, can respond to control and alleviate the health consequences of syndemics and ecosyndemics and the social conditions that produce them.

Beyond research, there is vital and pressing need for significant social action, including structural changes that facilitate the amelioration of the health consequences of global warming to the degree that that is still possible. Ecosyndemics promise to be among the killer plagues of the 21st century, joining other diseases of global warming in challenging human health and well-being.

7

Adaptation Versus Mitigation

Why Existing Climate Regimes and "Green Capitalism" are not Enough to Contain Global Warming

The grim reality of global warming has provoked the spilling of much ink on how best to adapt to it over the next several years and how to mitigate it over the long run. As Thompson et al. (2006:1) observe, *adaptation* is a "rather vague term, broadly defined as a process of modifying something to fit a new condition." While it is inescapable that over the short run human societies must try to adapt to global warming (or suffer the consequences), the more crucial issue is that of *mitigation*—that is, transcending global warming in order to ensure the survival of humanity as well as maintaining biodiversity. Indeed, a mere focus on adaptation poses the danger of political complacency, fatalism, and even cynicism.

Johansen (2006a:xi) asserts that failure to curtail fossil fuel consumption appreciably could result in the atmospheric carbon dioxide level reaching 800 to 1,000 ppm by 2100. Bearing such a possibility in mind, numerous strategies have been proposed to address global warming, most of which seek more or less to work within the parameters of the existing capitalist world system, and a few that seek to transcend it in one fashion or other. Some time ago, Andre Gorz (1973) made a useful distinction between *reformist reforms* and *nonreformist reforms*, or what Singer (1995) calls *system-correcting praxis*, to designate the conscious implementation of minor improvements that avoid any alteration of the basic structure in an existing social system, whether it be at the local, national, or global level. Whereas reformist reforms seek to stabilize the existing system, nonreformist reforms seek to pave the way for transcending it. Indeed, Nancy Scheper-Hughes (1995:415) has called upon anthropologists to adopt the "idea of an active, politically committed, morally engaged anthropology." Critical anthropologists, in seeking to develop a praxis that ultimately contributes to the transcendence of global capitalism, need to identify opportunities for nonreformist reform as part of the longer process of furthering global transformation, and with respect to this book, as part of a comprehensive program for mitigating global warming.

Bearing these thoughts in mind, it would be useful to distinguish between strategies that constitute reformist reforms, or what might be more loosely termed *muddling through* strategies, and those that constitute nonreformist reforms, or what might be called *transcendent* strategies, in terms of global warming. The former include 1) climate regime approaches; 2) neoliberal approaches; 3) sustainable development or social democratic approaches; and 4) *i*approaches. In reality, these approaches are not mutually exclusive but overlap considerably. We argue that for the most part, these minimal change strategies, while possibly leading to modest improvements, fail to come to grips with the ongoing commitment of global capitalism to unrestrained economic growth and its role in contributing to social and health inequities, international and domestic violence, population growth, and environmental degradation. We discuss transcendent strategies in the next and final chapter of this book, where we suggest the creation of a democratic ecosocialist global system as an authentic means of mitigating global warming.

Climate Regimes

Various scholars have argued that ultimately the problem of global warming or climate change will require "some kind of internationally coordinated response" (Rowlands 1995). Regimes refer to rules and decision-making processes in which nation-states agree to defer their sovereignty to a large international body. Indeed, since the late 1980s, a climate change regime has emerged at the international, regional, and even national and local levels. International and regional climate regimes include the United Nations Intergovernmental Panel on Climate Change, the United Nations Framework Convention on Climate Change, the 1997 Kyoto Protocol signatories, and the European Union. Climate regimes also include governments (national, state or provincial, and local); environmental nongovernmental organizations (ENGOs); indigenous people's organizations; research centers (such as the Pew Center on Climate Change in the U.S., the Tyndall Centre in the U.K., and the Potsdam Institute for Climate Research in Germany); and business and industrial nongovernmental organizations (BINGOs). The last category can be divided into "green business" bodies such as the U.S.-based Business Council for Sustainable Energy, the European Business Council for a Sustainable Future, and the World Business Council for Sustainable Development; and "gray businesses" bodies, such as the now-defunct Global Climate Coalition, which downplay or deny the reality of global warming (Yamin and DePledge 2004). At the national level, climate regime politics tends to be shaped by lead states, which promote efforts to mitigate global warming, such as most European Union nations and

Canada, and veto states, which seek to subvert or counteract efforts to mitigate global warming, such as the United States, Australia, and, perhaps to a lesser extent, China and India (Carter 2007:238).

International Climate Organizations and Agreements

United Nations–Related Bodies: The IPCC, the Framework Convention on Climate Change, and the Kyoto Protocol

In 1987 the UN Commission on Sustainable Development released a document entitled *Our Common Future* which emphasized that global warming constitutes a major environmental dilemma for the future of humanity (Skjaereth and Skodvin 2003:128). The following year the UN General Assembly passed a resolution stating that global warming constitutes a "common concern for mankind" (Yamin and DePledge 2004:22). The UN Commission met again in Villach, Austria, in 1990 and later in Bellagio, Italy. In 1988, Canada sponsored the Toronto Conference on the greenhouse effect, which recommended a 20 percent reduction in carbon dioxide emissions by 2005, an international treaty addressing global warming, and a fund in which developed countries would assist developing countries in reducing their greenhouse gas emissions. Davis (2007) asserts that the Toronto Conference shifted concern about global warming from a largely scientific focus to a more governmental one.

The First World Climate Conference occurred in 1979 and the Second World Climate Conference in 1990, which culminated in the 1992 UN Conference on Environment and Development in Rio de Janeiro, better known as the Earth Summit. The Intergovernmental Panel on Climate Change was created in 1988 and played a pivotal role at this conference. The Earth Summit resulted in the formation of the Framework Convention on Climate Change (FCCC), which took force in 1994. This body was modeled upon the 1996 Montreal Protocol, an international treaty that contributed significantly to the reduction of ozone-depleting chlorofluorocarbons (CFCs) used in various products, such as air conditioners and refrigerators. The Montreal Protocol, which is widely regarded as one of the most successful international environmental regimes, resulted in a reduction of CFC production from 1.2 million tons in 1986 to 164,000 tons in 1997 (Carter 2007). The FCCC meets more or less annually (see Table 7) in Conferences of the Parties (COPs), which are attended by thousands of delegates and observers, and are intended to discuss advances in climate science and details pertaining to implementation of the Kyoto Protocol.

In addition, since the Kyoto Protocol went into effect in February 2005, there have been three meetings of the parties to the Kyoto Protocol, the most recent one having taken place in Bali in December 2007.

Table 7. FCCC Conferences of Parties

Location	Year
Berlin	1995
Geneva	1996
Kyoto (Protocol signed)	1997
Buenos Aires	1998
Bonn	1999
Hague (Part 1)	2001
Bonn (Part 2)	2001
Marrekech	2001
New Delhi	2002
Milan	2003
Buenos Aires	2005

In its statement of principles, the FCCC emphasizes the following points: response to global warming should not be delayed until all scientific uncertainties can be resolved; and developed societies should take the lead in addressing climate change, and they should compensate developing countries for any additional costs incurred for taking action under the FCCC's guidelines. The FCCC has delineated voluntary goals for stabilizing greenhouse gas emissions. Industrialized countries agreed to voluntarily stabilize greenhouse gas emissions at 1990 levels by 2000. The FCCC requires its signatories to report regularly on their greenhouse gas emissions and to develop national programs to mitigate global warming.

The Kyoto Protocol has been ratified by 165 countries. It seeks to deliver upon Article 2 of the FCCC objective "to stabilise greenhouse gas concentrations in the atmosphere at a level that would prevent dangerous anthropogenic interference with the climate system." With Russia's ratification on February 16, 2005, the Kyoto Protocol became a binding treaty. The developed nations committed to a carbon dioxide reduction of 5.2 percent of 1990 levels by 2012. Some industrialized nations were permitted large increases in their emissions while others consented to large cuts. Whereas the agreement specified that the European Union would decrease its greenhouse gas emissions by eight percent, the United States by seven percent, and Canada and Japan by six percent, Australia was permitted to increase its greenhouse gas emissions by eight percent. Despite the fact that Australia has long been a major greenhouse gas emitter, it managed to obtain credit for having reduced its rate of land clearance due to increasing public concern about its environmental impact. Given that land clearance was a major source of Australian greenhouse gas emissions, the country was credited for its efforts with a permission to increase its emissions. Overall, as Carter summarizes:

> The EU "bubble" of 8 percent contains wide variations between member states: some richer states have to make large reductions, e.g., Denmark (21 percent), Germany (21 percent), UK (12.5 percent); others merely need to stabilise emissions, e.g., France and Finland; while less developed members can increase emissions, e.g., Portugal (27 percent), Greece (25 percent), Spain (15 percent) and Ireland (13 percent). [Carter 2007:253]

The Kyoto Protocol exempts developing nations, including China, India, and Brazil, from setting emissions reduction targets. It is intended to initiate a series of treaties that theoretically will be binding upon all countries, at least those that have signed it.

The only developed country that has not ratified the Kyoto Protocol is the United States. The Coalition Government under Prime Minister John Howard refused to ratify the Kyoto Protocol. Kevin Rudd, the new Prime Minister elected on November 24, 2007, in which the Australian Labor Party swept into power after 11 years of having been in the opposition to the conservative Coalition, made a pre-election pledge that his government would ratify the Kyoto Protocol, which he fulfilled in early 2008. While various factors contributed to Rudd's election, it is not inappropriate to conclude that global warming is beginning to have an impact on the political climate down under. In the U.S., the protocol was signed by the Clinton administration in 1998, but met with heavy opposition in the U.S. Senate, which opposed the decision by a vote of 95 to 0, with five abstentions, on the grounds that the protocol would harm the U.S. economy and did not include greenhouse gas reductions for developing societies. Numerous U.S. corporations engaged in intense lobbying opposing ratification and successfully influenced the Senate vote. In Australia, the Howard administration initially supported the Protocol but then backed off on the grounds that the developing countries had not signed the protocol and, like the U.S., claimed dictates of the protocol would interfere with the growth of the economy.

The more reluctant signatories of the Kyoto Protocol formed an umbrella group, consisting of the U.S., Canada, Japan, Russia, Australia, and a few smaller countries, committed to finding loopholes in the original agreement. The U.S. insisted that it be permitted to offset its emissions against its carbon sinks, particularly in the form of vast forests, since trees absorb carbon dioxide from the atmosphere. Opposition notwithstanding, many climate scientists have pointed out that the greenhouse gas emission reductions agreed to by many of the signatories are not being met and, even if they were, the proposed emissions reductions are far below what is needed to actually mitigate global warming.

The Intergovernmental Panel on Climate Change (IPCC) was created in 1988 by the World Meteorological Organization and the United Nations Environmental Program. The IPCC played a pivotal role at the Earth Summit in 1992 and bases its interpretations of global warming on the findings of climate models. It consists of three working groups: Group I is responsible for assessing the science of climate change; Group II is responsible for assessing the impacts of climate change on the environment and human societies; and Group III is responsible for developing response strategies to global warming. The IPCC released reports in 1991, 1996, 2001, and 2007, as well as a steady stream of occasional assessments and discussion papers, each of which has contributed to greater awareness of the nature and urgency of global warming. In 1995 the IPCC claimed that there was strong scientific evidence that global warming was related to human activities. In its 2001 report, the IPCC became more emphatic, noting that "Human activities . . . are modifying the concentration of atmospheric constituents . . . that absorb or scatter radiant energy . . . . [M]ost of the observed warming over the last 50 years is likely to have been due to the increase in greenhouse gas concentration" (McCarthy et al. 2001:21). The 2007 IPCC report uses even stronger language in its recognition of the contribution of anthropogenic activities, emphasizing that it is "extremely unlikely that the global climate changes of the past fifty years can be explained without invoking human activities" (Alley et al. 2007). Other than a few holdouts, the overwhelming majority of climate scientists maintain that human activities are a significant cause of global warming.

The European Union

European countries, acting in consort through the European Union, formed the Council of the First Action Programme on the Environment, which became involved in the mid-1980s in the formation of the Vienna Convention on the Protection of the Ozone Layer and the Montreal Protocol. The European Union has campaigned since 1989 for carbon dioxide stabilization by establishing reduction targets and time tables (Skjareth and Skodvin 2003). The European Union emissions trading scheme, which finally commenced operations on January 1, 2005, allows each member country to grant its largest industries the right to emit a specified among of carbon dioxide. These industries have the option of either cutting emissions or purchasing credits or the "right to pollute" from another company that has done better than targeted or a country outside Annex I or developed countries.

Baker (2007:297) maintains that the European Union is committed to a dual program of "sustainable development" and economic expansion, a combination that in large part is informed by ecological modernization. She asserts that ecological modernization, an approach that we discuss in greater detail later in this chapter, by and large does not address social justice concerns, the significant degree of mal-distribution of wealth around the globe, and the need for environmental sustainability strategies. Instead, ecological modernization focuses primarily on the role of corporate elites as implementers of environmentally sustainable business practices and technological fixes in mitigating global warming. Further, Baker (2007:310) asserts that "EU environmental policy does not impose threats to the competitiveness of European business, either [sic] by raising production costs, restricting what is produced or altering market opportunities." Furthermore, as Maslin (2004:123) notes, the "internal divisions within the EU [for example, between high and low energy-efficient countries] and its cumbersome internal decision-making procedures make it a frustrating negotiating partner." For the most part, the European Union has acted as united front during Kyoto Protocol negotiations. The downturn in emissions in the United Kingdom was in large part a result of that country's transition from coal to gas, and in Germany it was due largely to renovating and cleaning up heavily polluting industries in its new states carved out of what had been the German Democratic Republic.

The Group of Eight
The Group of Eight (G8), a powerful economic block of developed countries consisting of the governmental heads of Canada, France, Germany, Italy, Japan, Russia, the United Kingdom, and the United States, has made plans to implement the Global Earth Observation System of Systems (GEOSS) to thwart pollution and global warming. It created a Dialogue on Climate Change at its 2005 meeting in Gleneagles, Scotland, which was chaired by Tony Blair, then the prime minister of the United Kingdom. The G8 countries comprise about 13 percent of the world's population but are responsible for 45 percent of the world's greenhouse emissions. At the 2005 meeting, George W. Bush finally abandoned his assertion that the science of global warming was inconclusive and called for voluntary measures to contain global warming. The World Economic Forum issued a statement in June 2006 supporting Blair's call at the G8 to address global warming. Despite the G8's purported commitment to mitigation of global warming, its 2007 declaration in Rostock, Germany, indicates an ongoing emphasis on economic expansion as is indicated by its acceptance that "the number of motor vehicles will double from 1.2 billion by 2020" (Bello 2007). Instead, the G8 proposes to expand development of nonfossil fuels, such as hydrogen, for new cars.

The Asia-Pacific Partnership on Clean Development and Climate

The Asia-Pacific Partnership on Clean Development and Climate (also referred to as AP6) consists of the United States, Australia, China, Japan, India, and South Korea, countries that account for about half of the world's carbon dioxide emissions (Lowe 2005:178). The Bush administration took the lead on the creation of AP6, and the Howard government in Australia quickly jumped on board in respective efforts to deflect criticisms for the failure of these countries to ratify the Kyoto Protocol. According to Hamilton,

> China, India and South Korea needed some coaxing, but faced with promises of financial transfers to fund clean technology investments and promises that the new partnership would not jeopardise the Kyoto treaty, which the three had signed and ratified, they agreed to participate. Japan was more reluctant, suspecting that it was a plot to protect the United States and Australia from accusations of being internationally irresponsible. [Hamilton 2007:187]

The Asia-Pacific Partnership had its inaugural ministerial meeting in Sydney in January 2006 and stresses voluntary mitigation strategies, such as sharing technologies for renewable and reduced-carbon fuel sources.

The Group of 77 and the Alliance of Small Island States

A North-South or developed-developing world divide has emerged around the issue of global warming in that the rich countries have options that the poor countries do not have in terms of avoiding climate-related harm in the foreseeable future. The poor, including those who live in developed societies, lack access to air-conditioning when faced by heat waves and to medical facilities in case of climate-related emergences and more frequently to climate-sensitive diseases (Glantz 2003:172). In terms of climate politics, the developed-developing world divide plays itself out in part in the Group of 77 (established in 1964) and the Alliance of Small Island States (AOISIS, established in 1990). The Group of 77, which now consists of over 130 developing countries, represents differing interests on global warming issues. On the whole, its larger members, such as China and India, contend that emissions reductions could hinder economic development and that carbon trading should function as a mechanism for increasing their income. It stresses the importance of equity considerations in the creation of an international climate-governance mechanism, one that recognizes per capita emissions rather than emissions from specific countries or categories of countries. The AOSIS is a coalition of some 43 low-lying small island nations, some of which also belong to the Group of 77, that are highly vulnerable to sea level rise related to global warming. Included in this body are the Maldives, Mauritius, Singapore, Papua New Guinea, the Federated States of Micronesia, Tuvalu, the Marshall Islands, Vanuatu, Tonga, Samoa, Nauru, Fiji, and the Cook Islands. As Maslin (2004:121) observes, "the AOSIS position has always been to get the tightest control on global emissions as their countries seem to be most at threat from the impacts of global warming."

National Governments: The Cases of Germany, the United States, Australia, and China

At the national level, Agarwal (n.d.a) delineates three key climate regime camps: 1) nations that desire to take serious action on global warming (e.g., the AOSIS and some European countries); 2) nations that maintain that emissions reduction will entail high costs and seek low-cost solutions (e.g., the United States and Australia); and 3) poor nations that desire "environmental space" for future economic expansion (e.g., China and India). Sweden was the first country to take national action on global warming when it resolved to stabilize carbon dioxide emissions at the 1988 level by 2000, with Norway and the Netherlands making similar commitments shortly afterwards (Bulkeley and Betsill 2003). In this section, we discuss four key players in climate politics at the national level, namely Germany, the United States, Australia, and China.

Germany

Germany is often regarded as an international leader in global warming mitigation because it agreed to cutting back carbon dioxide emissions by 21 percent from 1990 to 2012 under the provisions of the Kyoto Protocol. In reality, however, as noted, much of Germany's initial advance toward this target has resulted from the closure of large sectors of the highly polluting East German industrial infrastructure. Despite Chancellor Angela Merkel's desire to reduce greenhouse gases by 40 percent by 2020 by increasing energy efficiency and expanding renewable energy, her coalition government has faced much opposition from German gas and electricity companies (Dempsey 2007). Germany is also actively developing renewable energy sources with the aim of having them account for 50 percent of all energy sources by 2050 (DiMento and Doughman 2007:112). The Federal Environment Agency has made plans to develop a "competency center" in order to adapt to global warming; it will coordinate efforts for more efficient energy use and the development of renewable energy sources, improved flood protection, and early-warning systems (Deutsche Welle 2006).

The United States

The U.S. government issued two contradictory reports on global warming in 1983. Whereas the National Academy of Sciences recommended no action until more scientific evidence indicated definitively the seriousness of global warming, the Environmental Protection Agency recommended immediate action (Davis 2007:185). Indeed, the EPA introduced an emissions trading scheme as early as 1976 (Lohmann 2006:57). McCright and Dunlap (2003) argue that the "conservative movement" played a key role in the U.S. government's failure to ratify the Kyoto Protocol. Organizations in the United States that have opposed efforts to mitigate global warming have included the now-defunct Global Climate Coalition (a coalition of some 50 trade associations and corporations), the Global Climate Information Project (a coalition of business, labor, and farm groups), the American Automobile Manufacturers Association, the Coalition for Vehicle Choice (a car manufacturers' front group), and the Information Council on Environment (a coal industry front group) (Beder 2000:237). The Heritage Foundation, the Heartland Institute, and the Cato Institute, three ultraconservative think tanks, also have attempted to undermine efforts to mitigate global warming. In 2002, for example, the Heritage Foundation asserted that rather than a consequence of greenhouse gases of anthropocentric origin "the recent surface warming trend may owe largely to changes in the sun's energy output" (Baliunus 2002).

In contrast to the earlier Clinton administration, the Bush administration has persistently engaged in a denial of the global warming crisis and only recently admitted its reality. It withdrew from the Kyoto Protocol on the alleged grounds that it is unfair to the United States because it exempted developing countries from the first rounds of emission cuts. The Bush administration placed pressure on the Environmental Protection Agency in summer 2003 to alter its 600-page report by editing out all references to dangerous impacts of global warming on the United States. It unsuccessfully instructed James Hansen, the director of NASA's Goddard Institute of Space Studies, not to speak publicly about the grave implications of global warming (Tidwell 2006). Various members of the Bush administration have strong ties with the fossil fuels industry: Vice President Dick Cheney had been the CEO of Halliburton, the largest oil-field services company in the United States; Secretary of State Condoleezza Rice had been a board member of Chevron Oil; Secretary of Commerce Donald L. Evans had been an employee of a Denver oil and gas company; White House Chief of Staff Andrew Card had been the president of the American Automobile Manufacturers Association (Gelbspan 2004:43); and while his father was president, George W. Bush was an executive at Harken Energy. Notably Texas, Bush's home state, produces more greenhouse gases than any other state.

The McCain-Lieberman bill, which became the Climate Stewardship Act, introduced in the U.S. Congress in October 2003 called for major greenhouse gas emitters to abide by mandatory emissions caps, but was rejected by the Senate in a vote of 43 to 55 (Hamilton 2007:183). The bill was resubmitted and on November 1, 2007, passed by the Senate Environment and Public Works subcommittee for further consideration in the Senate.

Conservative forces in the United States have played a major role in creating a great deal of public confusion about the seriousness of global warming. Polls in 2006 found that 64 percent of Americans thought there was "a lot" of scientific disagreement on global warming (Begley 2007). Only a third of those polled thought global warming is "mainly caused by things people do."

Jim Hansen, who is the U.S. government's leading climate scientist, started a public lecture a week before the 2004 U.S. presidential election with the following words: "I have been told by a high government official that I should not talk about dangerous anthropogenic interference with climate, because we do not know how much humans are changing the Earth's climate or how much change is dangerous. Actually we know quite a bit" (quoted in Pearce 2006:82).

Unfortunately, the Democrats have not been much better than the Republicans at tackling global warming. A Climate Stewardship Act, which would have placed a national cap on U.S. greenhouse gas emissions and introduced a cap-and-trade scheme, attracted the support of only 43 senators in October 2004. In August 2007 the Democratic leadership in the House of Representatives decided not to bring to a vote legislation designed to require automobile manufacturers to improve vehicle mileage. While all the Democratic presidential contenders for the 2008 presidential election admitted that global warming constitutes a serious threat to humanity and called for emissions cuts similar to those being passed in California and other states, John McCain was the only Republican hopeful in the 2008 election who adopted a similar position (Begley 2007).

In contrast to the federal government, numerous local and state governments have embarked upon efforts to mitigate global warming. The U.S. Conference on Mayors voted to meet or exceed Kyoto targets (Hertsgaard 2005:6). A substantial majority of U.S. states have enacted one or more laws or issued one or more executive mandates calling for greenhouse gas reductions. California has passed legislation requiring cars to emit 30 percent less greenhouse gas and joined eight states in suing electric utilities. On September 27, 2006, California Governor Arnold Schwarzenagger signed the California Global Warming Solutions Act, legislation designed to cap the state's greenhouse gas emissions at

1990 levels by 2020. In assessing such legislation, political scientist Barry Rabe (2004:151) observes that astute policy "entrepreneurs have tailored policies to the political and economic realities of their particular setting and have built coalitions that seem almost unthinkable when weighed against the past decade of federal-level experience." Ultimately, however, such legislative or executive acts are only as good as the ability to enforce them.

Australia

Certain segments of Australian society, ranging from politicians such as former Labor Prime Minister Bob Hawke to the Green Party, and a wide array of grass-roots environmental groups have exhibited an awareness of the potential impact of global warming on the environment and human societies. As early as 1981, the federal government's Office of National Assessments published *Fossil Fuels and the Greenhouse Effect* (Hamilton 2007:40). Australia adopted the Toronto Target in October 1990 and signed the Framework Convention on Climate Change in 1992. In 1995, the Labor government threatened industry with a carbon tax, which prompted the latter to accept the Greenhouse Challenge Program, a voluntary program accepted by John Howard, the leader of the coalition shortly after he assumed the Prime Ministership in 1996. Since that time, according to Hamilton (2007), a small "cabal" of lobbyists, self-described as the "greenhouse mafia" and consisting of executives from the oil, cement, aluminum, and electricity industries, had played a pivotal role in formulating the Howard government's climate change policies. Members of the "greenhouse mafia" regularly were consulted by government departments in the drafting of ministerial briefings on global warming or climate change. In a similar vein, Guy Pearse (2007), a Liberal Party member, lobbyist, and former Howard government advisor, asserted that the Prime Minister Howard allowed his climate policy to be shaped by the country's biggest polluters and lobbyists in Canberra.

Until 2006, the Howard government systematically either denied or downplayed the seriousness of global warming and refused to adopt any policies that would allegedly harm the Australian economy. Graeme Pearson, a former head of the Commonwealth Scientific and Industrial Research Organisation's (CSIRO) Division of Atmospheric Research, was instructed by his employer several times not to discuss the need to reduce greenhouse gas emissions (Hamilton 2007). Barrie Pittock (2005), an internationally renowned climate scientist and now retired CSIRO employee, was asked to remove a section from his book *Climate Change: Turning Up the Heat* in which he discussed the possibility of rising sea levels creating millions of climate refugees in the Asia-Pacific region. When the Science, Engineering, and Innovation Council urged the government to take a more proactive stance on global warming, Howard changed the membership of the group (Hamilton 2007:124). When Howard visited the United States in 2006, the Bush administration urged him to establish closer ties with the nuclear industry (Lowe 2007:75). Upon returning to Australia, he formed a task force to advise the government on the contribution that nuclear energy could allegedly play in terms of mitigating global warming. Beginning in 2006, in no small part because the effects of global warming are becoming part of everyday experience in Australia, climate politics became front-page news on a regular basis and Howard was forced to take the threat of global warming more seriously. He commissioned a task force, which recommended that Australia adopt an emissions trading scheme, one that should be in place by 2011 and that should set a low greenhouse gas emissions price (a somewhat arbitrarily determined cost allowing companies to emit greenhouse gas emissions by paying governments a fee) with deeper emissions cuts being required later on (Murphy 2007). Kevin Rudd, elected the Prime Minister of Australia in 2007, ratified the Kyoto Protocol and is committed to starting emissions trading by 2010 and setting an emissions reduction target of 60 percent at 2000 levels by 2050.

While only time will tell if Rudd follows through on his campaign promise of prioritizing global warming mitigation, it seems likely there will be difference in the new Labor government's stance on this issue from the 11 long years of coalition inaction under John Howard. With much of Australia being struck by a long drought and other parts being impacted by heavy rains and hurricanes, it appears that Australia no longer will serve as America's partner in thwarting mitigation efforts. The election in part is a political reflection of changing consciousness about global warming, as is former U.S. Vice President Al Gore's winning of the Nobel Peace Prize in 2007. Debate about global warming has been a factor in respective elections of the two countries.

As has been the case in the United States, in contrast to the federal government, various local and national governments in Australia have been more vigorous in legislating anti–global warming mitigation initiatives. The Australian Capital Territory (the national capital of Canberra), Brisbane, Adelaide, Melbourne, and various other municipalities have set local targets to limit greenhouse gas emissions (Lowe 2005:162). The Council of Australian Governments has criticized the Australian government for its cautious response to the dangers of global warming (Lowe 2005:178).

China

China's program of aggressive economic modernization and expansion is creating an ecological nightmare, not only in contributing to global warming but also in terms of air and water pollution, land degradation, and deforestation, desertification, flooding, and destruction of biodiversity. Bergsten and coauthors provide a sobering depiction of the consequences of these processes:

> Sixteen of the world's twenty most air-polluted cities are in China. Two-thirds of China's cities do not meet the country's own air emission standards. Nearly 200 cities fall short of the WHO standards for airborne particulates .... One SEPA [State Environmental Protection Agency] study revealed that in the 340 cities where air quality is monitored, 75 percent of the urban residents breathe unclean air. Air pollution in China is responsible for between 300,000 and 500,000 premature deaths annually. And yet the government is planning 562 new coal-fired power stations by 2012. [Bergsten et al. 2006:54]

Auto emissions, a major source of greenhouse emission, account for 79 percent of the air pollution in China. This is likely to worsen as the country is now adding some five million cars a year to its roads and highways.

While China claims to be committed to curtailing greenhouse gas emissions, it asserts that its primary objective is economic development, and thereby the eradication of poverty. China began to pass environmental protection laws in the late 1980s (Hatch 2003:46). It also began to monitor greenhouse gas emissions during the negotiations that eventually culminated in its ratification of the Framework Convention on Climate Change and the Kyoto Protocol. In 1990 China established the National Coordination Panel on Climate Change as a unit of the State Environmental Protection Commission (Zhang 2003:67). As a non–Annex I country, it is not obligated to reduce emissions under the first commitment period of 2008–2012. China, however, is an active participant in the Clean Development Mechanism under the Kyoto Protocol which provides emissions credits for verified reductions in developing nations. Credits can be purchased by developed countries, allowing them to meet their Kyoto targets without actually reducing their emissions (Pew Center for Global Climate Change 2007). Chinese officials claim that they plan to shift from the current heavy reliance upon coal to nuclear, hydroelectric, solar, and biomass power in order to curtail greenhouse gas emissions in the future (Pan 2005). Ironically, however, China reportedly "is planning to build more than five hundred new coal power plants by 2012 [while] looking to the Kyoto Protocol as well as the Asia Pacific Partnership on Clean Development and Climate . . . for foreign investment to reduce greenhouse gases from coal" (DiMento and Doughman 2007:115).

The Limitations of Climate Regimes

Global warming is clearly an international problem and will require an agreement by at least the majority of countries in the world, particularly those that are the largest greenhouse emitters, namely the United States, Germany, Japan, China, India, and Brazil. The least developed countries and small island nations, which will be the countries most adversely affected by global warming, are not crucial to mitigation efforts. Based upon an elaborate quantitative cross-national political analysis of international environmental agreements between 1963 and 1987, Roberts concludes:

> that wealthy, more powerful countries, and especially those without repressive governments and large military budgets, are those that tend to sign environmental treaties most often . . . . Furthermore, countries that are heavily in debt and that trade with relatively few other nations are likely to avoid agreeing to external limits for the protection of their environments. Contrary to prediction, however, countries with high levels of foreign direct investment were more likely to have ratified the nine major treaties ratified over the period of 1963–1987. [Roberts 1996:43]

In terms of global environmental governance, Roberts argues that it ultimately must be coupled with financial aid from developed to developing societies and redistribution of wealth in the world system. All environmental regimes face serious implementation difficulties. For example, only three European Union member states (the United Kingdom, Germany, and Luxembourg) reduced carbon dioxide emissions between 1990 and 1998 (Carter 2007).

Brunnengraeber (2006:226) assesses the limitation of the climate regime approach manifested in the Kyoto Protocol by noting, "It has not yet been possible to specify and implement the mechanisms for the reduction of greenhouse gases in such a way that a reduction of carbon dioxide measured in absolute figures can be guaranteed." Unfortunately, even if the targets of the Kyoto Protocol are fully met, they will only result in modest greenhouse gas emissions reductions. One atmospheric scientist has calculated that even if the protocol were to be fully implemented, a projected temperature increase of 3.6°F (2°C) by 2050 would be reduced by only 0.07°C (Wigley 2000). The United Kingdom and Germany have been the only large signatories that have come close to meeting their target emissions reductions. As noted earlier, however, much of these reductions are related to a shift from reliance on coal to gas in the United Kingdom, and the modernization of industries in the new German states. In Germany, environmentalists, particularly those affiliated with the Green Party, which has had a formidable presence in the *Bundestag*, have had a much greater institutional role shaping climate policies than in the United States or Australia. While environmentalists have had some successes in the United States and Australia, Germany has had a much stronger environmental movement, with left-wing, moderate, and right-wing factions, for a long time (Riordan 1997).

Despite the role it has played in alerting the world to the current state and risks of global warming, the IPCC has tended to privilege the physical and technical over the social implications of global warming. As Huckle and Martin (2001:144) observe, "even within its own ranks, Working Group I (science) is considered more solid and influential than Working Group III (socio-economic dimensions)." Unfortunately, according to Lohmann (2006:39), Working Group III's agenda is "captured in large part by orthodox economists who ignored the social roots of climate change as well as grassroots resources for tackling climate change." While the IPCC concedes that anthropogenic activities have been the primary cause of global warming, nowhere in its various reports has it acknowledged that global warming is a by-product of capitalism and its ever expanding levels of production and consumption. Indeed, Robert T. Watson, a World Bank scientist who directed the IPCC for a while, reportedly made a concerted effort to accommodate the body's scientific findings to U.S. corporate interests, including those of the oil companies, and World Bank interests (Lohmann 2006:40–41).

Some critics argue that the 2007 IPCC report is somewhat cautious in its assessment of the gravity of global warming but particularly in its recommendations on how to mitigate it. IPCC reports are carefully crafted consensus documents given that both governmental and scientific bodies have to sign off on them. Fred Pearce (2007) reports that various British scientists claimed that the IPCC report "was significantly watered down when governments became involved in it." The final version deleted references to growing concerns that global warming is accelerating the discharge of ice from major ice sheets, including the Greenland ice sheet. The 2007 IPCC report represents an uneasy alliance between climate science and mainstream economics. As Kovel argues,

> Economics stands over climate science insofar as it is the prime science of the ruling capitalist classes who control the state and the scientific establishment. The whole of modern industrial capital is inextricably wound up with the course of science, and so control over science is an absolute condition for accumulation. Therefore scientists today are bought and sold in the marketplace. They develop in tightly structured environments shot through with patronage, hierarchy and the tentacles of state and corporate power. [Kovel 2007:4]

In a similar vein, Kiely (2007:129) argues that conventional climate regimes "are too easily guilty of ignoring the uneven development of international capitalism, and therefore the unequal context in which rights, values, ethics and international institutions operate." In terms of the political economy of research funding, James Hansen (2007a:31) has gone so far as to suggest that those climate scientists who downplay the dangers of global warming are more likely to obtain research funding.

Neoliberal Approaches

Contemporary capitalism is being shaped by *neoliberalism*, a philosophical perspective (which to complicate matters, is neither new or liberal) embraced by conservative economists, policy makers, and corporate officials who urge the minimization of government regulation of the "free market," including supporting the free flow of goods and services across national boundaries. Inevitably, neoliberal solutions have come to pervade climate politics. Historically, corporations have tended to either deny or downplay the seriousness of global warming and their contribution to it. They often have been part and parcel of a category that has come to be termed *contrarians*, which includes: 1) those who deny the reality of global warming; 2) those who admit its existence but claim that anthropogenic forces are not primarily responsible for it, thus attributing it primarily to natural forces; and 3) those who admit that anthropogenic activities are partly responsible for global warming, but deny that it matters or argue that various social benefits may emanate from global warming (Diesendorf 2007:22). The Union of Concerned Scientists has conducted an analysis of contrarian groups and claims that the "great majority either belong to or are actively sponsored or funded by organizations such as the fossil fuel industries" (Hillman 2004:22). For example, Patrick J. Michaels, a leading contrarian scientist, receives funding from the Western Fuels Association and edits the *World Climate Report* (McCright 2000). Contrarian organizations include the Global Climate Coalition (now defunct), the Greening Earth Society (U.S.), Frontiers of Freedom (U.S.), the Cooler Heads Coalition (U.S.) the Cato Institute (U.S.), the Lavoisier Group (Australian), and the Institute of Public Affairs (Australian) (Beder 2000, Flannery 2006).

The Global Climate Coalition (GCC) was an energy industry lobby group that operated out of the Washington, DC, office of the National Association of Manufacturers (Linden 2006:273). Its mission was mounting a frontal attack on conclusions of the IPCC. The GCC, which included the American Highway Users Alliance, the American Petroleum Institute, the Edison Electric Institute, the National Association of Manufacturers, the National Mining Association, British Petroleum, and Shell Oil (Gelbspan 2004:40), began to fall apart in 1999, when the latter two corporations withdrew out of concern that their membership would damage their public image. Some of the members of the disbanded GCC joined the Pew Center's Business Environmental Leadership Council, a constituent unit of the Pew Center on Global Climate Change. Numerous corporations in the transport and energy fields especially, including Boeing, Lockheed-Marietta, Toyota, Whirlpool, 3M, British Petroleum, Sun Oil, American Electric Power, and International Energy, have lent their support to the Pew Center for Global Climate Change, which was launched in 1998 and views the Kyoto Protocol as the first step in addressing global warming (Hamilton 2007:85). The Pew Center provides information about global warming and associated climatic changes and proposes technological changes, such as increasing energy efficiency in buildings and appliances.

In recent years, many corporate elites around the world have come to recognize that denying the reality of global warming makes for poor public relations and contradicts claims of corporate responsibility. Reflecting the long history of capitalism's ability to adapt to new material circumstances, a small but growing number of corporations, in fact, have come to embrace some variant of what is called *green capitalism.* This approach involves the adoption of *sustainable development* and *environmental sustainability* as corporate slogans. Additionally "green capitalism" emphasizes schemes such as carbon trading and even carbon taxes as a means of controlling greenhouse gas emissions, but generally ignores the issue of environmental justice, The World Business Council for Sustainable Development, which consists of over 100 corporate members (such as Renault, Total, Fiat, British Petroleum, Shell Oil, Texaco, Mitsubishi, and Toyota), claims to be an advocate of *ecological modernization* (Gonzalez 2005). It is committed to "simultaneously improving environmental and financial performance" (quoted in Resistance 1999:84). This perspective, however, is premised on the notion that the globe has infinite resources and fails to address social disparities that are inherent in global capitalism. Inevitably the drive for profit overrides any alleged commitment to environmental sustainability.

Neoliberal economists have tended to view environmental damage and pollution as externalities or "entities that are external to economic markets and, therefore, not managed by them" (Huckle and Martin 2001:136). From this perspective, greenhouse emissions constitute factors that are not assigned a specified cost. Some neoliberal economists, however, have come to recognize that capitalism has the potential to kill the goose that laid the golden egg so to speak and, as a result, have begun to calculate the cost of greenhouse gas emissions.

Nicholas Stern (2006), for example, head of the U.K. Government Economic Service and a former chief economist of the World Bank, has proposed a celebrated neoliberal strategy for addressing global warming.

He argues "that if we don't act, overall costs and risks of climate change will be equivalent to losing at least 5 percent of global GDP each year, now and forever" (Stern 2007:xv). Stern asserts that the "risks from the worst impact of climate change" can be appreciably reduced if greenhouse gas levels in the atmosphere could be stabilized between 450 and 550 carbon dioxide equivalent. Bearing in mind that the currently carbon dioxide equivalent level (i.e., the conversion of all greenhouse gas emissions converted to an amount of carbon dioxide) is 430 and is rising at more than 2 ppm per annum, drastic actions are imminently required. Stern (2007: xv) asserts that the "costs of action—reducing greenhouse gas emissions to avoid the worst impacts of climate change—can be limited to around 1 percent of global GDP each year," a course of action that would lead to stabilization at around 500 to 550 ppm carbon dioxide by 2050. He maintains that all countries need to be involved in a massive effort to mitigate greenhouse gas emissions while none of them, whether developed or developing, need to "cap aspirations for growth" (Stern 2007:xvii). Stern proposes three basic strategies for cutting fossil fuel emissions: 1) reducing the demand for carbon-intensive products; 2) increasing energy efficiency; and 3) switching to low-carbon technologies."

Nowhere in his approach, however, is there a discussion of issues such as the constraint of finite global natural resources, ongoing global poverty and deepening poverty in some places, and the role of poverty as a catalyst of population growth, which in turn results in greater energy and resource demands. Stern's neoliberal approach seeks to make mitigation of global warming part and parcel of the market, an approach that the European Union has practiced since January 2005 with considerable fanfare (Lefevere 2005). However, this strategy has thus far failed because the cap on carbon dioxide emissions was so lenient that the price on carbon dioxide drastically decreased, thus eliminating the incentive to reduce emissions (Knobloch and Barnes 2006:4).

An emission trading scheme is embodied in the Kyoto Protocol, which includes a "cap and trade system" and imposes national caps on carbon dioxide emissions. Under this scheme, countries that exceed a designated cap can purchase credits from countries that do not exceed it. Various environmental groups have opposed emissions trading schemes because they grant the "right to pollute" (Hamilton 2001:153). Climate Action Network–Europe argues that the European Union's Emissions Trading Scheme, which commenced on January 1, 2005, was a "major disappointment" because it set lax national emission targets. Lohmann (2006) argues that current carbon-trading policies inadvertently encourage additional exploitation of fossil fuels and that new tree farms often drive people out of their traditional living grounds and destroy biological diversity. Under the dictates of the Kyoto Protocol, developed countries can circumvent emissions reductions by investing in forestation as a form of carbon sequestration (or capture), through soil conservation, or by investing in Clean Development Mechanism (CDM) projects in developing countries, which supposedly result in the transfer of more environmentally sustainable technologies to the latter (Lohmann 2006:49). Based upon a review of CDM projects, Sutter and Parreno (2007:84) report that they did not find any that are likely to meet the protocol's dual objectives of reducing greenhouse gas emissions and contributing to sustainable development.

Lohmann delineates fives reasons why emission trading constitutes a flawed approach to mitigation:

> *First*, in order to work, greenhouse gas trading has to create a special system of property rights in the earth's carbon-cycling capacity. This system sets up deep political conflicts and makes effective climate action exceedingly difficult. *Second*, pollution trading is a poor mechanism for stimulating the social and technical changes needed to address global warming. *Third*, the attempt to build new carbon-cycling capacity is interfering with genuine climate action. *Fourth*, global trading systems for greenhouse gases can't work without much better global enforcement regimes than are likely in the near future. And *fifth*, building a trading system reduces the political space available for education, movement-building and planned around the needed fair transition away from fossil fuels. [Lohmann 2006:72]

Various trading schemes, including those in the United States, the Kyoto Protocol, and the European Union Emissions Trading Scheme, grant corporations and developed countries property rights to emit greenhouse gases (Lohmann 2006:73). In its first phase, the European Union Emissions Trading Scheme granted 11,428 industrial facilities, most of them in the corporate sector, carbon dioxide emissions rights. When the scheme was first piloted in January 2004, the right to emit one ton of carbon dioxide cost about 12 euros, but by January it had dropped to about seven euros. Emission trading schemes have literally created billions of dollars in rights and assets. The World Bank, which functions as the largest provider of carbon trading finance, the London-based Climate Change Capital Bank and the U.S. Morgan Stanley Investment Bank have entered into the carbon trading market. Major corporate greenhouse emitters have sought carbon credits from other countries, and have passed the costs of carbon trading on to their customers (Lohmann 2006:119).

Carbon off-setting constitutes yet another neoliberal mitigation strategy, one that is also fraught with contradictions. Various corporations, such as Carbon Neutral Company, Offset My Life, and Climate Care seek to assuage the consciences of consumers who frequently fly around the globe or live in huge, energy-intensive dwelling units by suggesting that they can offset the environmental damage done by their affluent lifestyles by purchasing energy-efficient products, investing in renewable energy projects, using renewable energy sources, or planting trees. According to Smith (2007:6), "instead of encouraging individuals and institutions to profoundly change consumption patterns as well as social, economic, and political structures, we are asked to believe that paying a little extra for certain goods and services is sufficient." Offset schemes also inadvertently discourage people from becoming involved in the growing anti–global warming or climate change movement which is challenging the existing pattern of ever-growing production and consumption associated with global capitalism. In terms of tree plantating projects, it is difficult to calculate how much carbon dioxide is being absorbed and how quickly it will be absorbed from the atmosphere (Smith 2007).

Neoliberal approaches to mitigating greenhouse gas emissions also include various technological fixes, including renewable energy sources such as solar energy, wind energy, geothermal energy, marine energy, hydropower, tidal or wave power, and ocean currents power; the development of hybrid cars; and more technologically efficient appliances and lighting sources, such as fluorescent bulbs. Such technological fixes come under the rubric of *ecological modernization*, a stance that some environmentalists have embraced. This approach asserts that business can profit by protecting the environment. As Carter notes in laying out key components of ecological modernization:

> Ecological criteria must be built into the production process. On the supply side, costs can be reduced by improving productive efficiency in ways that have environmental benefits. Savings can be made by straightforward technological fixes to reduce waste, and hence pollution, but also through a more fundamental rethinking of manufacturing processes so that large-scale production systems such as "smoke-stack" industries, that can never be made ecologically sound, are gradually phased out. On the demand side, there are growing markets in green technologies such as air pollution abatement equipment and alternative forms of energy. The rise of "green consumerism" has stimulated demand for goods that minimise environmental damage both in the way they are made (by using recycled materials or minimising packaging) and in their impact when used (by containing less harmful chemicals such as phosphate-free washing powders). [Carter 2007:227–228]

Although ecological modernization concedes that environmental problems are a by-product of global capitalism, it rejects transcending the capitalist mode of production. It maintains that capitalism can be made more "environmentally friendly" through environmental regulations and technological changes managed by an ecologically sensitive government or "green state" that operates in concert with corporate interests (Clark and York 2005). Ecological modernization, which started in Northern European countries, particularly Germany, the Netherlands, Sweden, Norway, Austria, and Denmark, has quickly been adopted by corporate elites in various countries and even some moderate environmentalist groups in both developed and developing countries (Carter 2007).

The U.S. science-industrial complex, in particular, has proposed elaborate and incredibly expensive technological fixes, such as "seeding large areas of land with organisms genetically engineered to fix carbon 'more efficiently'; establishing floating kelp farms thousands of square kilometers in size which, growing heavier as they consumed carbon dioxide, would eventually sink to the ocean floor; and using fleets of C-130 military transport planes to bomb Scotland and other countries with millions of metal cones containing pine saplings" (Lohmann 2006:43). According to the Jevons paradox, "improvements in efficiency actually increase the use of natural resources under capitalist relations, thus diminishing the potential for developing ecological sustainability based on technological fixes" (Clark and York 2005:396).

Increasingly, as well, various governments, including Australia, and even noted environmental scientists such as James Lovelock and Tim Flannery, have come out in favor of using nuclear energy as a way of mitigating greenhouse gas emissions. Aside from the issues of the dangers posed by nuclear waste materials and the fact that uranium is not a renewable energy source, the construction of nuclear power plants creates significant greenhouse gases and pollution (Caldicott 2006). Other proposed measures for mitigating carbon dioxide include the development of carbon sink enhancement options entailing the capture and disposal of carbon dioxide. One problem with forestation as a carbon mitigation strategy is the difficulty in measuring the amount of carbon sequestered thereby (Drake 2000:211). Tropical forests are believed to sequester far more carbon than temperate forests. Ironically, much of the deforestation in the world is occurring in tropical areas, such as the Amazon Basin and Indonesia, rather than in temperate areas, which are situated in more developed countries, such as Canada. Already, for example, half of all tropical forests have been destroyed.

Sustainable Development or Social Democratic Approaches

Various segments of the environmental movement, particularly groups such as Greenpeace and Friends of the Earth, began to express alarm about the impact of global warming on the planet and human societies as early as the 1980s and played a key role in prompting climate scientists, the

United Nations, and even national governments to respond. Despite this, various scholars have argued that environmental organizations have lost influence and have become increasingly divided in terms of their positions on global warming (Skjaereth and Skodvin 2003). The dominant political strategy adopted by most environmental organizations has been to lobby politicians and governments to introduce regulations against environmental degradation, including global warming. Most environmentalists in one way or another are committed to the notion of *sustainable development* as a strategy for mitigating global warming. This concept was first formulated by the World Commission on Environment and Development (1987:8) in its report *Our Common Future* in which it states:

> The concept of sustainable development does not imply limits—not absolute limits but limitations imposed by the present state of technology and social organization on environmental resources and by the ability of the biosphere to absorb the effects of human activities. But technology and social organization can be both managed and improved to make way for a new era of economic growth.

Thus, sustainable development implies the possibility of a complementarity between economic expansion and environmental sustainability.

In an early summary of the Greenpeace perspective, Leggett (1990) argued that the principal avenues to mitigating global warming include adoption of energy-efficient technologies in developed countries and transfer of these technologies to developing countries, renewable forms of energy production, less greenhouse gas–intensive agriculture, curtailment of deforestation, reforestation, reduction of nuclear energy production, and grass-roots anti-greenhouse actions. Various environmental groups, such as the Natural Resources Defense Council, the Union of Concerned Scientists, and the World Wildlife Federation, have agreed to accept what they regard to be a "politically feasible target" of 450 ppm of carbon dioxide. In assessing this stance, Athanasiou and Baer (2002:130) assert that "climate people" tend to be naïve about the growing alliance between multilateral climate regimes and neoliberal institutions. For the most part, large international environmental organizations, such as Friends of the Earth, the World Wide Fund for Nature, and even Greenpeace, have accommodated their campaigns in such a way that they avoid a direct critique of the role of global capitalism in contributing to the global warming crisis (Arts and Cozijnsen 2003, Carter 2007). According to Huckle and Martin (2001:151), "it has largely been left to smaller groups, and especially networks of Third World activists, to employ issues of atmospheric pollution [including global warming] as part of a challenge to paradigms of technocentrism, neoliberalism, and globalization."

Athanasiou and Baer (2002) contend that mitigation will require a total drop to 60 to 80 percent below 1990 levels of greenhouse gas emissions and advocate the implementation of a "precautionary global emissions cap." They maintain that the developed countries need to assist the developing countries to engage in a rapid process of "leapfrogging" that will allow them to adopt more environmentally sustainable technologies. While not advocating an end to global capitalism per se, Athanasiou and Baer (2002:113) propose substituting "privatization of the commons by establishing the institutions and politics of communal ownership" with respect to the atmosphere. They agree with the position of the International Forum on Globalization, which argues: "There is an appropriate place for private ownership and markets to play in the management, allocation, and delivery of certain common heritage resources, as for example land, within a framework of effective democratically accountable public regulation that guarantees fair pricing, equitable access, quality, and public stewardship" (quoted in Athanasiou and Baer 2002:113). Unfortunately, despite their commitment to poverty alleviation, environmental sustainability, and democracy, Athanasiou and Baer (2002:142) fail to make clear how these ideals will be achieved within the parameters of even a regulated global capitalist system. In contrast to mainstream environmentalists, radical environmentalists, such as Vandana Shiva (2005), have come to reject the notion of sustainable development because of its close association with ecological modernization.

In the early 1990s, the Global Commons Institute, under the directorship of Aubrey Meyer, formulated a contraction and convergence scheme. Contraction would entail determining an international agreement on an tolerable level of carbon dioxide, possibly somewhere between 350 and 450 ppm, and then calculating the rate at which present emissions must be cut back in order to achieve this level (Hillman 2004:180). In terms of convergence, Hillman and Meyer propose a "fair shares for all" scheme which includes the following features: 1) equal allowances of greenhouse gas emissions for all individuals with only rare exceptions; 2) an annual reduction of the allowance with considerable forewarning; 3) all personal transportation and household energy would be included; and 4) provision for trading of allowances (Hillman 2004). Individuals would be issued a "Carbon Allowance Card." This contraction and convergence scheme has received the support of various European environmental ministers and the vast majority of elected representatives in the European Parliament; the All-Party Parliamentary Climate Change Group of Members of Parliament in the United Kingdom; the World Bank; the United Nations Environmental Program Financial Initiative; numerous NGOs, including the IPCC Third Policy Assessment; the

World Council of Churches; most governments in developing countries; various political parties in developed countries; and certain prominent individuals (Hillman 2004, Lohmann 2006).

Austerity Approaches

Monbiot (2006) maintains that the campaign against global warming or climate change is a "campaign not for abundance but for austerity." Obviously, this assertion applies more to the majorities in developed countries and the affluent in developing countries than the poor in both, groups that already experience a daily austerity program. Monbiot (2006) calls for a 90 percent reduction in carbon dioxide emissions and argues that governments need to require people to alter their lifestyles, which would include measures such as relying less on private motor vehicles and more on mass transportation, drastically reducing air travel, adopting low-carbon technologies, better insulating buildings and dwelling units, using less and more energy-efficient lighting, and shopping on the Internet. He does not discuss how some of these measures will be achieved in a global economic order committed to consumption and in which multinational corporations shape many government policies to fit their economic interests rather than environmental concerns.

In sum, while numerous strategies, including carbon trading, carbon sequestration, and the contraction and convergence model, have been proposed as ways of mitigating global warming, virtually all of them are framed within the existing parameters of global capitalism and ultimately fail to fully address the costly engine of ever expanding production and consumption that has driven global warming

By its own logic, capitalism must grow or die out. As Pepper (1993:218–219) asserts, "sound capitalist development is a contradiction in terms . . . Capitalism is growth-oriented—growth in real values resting on the exploitation of nature, including human labour." While green capitalism seeks to incorporate environmental factors, including greenhouse gas emissions, into its economic calculations, it is oblivious to issues of social equity, population growth driven by poverty, and the reality of limited natural resources. Obviously production and consumption are an integral part of any society, starting out historically with foraging societies. But the rules of capitalism encourage the production of numerous consumer items that are not essential for human subsistence and often serve as a compensation for alienation from mundane and tedious work and social isolation in an increasingly urbanized and socially fragmented world. Through the development of bigger and better variants of the same products, intensive advertising, and effective marketing, capitalism has contributed to the emergence, first within what are now developed countries and increasingly in developing countries, of what might be called a *global sumptuary culture*. In developed countries, this culture is seen in the practice of shopping as recreation, in competitive purchasing (known in the folk idiom as outdoing "the Joneses"), and in the validation of self-worth and achievement through ownership. In developing countries, Western products have taken on an "aura of modernity," in that merely having or consuming them allows individuals to feel like are participating in the good life of the developed world.

Green capitalism in the developed world generally does not address the issue of growing industrial production in the developing world, particularly in China and India. Yet multinational corporations are in the habit of relocating their most polluting operations to developing countries where environmental protection laws are weakest. Thus, as Biel argues,

> if . . . all that happens is a change of [industry's] *location*, any "greening" would be merely cosmetic: for example, pollution of the immediate living environment could be reduced in the core (by shifting industry to the periphery) but without reducing the physical-environmental entropy of the system as a whole. It might well get worse, because of the huge transportation costs associated with globalized industry. [Biel 2006:131]

In a somewhat different vein, Podobnik maintains:

> In order for most core nations to approach their per capita emissions norm, they would have to reduce their commercial energy consumption levels by factors of 3, 4, or 5. Moreover, these reductions would have to be achieved in a context in which per capita emissions from peripheral nations were allowed to rise toward the global threshold. In other words, the historically ingrained transfer of resources characteristic of the world energy system would have to be reversed. Nothing short of a fundamental change in the material structures and political culture of the world-system itself would be required to attain an equitably distributed allotment of consumption rights. [Podobnik 2002:265]

Bearing this in mind, in our concluding chapter we propose a vision for an alternative to the existing capitalist world system and some strategies for transcending "business as usual."

8

Toward a Healthier Planet

The Creation of a Democratic Ecosocialist World System

While global capitalism has resulted in impressive technological innovations, including ones in biomedicine and health care delivery, it is a system fraught with contradictions, including an incessant drive for economic expansion, growing social disparities, undemocratic practices that undermine its claims of equality, militarist and imperialist practices, depletion of natural resources, and environmental degradation (including global warming and associated climatic changes). All of these contradictions entail numerous consequences for people's health and access to health care. The contradictory features of global capitalism are intertwined (e.g., military ventures wreck havoc on the environment and significantly deplete natural resources while promoting global social inequality), and hence it is hard to fully analyze one contradiction separate from the others. Each is so complex in its relationship to health, however, that it requires the kind of detailed single-issue examination presented in this book.

Based on the assessment presented, it is clear that human societies will have to adapt to the reality of global warming in a variety of ways, including technological fixes, reliance upon alternative forms of energy, significant expansion and improvement in mass transit systems, more efficient forms of heating and cooling, the development of buildings and dwelling units that are more energy efficient, the redesign of cities to control their energy demands and heat outputs, restoration of degraded environments, protection of biodiversity, and less reliance upon airplanes as a form of travel. Yet, it is the argument of this book that while these kinds of *reformist reform strategies* will help to limit future greenhouse gas emissions, they are insufficient to reverse global warming if they are implemented within the reigning productivist and consumptionist ethics of global capitalism. Adopting capitalist solutions to the contradictions of capitalism—such as green capitalism and neoliberal approaches—we argue, is a kind of fool's paradise that misdiagnosis both the extent and the ultimate source of the threat facing the ecohealth of the planet and its occupants.

Consequently, we believe it is necessary to adopt *nonreformist reform* transcendent approaches to global warming that move toward the development of a new global system, one committed to social equality, social democracy, and environmental sustainability at local, national, and global levels. In the 19th century, various revolutionaries and reformers, particularly Karl Marx and Frederich Engels, sought to develop alternatives to an increasingly globalizing capitalist world system. Efforts at the national level to create an alternative started out with the Bolshevik Revolution in Russia in 1917 and included subsequent revolutions in other countries, including China in 1949, Vietnam in 1954, Cuba in 1959, Laos in 1975, and Nicaragua and Afghanistan in 1979. Academics and political activists have engaged in considerable discussion and debate in their efforts to determine whether these societies constituted examples of "state socialism" or "actually existing socialism," transitions between capitalism and socialism that needed to undergo democratization, state capitalism, or new class societies. They also have asked why these societies, such as the Soviet Union and China, in different ways failed to transcend the reigning global economic structure and were eventually fully reincorporated into the capitalist world system.

Ultimately, the failure of these societies to develop democratic ecosocialism was related to both internal forces specific to each society (including their initial lower level of technological development) and external forces that created a hostile environment (both economically and politically) which impeded progressive changes and pushed their systems away from democracy toward centralization.

A Vision of Global Democratic Ecosocialism

The collapse of communist regimes created a crisis for people on the left throughout the world. Many progressives had hoped that somehow these societies would undergo changes that would transform them into democratic and environmentally sustainable egalitarian societies. This did not occur. In the aftermath, some politically progressive analysts began advocating shedding the concept of socialism and replacing it with terms such as *radical democracy* and *economic democracy*. While such efforts are understandable given the fate of postrevolutionary or socialist-oriented societies, we believe that it is necessary to come to terms with both the achievements and flaws of these societies and to reformulate the concept of socialism. For example, the tiny country of Cuba, some 90 miles (145 km) offshore from the United States, exhibits health statistics on par with those of highly developed and wealthy societies, exports physicians to various developing countries around the world (particularly those facing crisis situations), and, according to the mainstream World Wildlife Fund, is the only country in the world that meets the criteria of *sustainable development.*

The creation of what we term *democratic ecosocialism,* or what world systems theorists Terry Boswell and Christopher Chase-Dunn (2000) term *global democracy,* would entail the following components: 1) an increasing movement toward public ownership of productive forces at local, regional, national, and international levels; 2) the development of an economy oriented toward meeting social needs, such as basic food, clothing, shelter, and health care, and environmental sustainability rather than profit making; 3) a blending of both representative and participatory democratic processes; 4) the eradication of health and social disparities and redistribution of human resources between developed and developing societies and within societies in general; 5) the curtailment of population growth that in larger part would follow from the previously mentioned condition; 6) the conservation of finite resources and the development of renewable energy resources, such as wind, solar, and thermal energy, all of which would counteract the present trend toward rapidly accelerating global warming; 7) the redesign of settlement and transportation systems to cut energy demands and greenhouse gas emissions; and 8) the reduction of wastes through recycling and transcending the reigning culture of consumption.

On a global level, democratic ecosocialism also seeks to address not only the matter of environmental sustainability but also social justice (including environmental justice), both within developed societies, where large numbers of people continue to suffer from poverty, but particularly in developing societies. To achieve these goals, there is no escaping the difficult fact that the majority of people in developed societies will need to scale back their consumption of material goods. In one of his ongoing popular commentaries, Immanuel Wallerstein (2007:1), a principal architect of world systems theory, delineates three powerful obstacles to overcoming global warming: 1) the "interests of producers/entrepreneurs" who function as the purveyors of the constant cycle of production and consumption; 2) the "interests of less wealthy nations," like China and India, that seek to catch up with the core nations, and 3) the "attitudes of you and me," that is ordinary people like the authors and readers of this book who consciously or unconsciously find ourselves embedded in the contradictions of global capitalism wherever we live, including the enculturated needs we feel for acquiring "more things." As Wallerstein asserts, mitigation of global warming starts at the individual level, a notion that applies to most people in developed societies, depending on their class status, and the more affluent social classes in developing countries. While poorer regions of the world are in need of economic development—that is, access to basic resources and health care—much of the developed world and parts of the developing world are, in a sense, overdeveloped (although the products of this overdevelopment are not equitably distributed). As Foster argues,

> Sustained economic development over decades . . . is . . . not the same thing as environmentally sustainable development . . . . Any discussion of the global ecological crisis must therefore concentrate on the excesses of the advanced capitalist states, and their impact on the periphery of the world economy. It is here at the heart of the capitalist world system that the problem of unsustainable development arises in its acute form. [Foster 2002:82]

Further, as Loewy observes,

> The countries of the South, where . . . [basic material] needs are very far from being satisfied, will need a much higher level of "development"—building railroads, hospitals, sewage systems, and other infrastructures—than the advanced industrial ones. But there is no reason why this cannot be accomplished with a productive system that is environmentally-friendly and based on renewable energies. [Loewy 2006:303]

Democratic ecosocialism rejects a statist, growth-oriented, or productivist ethic and the enshrinement of possession and consumption as pathways to emotional satisfaction and as markers of personal achievement. Instead, it recognizes that we live on an ecologically fragile planet with limited resources and endangered wildlife and plants that must be sustained and renewed for future generations. According to Pepper (1993:234), "the basic socialist principles—egalitarianism, eliminating capitalism and poverty, resource distribution according to need and democratic control of our lives and communities—are also environmental principles." Public ownership of the means of production would blend elements of centralism and decentralism. For example, large-scale operations such as telecommunications or a railway system could be owned and operated by the national government whereas a small-scale operation such as a shoe factory or publishing house could be owned by a local community.

Socialism has the potential to place constraints upon resource depletion and attacks upon biodiversity. As McLaughlin (1990:80–81) maintains, "Socialism provides the conscious political control of those processes of interacting with nature which are left to the unconscious market processes under capitalism." The construction of democratic ecosocialism needs to be based upon a commitment to a long-term sustainable balance between sociocultural systems and the natural environment. As Foster (2005b:9) argues, a *global ecological transformation* requires a socialist transformation. Part and parcel of the transformation to a safer and sustainable way of life is the movement away from the narrow self-interested focus on personal (and familial) wealth that is promoted by global capitalism toward a focus on social responsibility. As Lohmann (2006:339) observes, "no aspect of the discussion on global warming can be disentangled from debates about colonialism, racism, gender, exploitation and the democratic control of technology."

Nonreformist Reforms for Mitigating Global Warming: Pathways to Social Transformation

The types of transformations suggested above require the development of concrete plans and pathways to lead us away from the limited programs of mitigation now being offered by corporate elites, the governments of developed nations, and even some environmentalists as the "solution" to global warming. The Socialist Alliance (2007), an Australian political party, has delineated a 10-Point Climate Action Plan for Australia that could be modified for other countries, both developed and developing countries:

1. "Aim for 60 percent overall emissions reduction, including 95 percent power station reduction by 2020, and 90 percent overall emissions reduction by 2030;
2. Ratify the Kyoto treaty and initiate a further international treaty and mutual assistance program to bring other countries together to meet a global target of 90 percent emissions by 2030;
3. Start the transition to a zero-waste economy, [starting out with a program of energy auditing];
4. Set a minimum 10-star energy efficiency rating for all new buildings;
5. Bring all power industries under public ownership and democratic control;
6. Bring the immense manufacturing potential of the auto industry under public control;
7. Immediately begin constructing wind farms in suitable areas;
8. End industrial farming based on fossil-fuel fertilisers, pesticides and fuels;
9. Stop logging old-growth forests and begin an urgent program of re-forestation and protecting biodiversity to ensure a robust biosystem that can survive the stress of climate change and provide an increased carbon sink; and
10. Make all urban and regional public transport free and upgrade the network to enable all urban residents to use it for all their regular commuting."

While the climate action plan may strike many people as being utopian, like the notion of democracy, it constitutes a vision for an alternative to flawed "business as usual" or existing climate regimes and green capitalism.

While we view the creation of a democratic ecosocialist world order as the ultimate mitigation strategy for addressing global warming, we are not under any illusions that this vision will be implemented any time soon, if ever for that matter, and certainly not without a mass, grass-roots and global social movement to promote it. In the meantime, those concerned above the grave threats of global warming and other contradictions of global capitalism need to identify and push for nonreformist reforms. As Pittock (2005:151) observes, "mitigation action taken now will have its most significant effects decades into the future."

Some shorter-term nonreformist reforms might include: lobbying national, regional, and state governments to adopt and implement strong mitigation plans; voluntary personal lifestyle changes, such as relying more on mass transit, cycling, and walking as modes of transportation and traveling more within one's region than over long distances; and supporting progressive social movements that critically challenge the political, economic, and social forces that contribute to global warming and promote narrow solutions for overcoming its dire effects.

Theoretically, a tax on greenhouse gas emissions could also constitute a nonreformist reform. Climate-related regulation and climate-relaxed tax codes already exist in various countries (Lohmann 2006:334). Unfortunately, efforts to impose a carbon tax in the European Union have met with failure because certain member states, such as the United Kingdom, capitulated to the claims of various industries that they would not be able to compete with non–European Union industries (O'Riordan and Jordan 1999:84). Conversely, carbon tax schemes emanating from social movements could incorporate measures to resist capitulation to corporate lobbying, bullying, and nationalist propaganda campaigns.

Various other plans that contain valuable ideas also have been suggested. Ian Angus, the late director of the Centre for Science and Environment in India, for example, recommended the following reforms as key components of a socialist agenda for global warming mitigation:

- Establish and enforce rapid mandatory reductions in CO_2 emissions: real reduction, not phoney trading plans.
- Make the corporations that produce greenhouse gases pay the full cost of cutting emissions.
- End all subsidies to fossil fuel producers.
- Redirect the billions now being spent on wars and debt into public transit, into retrofitting homes and offices for energy efficiency, and into renewable energy projects. [Angus 2007]

Alternately, Firor and Jacobsen (2002) propose an approach to mitigation of global warming that contains a hybrid of the social democratic approach that we discussed in the previous chapter and the democratic ecosocialist approach set forth in this chapter. In contrast to green capitalism advocates, who adhere to the notion that the levels of production must continually grow in order to ensure a robust national economy, Firor and Jacobsen (2002) acknowledge that GDP is an artificial and misleading measure of economic and social well-being in that it does not measure quality of life and environmental sustainability. In line with our discussion above, they argue that there are two needed social revolutions if humans are to flourish on earth: 1) an equity revolution (including in the area of health) across social classes within societies and between societies and 2) an efficiency revolution that would change the relationship between economic activities and the planetary ecosystem. Whereas they argue that "business and industry," which have contributed heavily to environmental degradation, must play a role in saving the environment, we argue that ultimately both activities need to be subsumed within an alternative global political economy.

Finally, Ted Trainer (1989, 1995), an Australian environmental scientist, provides several proposals that might be termed nonreformist reforms in that they could serve as transition points between the present global system and a newer, planet-friendly alternative. Trainer calls for "appropriate development" for both "rich" and "poor" countries. In terms of the former, this would entail an enormous reduction in consumerism (Trainer 1989:196) and essentially reversion to a "zero-growth economy" in which societies "will work hard at reducing the amount of producing and consuming going on" (Trainer 1995:108). In terms of the latter, this would include a focus on local economic self-sufficiency; the utilization of "low, intermediate, and alterative technologies processing locally available resources"; and a commitment to environmental sustainability (Trainer 1989:199–201). Unfortunately, Trainer, who views excessive consumption as the root of global environmental crisis, fails to analyze consumption as an inevitable component of capitalism's insatiable need for ever-expanding economic growth.

Challenging Global Warming at the Grass-Roots Level

Achieving a just, democratic, and environmentally safe world will not be easy, at either the individual or group levels, especially given the fate of earlier efforts to create more equitable and just social systems (e.g., the Soviet Union and the People's Republic of China), but ultimately it is mandatory to mitigate the significant adverse impacts of global warming. The creation of an alternative global social order will require a multifaceted effort drawing upon expertise from many quarters, including not only mainstream political and economic institutions but also progressive social movements. Already there are voices from many quarters bucking the existing global political economy, including the anti-corporate globalization, environmental, labor, indigenous and ethnic rights, peace, and social justice movements. As a result of grass-roots pressure, various city and state governments in developed societies, including the United States and the United Kingdom, have been passing ordinances and implementing programs of greenhouse gas abatement (Bulkeley and Betsill 2003). Indeed, some of these measures may qualify as local nonreformist reforms in that they empower local groups to counteract measures on the part of national governments that capitulate to corporate demands, that undermine mitigation of global warming, and provide these local groups with leverage to mobilize broader national and international campaigns against global warming.

Indeed, an anti–global warming movement has begun to crystallize since the turn of the 21st century, and has built upon warnings about the dangers of global warming emanating over the past two decades from climate scientists, environmental groups, small island states, indigenous groups in the Arctic and South Pacific, other Third World peoples, and some mainstream and even some evangelical churches. Indeed, the anti-global or climate movement exhibits huge overlaps with the anti-corporate globalization or global justice movement, in that they both struggle against corporate control of the global economy and for environmental sustainability. Agyeman, Doppelt, Lynn, and Hatic (2007:121) assert that the "emerging climate-justice movement shifts the discursive framework of climate change from a scientific-technical debate to one about ethics focused on human rights and justice."

The small island states formed the Alliance of Small Island States (AOSIS) during the Second World Climate Conference in 1992 in Geneva. Most Pacific island nations have ratified the Framework Convention on Climate Change (FCCC). On August 28, 2002, the International Climate Justice Network delineated 26 points in its Bali Principles of Climate Justice (Agyeman, Doppelt, Lynn, and Hatic 2007:122–124). Various bodies from around the world issued a declaration at the Climate Justice Summit in New Delhi on October 26–27, 2002 which included the following words:

> We, representatives of the poor and the marginalized of the world, representing fishworkers, farmers, Indigenous Peoples, Dalits, the poor and the youth, resolve to actively build a movement from the communities that will address the issue of climate change from a human rights, social justice and labour perspective. We affirm that climate change is a human rights issue. . . . We reject the market based principles that guide the current negotiations to solve the climate crisis: Our World is Not for Sale! [Indian Climate Forum 2002:1].

This statement reflects an often overlooked perspective that has been emphasized by various indigenous organizations and spokespersons.

For example, the Second International Indigenous Forum on Climate Change, which was held in The Hague, drafted a declaration on November 11–12, 2000, which included the following points:

> Earth is our Mother .... [It] is not a commodity, but a sacred space .... Our traditional knowledge on sustainable use, conservation and protection of our territories has allowed us to maintain our ecosystems in equilibrium .... Our cultures, and the territories under our stewardship, are now the last ecological mechanisms remaining in the struggle against climate devastation.... Climate change is a reality and is affecting hundreds of millions of our peoples and our territories, resulting in famine, extreme poverty, disease, loss of basic resources in our traditional habitats and provoking involuntary displacements of our peoples as environmental refugees. The causes of climate change are the production and consumption patterns in industrialised countries and are therefore, the primarily responsibilities of these countries. [www.c.3.hu/~bocs/eco-a-/htm, accessed August 6, 2008]

Similarly, the Third International Forum of Indigenous Peoples and Local Communities on Climate Changes, in its declaration in Bonn on July 14–15, 2001, denounced the UNFCCC and the Kyoto Protocol for not recognizing the "existence or the contributions of Indigenous Peoples," noting that

> Indigenous Peoples, as part of the international community, have the right to self-determination over our lives, our territories and our resources. Self-determination includes, inter alia, the right to possess, control, and administer our territories .... The discussions under the UNFCCC and the Kyoto Protocol have totally excluded the indigenous peoples to the extent that neither recognizes the right of indigenous peoples to full and effective participation and to contribute to discussions and debates. [International Indian Treaty Council 2001]

Pointing to the important role of indigenous communities in arctic environments in monitoring climate change, Sheila Watt-Cloutier, president of the Inuit Circumpolar Conference, stated the following in her address before a U.S. Senate Commerce Committee hearing in August 2004: "The Earth is literally melting .... Protect the Arctic and you will save the planet. Use us as your early-warning system. Use the Inuit story as a vehicle to reconnect us all so that we can understand the people and the planet are one" (quoted in Johansen 2006b). She submitted a petition to the Inter-American Commission on Human Rights on behalf of her people, requesting relief from "violations resulting from global warming caused by acts and omissions of the United States" (quoted in Lynas 2007:84). Native Alaskans, who constitute 17 percent of the state's population, have established a website (www.nativeknowledge. org) to share their experiences with global warming with the world community.

Other opponents of a market approach to addressing global warming have appeared around the world. The Dag Hammarskjoeld Foundation, for example, in collaboration with various civil society groups organized a seminar in South Africa in October 2004 (Lohmann 2006:3). The seminar resulted in the Durban Declaration on Climate Justice, which in turn led to the creation of the Durban Group for Climate Justice. The latter describes itself as "an international network of independent organisations, individuals and peoples' movements who reject the market approach to climate change" and which is "committed to help build a global grassroots movement for climate justice, mobilize communities around the world and pledge our solidarity with people opposing carbon trading on the ground" (www.carbontradewatch.org/durban, accessed September 29, 2007). Other organizations that are part of a growing anti–global warming or climate movement include the Global Justice Ecology Project, the Transnational Institute, and Climate Indymedia (a media activist organization). In April 2001, Redefining Progress, an Oakland, California–based think tank, formed the Environmental Justice and Climate Change (EJCC) initiative, a coalition of 28 environmental justice, climate justice, religious, policy, and advocacy groups (Agyeman, Bulkeley, and Nochur 2007). EJCC released its 10 Principles for Just Climate Change Policies in the U.S. at the 2002 World Summit on Sustainable Development in Johannesburg, South Africa. These principles are: "1) stop cooking the planet; 2) protect and empower vulnerable individuals and communities; 3) ensure just transition for workers and communities; 4) require community participation; 5) global problems need global solutions; 6) the United States must take the lead; 7) stop exploration for fossil fuels; 8) monitor domestic and international carbon markets; 9) use caution in the face of uncertainty; and 10) protect future generations" (Environmental Justice and Climate Initiative n.d.). At the regional and local levels, the climate movement has come to include numerous grass-roots groups, such as the Massachusetts Climate Action Network, the Chesapeake Climate Action Network, the Green House Network, the New England Grassroots Environment Fund, Clean Air-Cool Planet in New England, Grand Canyon Trust, Climate Solutions in the Pacific Northwest, and West Harlem Environmental Action (Agyeman, Bulkeley, and Nochur 2007:141, Finley 2007:39).

The climate movement can now be found worldwide, even in seemingly isolated settings, such as New Zealand. The latter (as well as Tasmania) is sometimes viewed as a place where mainland Australians could potentially retreat if their country becomes too hot and dry. Outsiders often regard New Zealand as either a semi-tropical or temperature paradise, depending upon the location (whether on the North Island or the South Island); a remote place in the South Pacific that, according to some, is the victim of the "tyranny of distance" (i.e., it is geographically quite isolated), and, according to others, is a retreat "far away from the maddening crowd." Despite these perceptions, this country of some 4.2 million people, which is one of the first places on the globe to welcome the new day, is not immune from the contradictions of the global capitalism. New Zealanders (or Kiwis as they are known) have been subjected to two decades of neoliberal policies under both conservative National and social democratic Labour governments. Housing prices are sky-rocketing as affluent Americans are choosing to relocate or establish second homes there. Even in this remote corner of the world, one finds the emergence of the climate movement. Daphne Lawless, a member of Socialist Worker, reports:

> ClimAction, a climate change action coalition, sprang up in Auckland in October 2006. A broad grouping of ecologists, socialists, anarchists, unionists and other activists, ClimAction has already made a name for its feisty and innovative campaigning style. High-profile activities to date include an occupation-cum-carnival in Queen Street and a "call out" when Al Gore swept into town to Sweet-talk the local elite. [Lawless 2006:10]

ClimAction was created only a month before the International Day of Action on Climate Change on November 4, 2006. The organizers made two demands: the creation of a free and frequent public transport system in the Auckland metropolitan area, and the reduction of greenhouse gas emissions by 90 percent by 2030 (Carolan 2006). ClimAction has embarked upon a campaign to spotlight New Zealand's biggest greenhouse gas, namely methane from sheep and cattle farming, which accounts for over half of the country's emissions, as opposed to about a quarter for carbon dioxide.

As the account above suggests, for the most part, the global climate movement is a rather disparate phenomenon that includes not only grass-roots environmental, liberal, and leftist groups, but also religious organizations and even small business organizations. There is always the danger that the climate movement will devolve into a fragmented set of single-issue groups, such as was the case earlier in the anti–nuclear arms movement. Already, as we have seen, the climate movement has splintered into a reformist faction that seeks to work within the parameters of capitalism by relying upon a limited program of carbon trading and other market mechanisms and a radical faction that seeks to transcend capitalism. Green parties around the world appear to have assumed a middle-ground position between these two polar factions. The climate justice segment of the anti–global warming movement exhibits an authentically progressive impetus. According to Agyeman, Bulkeley, and Nochur,

> Climate justice activists contend that the only way to address the climate crisis is through actual emissions reductions on the part of the developed world. They emphasize the need for participation of vulnerable communities in developing policies that incorporate social and environmental justice concerns, such as equal per capita emissions rights. They also call upon mainstream environmental groups to develop climate justice analyses and to not settle for policies that merely make incremental progess. [Agyeman, Bulkeley, and Nochur 2007:138]

In short, the climate justice movement seeks to identify nonreformist reform strategies for change as it seeks to move step by step toward a broader and enduring social transformation.

An Engaged Anthropology, Global Warming, and the Future of Humanity and the Planet

As researchers committed to understanding life experience, social behavior, and contextual influences on human communities, as well as human biological development, diversity, and health, anthropologists, both at the theoretical and the applied levels, are in a unique position to help assess the human impact of global warming. This impact will be significant but will vary among the diverse peoples traditionally studied within anthropology, such as the Inuit of the Arctic, cattle pastoralists in East Africa, horticultural villagers in the South Pacific and Southeast Asia, and Andean peasants, as well as among peoples that the discipline been more recently studying, such as urbanites in both the developed and developing worlds. There is a critical need for anthropologists to examine in detail ways in which local populations can both adapt to and even circumvent the potentially destructive impact of global warming. Another contribution that anthropologists can make is in the examination of the emergence of an anti–global warming movement and its relationship to other social movements, particularly the social justice, anti-corporate globalization, indigenous and Third World peoples' rights, and environmental movements. No less important is "studying up," namely conducting research on the corporations that most contribute to global warming, their leaders, and their strategies for pushing a productivist program. Beyond research, applied projects involving anthropologists test and disseminate environmentally sound alternative ways of life, settlement patterns, and transportation and other technologies.

The effort to examine and respond to the adverse impacts of global warming on humanity is likely to be most effective as an interdisciplinary effort, one that involves collaboration with climate scientists, physical geographers, environmental studies scholars, and other social scientists, including sociologists, political scientists, and human geographers. Indeed, other social scientists, particularly human geographers, political scientists, and sociologists, already have addressed various aspects of global warming, including adaptations by local populations (Becken 2005, Parish and Funnell 1999, Thompson et al. 2006), international and regional climate change regimes (Liberatore 1994, O'Riordan and Jordan 1999), and corporate and neoconservative stances toward global warming (McCright and Dunlap 2003).

As critical anthropologists, influenced by Wallerstein (1979:ix–xii), we realize that social systems, either local, regional, or global, do not last forever. Global capitalism has been around for some 500 years but we believe that it has so many inherent contradictions that ultimately it must be transcended if humanity and the planet are going to survive in some reasonable fashion. Anthropologists can contribute to a larger effort not only to mitigate the impact of global warming on humanity but also to help devise an alternative global system, one committed to meeting people's basic needs, struggling for social equity and justice, building democracy, and achieving environmental sustainability. As part of this endeavor, it is imperative that anthropologists become politically engaged and work in solidarity with progressive movements that in various ways, some of which are cumbersome and even contradictory, are seeking to create a less damaging substitute to the present world order. Some would even argue that environmentally engaged anthropologists need to be passionate and even boldly outrageous given that we live in outrageous times.

Going from the present capitalist world system to an alternative global political economy, whether it be defined as global democracy, economic democracy, earth democracy, or democratic ecosocialism, will require much effort, and there are no guarantees that we will be able to create a more equitable and environmentally sustainable world. Conversely, the question must be continually asked: Do we really have any choice if we are to avoid an accelerating downward spiral that culminates in the destruction of much of humanity and vast environmental degradation? While this choice of words may seem overly dramatic to some, there is considerable data now available to affirm a potentially disastrous future for humanity and planet earth. As noted scientist, author, inventor, and environmentalist James Lovelock warns, "Our future . . . is like that of the passengers on a small pleasure boat sailing quietly above the Niagara Falls, not knowing that the engines are about to fail" (quoted in Goodell 2007). Lovelock believes that by the year 2100 the earth's population will be cut down by global warming from the 6.6 billion people living today to as few as 500 million. Moreover, he emphasizes, limited efforts will have little effect in avoiding this disaster. Ultimately, mitigating global warming, we believe, will require nothing less than what Foster (2005b:9) terms an "ecological revolution"—one that draws upon the "struggles of working populations and communities at the bottom of the global capitalist hierarchy."

It is crucial that anti-systemic movements act as counter-hegemonic forces in both developed or core countries and in developing countries. As Chase-Dunn and Hall observe,

> Seen in a long run comparative perspective, the struggle for democratic socialism within the core states, though currently in the doldrums, is crucial for eventual systemic transformation . . . . The continuation of capitalist uneven development will likely spur new broad populist, anti-systemic movements. World socialists should be prepared to provide direction and leadership to these, lest they be harnessed by reactionaries or neo-fascists, a frightening prospect. Building ties of cooperation and friendship among peoples, institutions based on democratic and collectively rational (i.e., planned) economic organization and exchange, and a more ecologically balanced and egalitarian form of global development are important both as immediate and as long term means for reducing the probability of systematically-produced warfare. [Chase-Dunn and Hall 1997:420]

Over the past few decades, anthropologists and other social scientists have often alluded to a cavalcade of "posts": postcolonialism, post-industrialism, post-Fordism, postsocialism, post-Marxism, postfeminism, etc. Anthropologists might entertain the possibility of two other new "posts," namely postcapitalism and post–global warming. In doing so, we need to further develop an anthropology of the future. Perhaps one place to start such an effort is with perusing William Wager's enthralling book, *A Short History of the Future*, which was published in 1992, two years after the collapse of Soviet bloc and at a time when various climate scientists and environmentalists, but unfortunately virtually no social scientists, were taking note of global warming. Relying upon world systems theory, he presents a science-fiction account of the history of humanity into the 21st and 22nd centuries. In his account, the period of 2001 to 2032 is characterized by an economic boom "hinged in great part on advances in the production and cheapness of energy" (Wager 1992:63). Whereas 82 percent of the world's energy resources came from oil, gas, and coal in 1973 (the time of the famous OPEC oil embargo), technological innovations, including the creation of expensive fusion nuclear power plants, allowed reliance on fossil fuels to drop to 71 percent by

2030. Nevertheless, despite various techno fixes, the capitalist treadmill of production and consumption continued to contribute to global warming at the time. Thus, by 2040, the atmosphere contained 555 ppm of carbon dioxide and even more alarming increases in methane and CFCs due to burning of fossil and biomass fuels, fertilizer use, and the decay of organic matter in rice paddies necessitated by an ongoing global population (Wager 1992:67). The average global temperature increased 7.56°F (4.2°C) between 1980 and 2040 and the sea level increased by six and a half feet (2 m) due to the melting of ice caps and glaciers. In addition to a major flooding disaster in Bangladesh in 2039, "in the early 2040s, other areas gradually went under: much of coastal Florida, the delta of the Mississippi [River] in Louisiana, other deltalands that undermine its claims of equality in Egypt, Pakistan, China, and Colombia, and large stretches of coastal southern Australia, Burma, Vietnam, and Mexico" (Wager 1992:68). Due to climatic changes, food production in 2043 fell to its lowest level in the 21st century, making the feeding of all of the over nine billion people on the planet impossible. These developments resulted in the Catastrophe of 2044, which was marked by the outbreak of worldwide nuclear warfare and a sudden shift to arctic cold. The global war of 2044–2046 resulted in the devastation of most of the cities of North America, Europe, Japan, China, and the Indian subcontinent and to rampant epidemics. In the aftermath of the war, the power center of the world fell to countries south of the 25th parallel. The remainder of the book describes the creation of two alternative world systems, the first of which was a bureaucratic, technocratic, socialist world government with its capital in Melbourne, and the second an anarchistic global system committed to ecological, mysticism, and small-scale technology.

Science fiction allows us to speculate about the future, about its grim realities and possibilities for better alternatives. Ironically, the made-up future envisioned by Wager is arriving far ahead of his fictional time frame. Changes that were thought to be decades away have already begun, making Wager's future our present. Perhaps more than any other issue, global warming allows us, as critical anthropologists, to contemplate the contradictions of the existing capitalist world system, including its implications for health, and to ponder the creation of an alternative world system, one committed to social equality, democracy, environmental sustainability, and a cooler planet; one world, in other words, in which humans live in balance with their home.

References

Aaheim, A., and L. Sygna. 2000. Economic Impacts of Climate Change on Tuna Fisheries in Fiji Islands and Kiribati. Report 2000–4. Oslo: Centre for International Climate and Environmental Research.

Abecasis, Ana, Philippe Lemey, Nicole Vidal, Tulio de Oliveira, Martine Peeters, Ricardo Camacho, Beth Shapiro, Andrew Rambaut, and Anne-Mieke Vandamme. 2007. Recombination Is Confounding the Early Evolutionary History of HIV-1: Subtype G Is a Circulating Recombinant Form. Journal of Virology. Electronic document in advance of publication at http://www.ncbi.nlm.nih.gov/sites/entrez?Db=pubmed&Cmd=ShowDetailView&TermToSearch=17553886&ordinalpos=3&itool=EntrezSystem2.PEntrez.Pubmed.Pubmed_ResultsPanel.Pubmed_RVDocSum. Accessed April 22, 2008.

Abrahamowicz, M., T. Schopflocher, K. Leffondre, R. du Berger, and D. Krewski. 2003. Flexible Modeling of Exposure-Response Relationship Between Long-Term Average Levels of Particulate Air Pollution and Mortality in the American Cancer Society Study. Journal of Toxicology and Environmental Health 66:1625–1654.

Abt Associates, Inc. 2004. Gilbert Kombe. Abstracts Newsletter 2(2):1–4.

Agarwal, Anil. N.d. a. Making the Kyoto Protocol Work: Ecological and Economic Effectiveness and Equity in Climate Regimes. New Delhi: Centre for Science and Environment.

———. N.d. b. Climate Change: A Challenge to India's Economy—Briefing Paper for Members of Parliament. New Delhi: Centre for Science and Environment.

Agyeman, Julian, Harriet Bulkeley, and Adita Nochur. 2007. Climate Justice. In Ignition: What You Can Do to Fight Global Warming and Spark a Movement. Jonathan Isham, Jr., and Sissel Waage, eds. Pp. 135–144. Washington, DC: Island Press.

Agyeman, Julian, Bob Doppelt, Kathy Lynn, and Halida Hatic. 2007. The Climate-Justice Link: Communicating Risk with Low-Income and Minority Audiences. In Creating a Climate for Change: Communicating Climate Change and Facilitating Social Change. Susan C. Moser and Lisa Dilling, eds. Pp. 119–138. Cambridge: Cambridge University Press.

Akinbami, Laura. 2006. The State of Childhood Asthma, United States, 1980–2005. Advance Data from Vital and Health Statistics; no. 381, Hyattsville, MD: National Center for Health Statistics.

Alcamo, Joseph, Nikolai Dronin, Marcel Endejan, Genady Golubev, and Andrei Kirilenko. 2007. A New Assessment of Climate Change Impacts on Food Production Shortfalls and Water Availability in Russia. Global Environmental Change 17:429–444.

Alley, Richard, et al. 2007. Climate Change 2007: The Physical Science Basis: Summary for Policymakers. Intergovernmental Panel on Climate Change. Geneva: IPCC Secretariat.

Alston, Margaret, and Jenny Kent. 2004. Social Impacts of Drought: A Report to NSW Agriculture. Wagga Wagga, NSW: Centre for Rural Social Research, Charles Stuart University.

American Lung Association. 2007. Particle Pollution Fact Sheet. Electronic document, http://www.lungusa.org/site/pp.asp?c=dvLUK9O0E&b=50324. Accessed August 4, 2008.

Anderson, Sarah, and John Cavanaugh. 2005. Field Guide to the Global Economy New York: New Press.

Andrus, C.F.T., D. H. Sandweiss, and E. J. Reitz. 2008. Climate Change and Archaeology: The Holocene History of El Niño on the Coast of Peru. In Case Studies in Environmental Archaeology. 2nd edition. E. J. Reitz, C. M. Scarry, and S. J. Scudder, eds. Pp. 143–157. London: Springer Science Business Media.

Angus, Ian. 2007. Confronting the Climate Change Crisis. Electronic document, http://climateandcapitalism/?p=6#more-6. Accessed July 25, 2008.

Antilla, Lisa. 2005. Climate of Scepticism: US Newspaper Coverage of the Science of Climate Change. Global Environmental Change 15:338–352.

Antonucci, G., E. Girardi, H. Raviglioni, and G. Ippolito. 1995. Risk Factors for Tuberculosis in HIV-infected Persons. A Prospective Cohort Study. Journal of the American Medical Association 274:143–148.

Anzaldúa, Gloria. 1987. Borderlands/La Frontera: The New Mestiza, San Francisco: Aunt Lute Book Company.

Appel, Addrianne. 2005a. Gulf Wracked by Katrina's Latest Legacy—Disease, Poisons, Mold. National Geographic News, September 30. Electronic document, http://news.nationalgeographic.com/news/2005/09/0930_050930_katrina_health.html. Accessed August 8, 2008.

———. 2005b. New Orleans Floodwater Fouled with Bacteria, Chemicals. National Geographic News, September 30. Electronic document, http://news.nationalgeographic.com/news/2005/09/0907_050907_floodwater.html. Accessed April 12, 2008.

Arts, Bas, and Jos Cozijnsen. 2003. Between "Curbing the Trends" and "Business-as-Usual": NGOs in International Climate Change Policies. In Issues in International Climate Policy: Theory and Policy. Ekko C. van Ierland, Joyeeta Gupta, and Marcel T.J. Kok, eds. Pp. 243–261. Cheltenham, UK: Edward Elgar.

Athanasiou, Tom, and Paul Baer. 2002. Dead Heat: Global Justice and Global Warming. New York: Seven Stories Press.

Baer, Hans. 1996. Bringing Political Ecology into Critical Anthropology. Medical Anthropology 17:129–141.

———. 2007. Global Warming, Human Society and Critical Anthropology: A Research Agenda. Social of Social and Environmental Enquiry Working Papers in Development. Melbourne: University of Melbourne.

———. 2008a. Global Warming as a By-product of the Capitalist Treadmill of Production and Consumption: The Need for an Alternative Global System. Australian Journal of Anthropology 19:58–62.

———. 2008b. Toward a Critical Anthropology on the Impact of Global Warming on Health and Human Societies. Medical Anthropology 27:2–8.

Baer, Hans, Merrill Singer, and Ida Susser. 2003. Medical Anthropology and the World System. 2nd edition. Westport, CT: Praeger.

Baker, Susan. 2007. Sustainable Development as Symbolic Commitment: Declaratory Politics and the Seductive Appeal of Ecological Modernisation in the European Union. Environmental Politics 16:297–317.

Baliunus, Sallie. 2002. Warming Up the Truth: The Real Story About Climate Change, Heritage Lecture #758. The Heritage Foundation. Electronic document, http://www.heritage.org. Accessed July 15, 2007.

Barnett, Jon. 2006. Climate Change, Insecurity, and Injustice. In Fairness in Adaptation to Climate Change. W. Neil Adger, John Paavola, Saleemul Huq, and M. J. Mace, eds. Pp. 115–129. Cambridge, MA: MIT Press.

Barnett, Jon, Suraje Desai, and Roger N. Jones. 2005. Vulnerability to Climate Variability and Change in East Timor. Working Paper No. 05/05, May. School of International Development, Melbourne University Private.

Barry, John. 2004. The Virus Next Time. The Hartford (Connecticut) Courant, October 24: C1 & C6.

Bartley, Tim, and Albert Bergsen. 1997. World-System Studies of the Environment. Journal of World-Systems Research 3(3):1–11.

BBC News. 1999. Global Warming Disease Warning. Electronic document, http://news.bbc.co.uk/1/hi/sci/tech/372219.stm. Accessed August 8, 2008.

Bean, W., M. Schell, J. Katz, Y. Kawaoka, C. Naeve, O. Gorman, and R. Webster. 1992. Evolution of the H3 Influenza Virus Hemagglutinin from Human and Nonhuman Hosts. Journal of Virology 66:1129–1138.

Becken, Susanne. 2005. Harmonising Climate Change Adaptation and Mitigation: The Case of Tourist Resorts in Fiji. Global Environmental Change 15:381–393.

Beder, Sharon. 2000. Global Spin: The Corporate Assault on Environmentalism. Melbourne: Scribe Publications.

Beer, Linda, and Terry Boswell. 2002. The Resilience of Dependency Effects in Explaining Income Inequality in the Global Economy: A Cross-National Analysis, 1975–1995. Journal of World-Systems Research 13:30–59.

Begley, Sharon. 2007. Global-Warming Deniers: A Well-Funded Machine, Newsweek, August 13.

Bello, Walden. 2007. Climate Change Flap at the G8. ZNet, July 7. Electronic document, www.zmag.org. Accessed October 9, 2007.

Belshie, Robert. 2005. The Origins of Pandemic Influenza—Lessons from the 1918 Virus. New England Journal of Medicine 353(21):2209–2211.

Berger, John J. 2000. Beating the Heat: Why and How We Must Combat Global Warming. Berkeley, CA: Berkeley Hills Books.

Bergsten, C. Fred, Bates Gill, Nicholas R. Lardy, and Derek Mitchell. 2006. China: The Balance Sheet: What the World Needs to Know Now About the Emerging Superpower. New York: Public Affairs.

Berzon, Alexandra. 2007. Tuvalu Is Drowning. Salon.com. Electronic document, http://www.salon.com/news/feature/2006/03/31/tuvalu. Accessed August 8, 2008.

Biel, Robert. 2006. The Interplay between Social and Environmental Degradation in the Development of the International Political Economy. Journal of World-Systems Research 12(1):109–147.

BlackHealthcare.com. 1999. Hypertension Description. Electronic document, http://www.blackhealthcare.com/BHC/Hypertension/Epidemiology.asp. Accessed July 10, 2006.

Bodley, John H. 2008. Anthropology and Contemporary Human Problems. 5th edition. Walnut Creek, CA: Altamira Press.

Bord, Richard, Ann Fisher, and Robert O'Connor. 1998. Public Perceptions of Global Warming: United States and International Perspectives. Climate Research 11:75–84.

Boswell, Terry, and Christopher Chase-Dunn. 2000. The Spiral of Capitalism and Socialism. Boulder, CO: Lynne Rienner.

Boykoff, Maxwell T., and Jules M. Boykoff. 2004. Balance as Bias: Global Warming and the US Prestige Press. Global Environmental Change 14:125–136.

Brandon, J., F. Crespin, C. Levy, and D. Reyna. 1997. Border Health Issues. In Border Health: Challenges along the U.S.-Mexico Border. J. Bruhn and J. Brandon, eds., 37–72. New York: Garland Press.

Brander, Keith. 2003. Marine Ecosystems–Fisheries. Intergovernmental Panel on Climate Change, Workshop on the Detection and Attribution of the Effects of Climate Change, Pp. 43–44. New York: Goddard Institute for Space Studies and the World Health Organization.

Brandt, Mary, Clive Brown, Joe Burkhart, Nancy Burton, Jean Cox-Ganser, Scott Damon, Henry Falk, Scott Fridkin, Paul Garbe, Mike McGeehin, Juliette Morgan, Elena Page, Carol Rao, Stephen Redd, Tom Sinks, Douglas Trout, Kenneth Wallingford, David Warnock, and David Weissman. 2006. Mold Prevention Strategies and Possible Health Effects in the Aftermath of Hurricanes and Major Floods. Morbidity and Mortality Weekly Reports 55:1–27.

Brandt, Mary, and David Warnock. 2003. Laboratory Aspects of Medical Mycology. In Clinical Mycology. W. Dismukes, P. Pappas, and J. Sobel, eds. Pp. 1–22. New York: Oxford University Press.

Brecher, J., and T. Costello. 1998. Global Village or Global Pillage: Economic Reconstruction from the Bottom Up. Boston: South End Press.

Brink, Susan. 2007. Black Men's Shorter Life Span May Be Attributable in Part to the Stresses of Their Position in Society. Los Angeles Times, September 24:1.

Brinkley, Douglas. 2006. The Great Deluge: Hurricane Katrina, New Orleans, and the Mississippi Gulf. New York: Harper.

Britt, Robert Roy. 2005. Insurance Company Warns of Global Warming's Costs. Electronic document, htpp//:www.livescience.com/environment/051101_insurance_warming.html. January 21, 2008.

Broinowski, Alison, and James Wilkinson. 2005. The Third Try: Can the UN Work? Melbourne: Scribe.

Brown, Donald A. 2003. American Heat: Ethical Problems with the United States Response to Global Warming. Berkeley, CA: Berkeley Hills Books.

Brown, Kathyrn S. 1999. Climate Anthropology: Taking Global Warming to the People. Science 283(5407):1440–1441.

Brown, Lester. 2005. Outgrowing the Earth. New York: W. W. Norton & Company.

Brownstein, J., T. Holford, and D. Fish. 2005. Effect of Climate Change on Lyme Disease Risk in North America. EcoHealth 2:38–46.

Brunkard, Joan Marie, Jose Robles, Josue Ramirez, Enrique Cifuentes, Stephen Rothenberg, Elizabeth Hunsperger, Chester Moore, Regina Brussolo, Norma Villarreal, and Brent Haddad. 2007. Dengue Fever Seroprevalence and Risk Factors, Texas–Mexico Border, 2004. Emerging Infectious Diseases 13(10). Electronic document, http://www.cdc.gov/eid/content/13/10/1477.htm. January 22, 2008.

Brunnengraeber, Achim. 2006. Political Economy of the Kyoto Protocol. In Coming to Terms with Nature: Socialist Register 2007. Leo Panitch and Colin Leys, eds. Pp. 213–230. London: Merlin Press.

Buan, R., A. Maglinao, P. Evangelista, and B. Pajuelas. 1996. Vulnerability of Rice and Corn to Climate Change in the Philippines. In Climate Change Vulnerability and Adaptation in Asia and the Pacific. L. Erda, W. Bolhofer, S. Huq, S. Lenhart, S. Mukherjee, J. Smith, and J. Wisniewski, eds. Pp. 41–51. Dordrecht, the Netherlands: Kluwer Academic Publishers.

Budrys, Grace. 2003. Unequal Health: How Inequality Contributes to Health or Illness. Lanham, MD: Roman & Littlefield Publishers.

Bulkeley, Harriet, and Michele M. Betsill. 2003. Cities and Climate Change: Urban Sustainability and Global Environmental Governance. London: Routledge.

Burns, Thomas, Byron L. Davis, and Edward L. Kick. 1997. Position in the World System and National Emissions of Greenhouse Gases. Journal of World-Systems Research 3:432–466.

Burroughs, William James. 2001. Climate Change: A Multidisciplinary Approach. Cambridge: Cambridge University Press.

Byrne, David. 2004. Combating Emerging Zoonoses: Challenges and Prospects at Community Level. Presented at the Conference on Infectious Disease: European Response to Public Health Risks from Emerging Zoonotic Diseases, the Hague. Electronic document, http://europa.eu/rapid/pressReleasesAction.do?reference=SPEECH/04/405&format=PDF&aged=0&language=en. Accessed July 3, 2007.

Cakmak, S., R. Dales, and S. Judek. 2006. Respiratory Health Effects of Air Pollution Gases: Modification by Education and Income. Archives of Environmental and Occupational Health 61(1):5–10.

Caldicott, Helen. 2006. Nuclear Power Is Not the Answer to Global Warming or Anything Else. Melbourne: Melbourne University Press.

Campbell, B., and M. Little. 1988. The Finding of Angiostrongylus Cantonensis in Rats in New Orleans. American Journal of Tropical Medicine and Hygiene 38(3):568–573.

Campbell, Grant, and James Hughes. 1995. Plague in India: A New Warning from an Old Nemesis. Annals of Internal Medicine 122(2):151–153.

Canziani, Osvaldo. 2003. Extreme Precipitation Events and Floods in the Pampas Flatlands. In the Province of Buenos Aires. New York: Intergovernmental Panel on Climate Change, Workshop on the Detection and Attribution of the Effects of Climate Change, Pp. 36–38. Goddard Institute for Space Studies and the World Health Organization.

Caribbean Compass. 2004. Ivan Hits Below the Belt. Electronic document, http://www.caribbeancompass.com/hurricanegren.htm. Accessed June 2, 2008.

Carolan, Joe. 2006. ClimAction Is Moving. In System Change Not Climate Change. Auckland: Socialist Worker.

Carter, Neil. 2007. Politics of the Environment: Ideas, Activism, Policy. 2nd edition. Cambridge: Cambridge University Press.

Casa, Douglas, Brendon McDermott, Elaine Lee, Susan Yeargin, Lawrence Armstrong, and Carl Maresh. 2007. Cold Water Immersion: The Gold Standard for Exertional Heatstroke Treatment. Exercise and Sport Sciences Reviews 35(3):141–149.

Castello, J., S. Rogers, W. Starmer, C. Catranis, L. Ma, G. Bachand, Y. Zhao, and J. Smith. 1999. Detection of Tomato Mosaic Tobamovirus RNA in Ancient Glacial ice. Polar Biology 22:207–212.

CBS News. 2002. Global Warming May Spread Diseases: Pathogens Invade New Areas as Temperatures Rise. Electronic document, http://www.cbsnews.com/stories/2002/06/20/tech/main512920.shtml. Accessed March 3, 2008.

Centers for Disease Control and Prevention (CDC). 2003. Resources for TV Writers and Producers: Lyme Disease. Electronic document, http://www.cdc.gov/healthmarketing/entertainment_education/tips/lyme.htm. Accessed January 24, 2008.

———. 2005. AIDS Public Information Data Set, 2001. Electronic document, http://www.cdc.gov/hiv/softward/apids.htm. Accessed January 24, 2008.

———. 2006a. Dengue Fever. Electronic document, http://www.cdc.gov/ncidod/dvbid/dengue. Accessed January 27, 2008.

———. 2006b. Hantavirus Pulmonary Syndrome. Electronic document, http://www.cdc.gov/ncidod/diseases/hanta/hps/index.htm. Accessed January 21, 2008.

———. 2007. West Nile Virus Activity—United States, 2006. Morbidity and Mortality Weekly Reports 56(22):556–559.

Chadee, Dave, Samuel Rawlins, and T. Tiwaris. 2003. Short Communication: Concomitant Malaria and Filariasis Infections in Georgetown, Guyana. Tropical Medicine and International Health 8(2):140–143.

Chadwick, Douglas. 2003. Pacific Suite. National Geographic 203(2):104–127.

Chase-Dunn, Christopher. 1989. Global Formation: Structures of the World-Economy. Oxford: Basil Blackwell.

Chase-Dunn, Christopher K., and Thomas D. Hall. 1997. Ecological Degradation and the Evolution of World Systems. Journal of World-Systems Research 3(3):1–30.

Chernomas, Rober, and Ian Hudson. 2007. Social Murder and Other Shortcomings of Conservative Economics. Winnepeg: Arbeiter Ring Publishing.

Chernov, Ron. 2004. Alexander Hamilton. New York: Penguin Books.

Chesson, H., S. Pinkerton, R. Voight, and G. Counts. 2003. HIV Infections and Associated Costs Attributable to Syphilis Coinfection among African Americans. American Journal of Public Health 93(6):943–948.

Chowers, M., R. Lang, F. Nassar, D. Ben-David, M. Giladi, E. Rubinshtein, A. Itzhaki, J. Mishal, Y. Siegman-Igra, R. Kitzes, N. Pick, Z. Landau, D. Wolf, H. Bin, E. Mendelson, S. Pitlik, and M. Weinberger. 2001. Clinical Characteristics of the West Nile Fever Outbreak, Israel, 2000. Emerging Infectious Diseases 7(4):675–678.

Chretien, J. 1990. Tuberculosis and HIV: The Cursed Duet. Tuberculosis and Lung Disease 65(1):25–28.

Chua, K. 2003. Nipah Virus Outbreak in Malaysia. Journal of Clinical Virology 26(3):265–275.

Chua, K., B. Chua, and C. Wang. 2002. Anthropogenic Deforestation, El Niño and the Emergence of Nipah Virus in Malaysia. The Malaysian Journal of Pathology 24(1):15–21.

Chua, K., K. Goh, K. Wong, A. Kamarulzaman, P. Tan, T. Ksiazek, S. Zaki, G. Paul, S. Lam, and C. Tan. 1999. Fatal Encephalitis due to Nipah Virus Among Pig-farmers in Malaysia. Lancet 354:1257–1259.

Clark, Brett, and Richard York. 2005. Carbon Metabolism: Global Capitalism, Climate Change, and Biospheric Rift. Theory and Society 34:391–428.

CNA Corporation. 2007. National Security and the Threat of Climate Change. Alexandria, VA: SecurityAndClimate.cna.org.

Cogo, Paola, Massimo Scaglia, Simonetta Gatti, Flavio Rossetti, Rita Alaggio, Anna Maria Laverda, Ling Zhou, Lihua Xiao, and Govinda S. Visvesvara. 2004. Fatal Naegleria fowleri Meningoencephalitis, Italy. Emerging Infectious Diseases 10(10). Electronic document, http://www.cdc.gov/ncidod/EID/vol10no10/04-0273.htm. Accessed on February 16, 2008.

Cohen, Robin, and Paul Kennedy. 2000. Global Sociology. New York: New York University Press.

Cohen, Mitchell. 1998. Resurgent and Emergent Disease in a Changing World. British Medical Bulletin 54:523-532.

Collier, Paul. 2003. Natural Resources, Development and Conflict: Channels of Causation and Policy Interventions. Development Research Group, World Bank Working Papers, Document 28739.

Collier, Paul, and Anke Hoeffler. 2004. Greed and Grievance in Civil War. Oxford Economic Papers 56(4):563-595.

Colorado Department of Public Health and Environment. 2004. Two West Nile Virus Death Reported. Public Health News. Electronic document, http://www.co.boulder. co.us/health/pr/2003/0929WNV42ndHumanDeath.htm. Accessed July 28, 2008.

Colwell, Rita. 1996. Global Climate and Infectious Diseases: The Cholera Paradigm. Science 274(5295):2025-2031.

Combes, Stacey. 2006. Are We Putting Our Fish in Hot Water? Gland, Switzerland: World Wildlife Fund.

Comrie, Andrew. 2007. Climate Change and Human Health. Geography Compass 1(3):325-339.

Contenau, G. 1954. Everyday Life in Babylon and Assyria. New York: St. Martin's Press.

Coreil, Robert W. 2004. Statement to the Committee on Commerce, Science, and Transportation, United States Senate, November 16. In Arctic Climate Impact Assessment. Carolyn Symon, Lelani Arris, and Bill Heal, eds. Pp. 1-7. Cambridge: Cambridge University Press.

Cowie, Jonathan. 1998. Climate Change and Human Change: Disaster or Opportunity? London: Parthenon Publishing Group.

Cox, John D. 2005. Climate Crash: Abrupt Climate Change and What It Means for Our Future. Washington, DC: Joseph Henry Press.

Crosby, Alfred W. 2003. America's Forgotten Pandemic: The Influenza of 1918. Cambridge: Cambridge University Press.

———. 2004. Ecological Imperialism: The Biological Expansion of Europe, 900-1900. Cambridge: Cambridge University Press.

Cross, Eleanor and Kenneth Hyams. 1996. The Potential Effect of Global Warming on the Geographic and Seasonal Distribution of Phlebotomus papatasi in Southwest Asia. Environmental Health Perspectives 104:724-727.

Crowe, Cathy. 2006. Toronto Cool to Heat Wave Planning. Toronto Star, July 31:1.

Cruikshank, Julie. 2001. Glaciers and Climate Change: Perspectives from Oral Tradition. Artic 54(4):377-393.

———. 2007. Melting Glaciers and Emerging Histories in the Saint Elias Mountains. In Indigenous Experience Today. Marisol de la Cadena and Orin Starn, eds. Pp. 355-378. Oxford: Berg.

Cubillos-Garzon, L., J. Casas, C. Morillo, and L. Bautista. 2004. Congestive Heart Failure in Latin America: The Next Epidemic. American Heart Journal 47(3):386-389.

Curriero, Frank, Jonathan Patz, Joan Rose, and Subhash Lele. 2001. The Association Between Extreme Precipitation and Waterborne Disease Outbreaks in the United States, 1948-1994. American Journal of Public Health 91(8):1194-1199.

Cypher, James M. 2007. From Military Keynesianism to Global-Neoliberal Mlitarism. Monthly Review (June):37-55.

Davidson, I., R. Borenshtain, H. Kung, and R. Witter. 2002. Molecular Indications for In Vivo Integration of the Avian Leukosis Virus, Subgroup J-Long Terminal Repeat into the Marek's Disease Virus in Experimentally Dually-infected Chickens. Virus Genes 24(2):173–180.

Davis, David Howard. 2007. Ignoring the Apocalypse: Why Planning to Prevent Environmental Catastrophe Goes Astray. Westport, CT: Praeger.

Dawdy, Shannon Lee. 2006. The Taphonomy of Disaster and (Re)Formation of New Orleans. American Anthropologist 108(4):719–730.

Daza, E., V. Frias, A. Alcola, I. Lopez, I. Bruzon, J. Montero, G. Alvarez, M. Garcia, R. Rodriguez, J. Boschell, F. de la Hoz, F. Rivas, V. Olano, L. Diaz, F. Caceras, G. Aristizabal, V. Cardenas, J. Cuellar, E. Gonzalez, A. Ruiz, F. Pinheiro, R. Gusmao, S. Weaver, R. Tesh, and R. Ricco-Hesse. 1995. Venezuelan Equine Encephalitis—Colombia, 1995. Morbidity and Mortality Weekly Reports 44(39):721–724.

De Waal, A., and A. Whiteside. 2003. New Variant Famine: AIDS and Food Crisis in Southern Africa. Lancet 363(9399):1938–1939.

Dear, K., G. Ranmuthugala, T. Kjellström, C. Skinner, and I. Hanigan. 2005. Effects of Temperature and Ozone on Daily Mortality during the August 2003 Heat Wave in France. Archives of Environmental and Occupational Health 60(4):205–212.

De Cock, K. 1994. The New Tuberculosis. African Health 16(3):8–10.

De Jonckheere, J., and S. Brown. 1997. Primary Amebic Meningoencephalitis in a Patient with AIDS: Unusual Protozoological Findings. Clinical Infectious Disease 25(4):943–944.

Dempsey, Judy. 2007. Letter from Europe: Climate Change. International Herald Tribune, July 13. Electronic document, http://www.iht.com. Accessed March 3, 2008.

Denning, D. 1998. Invasive Aspergillosis. Clinical Infectious Disease 26:781–803.

Denning, D., and D. Stevens. 1990. Antifungal and Surgical Treatment of Invasive Aspergillosis: Review of 2,121 Published Cases. Review of Infectious Diseases 12:1147–1201.

Dessler, Andrew E., and Edward A. Parson. 2006. The Science and Politics of Global Climate Change: A Guide to Debate. Cambridge: Cambridge University Press.

Deutsche Welle. 2006. Germany in Top Five Countries Fighting Climate Change, November 11. Electronic document, http://www.dw-world.de. Accessed September 12, 2007.

Diamond, Jared. 2005. Collapse: How Societies Choose to Fail or Succeed. London: Penguin.

Diaz, Madeline Bar. 2005. Hospital Crisis: Harrowing Five Days Until Rescue. Fort Lauderdale Sun Sentinel, September 7.

Diaz-Sanchez, D., A. Tsien, J. Flemming, and A. Saxon. 1997. Combined Diesel Exhaust Particulate and Ragweed Allergen Markedly Enhances In Vivo Nasal Ragweed-specific IgE and Shows Cytokine Production to a TH2-type Pattern. Journal of Immunology 158(5):2406–2413.

Dietz, Thomas, and Eugene A. Rosa. 1997. Effects of Population and Affluence on CO_2 Emissions. Proceedings of the National Academy of Sciences 94:175–179.

DiMento, Joseph F.C., and Pamela Doughman. 2007. Climate Change: How the World Is Responding. In Climate Change: What It Means for Us, Our Children, and Our Grandchildren. Joseph F.C. Dimento and Pamela Doughman, eds. Pp. 101–138. Cambridge, MA: MIT Press.

Diesendorf, Mark. 2007. Greenhouse Solutions with Sustainable Energy. Sydney, NSW: UNSW Press.

Dobson, Andrew, and Robin Carper. 1992. Global Warming and Potential Changes in Host-Parasite and Disease-Vector Relationships. In Global Warming and Biodiversity. R. Peters and T. Lovejoy, eds, Pp. 201–220. New Haven, CT: Yale University Press.

Dolin, P., M. Raviglione, and A. Kochi. 1994. Global Tuberculosis Incidence and Mortality during 1990–2000. Bulletin of the World Heatlh Organization 72:213–220.

Dorn, Patricia, Leon Perniciaro, Michael Yabsley, Dawn Roellig, Gary Balsamo, James Diaz, and Dawn Wesson. 2007. Autochthonous Transmission of Trypanosma cruzi, Louisiana. Emerging Infectious Diseases 13(4). Electronic document, http://www.cdc.gov/EID/content/13/4/605.htm. Accessed April 19, 2008.

Douglen, Leonard. 2005. Hurricane Katrina—Pest Population Set to Explode. Pest Control Portal. Electronic document, http://www.pestcontrolportal.com/industry/news/showNewsArticle.asp?id=92. Accessed February 3, 2007.

Dow, Kirstin, and Thomas E. Downing. 2006. The Atlas of Climate Change. Brighton, UK: Earthscan.

Downing, T. 1991. Vulnerability to Hunger and Coping with Climate Change in Africa. Global Environmental Change 1(5):365–380.

———. 1992. Climate Change and Vulnerable Places: Global Food Security and Country Studies in Zimbabwe, Kenya, Senegal and Chile. Oxford: University of Oxford, Environmental Change Unit.

Doyle, M. Ellin. 1998. Non-Cholera Vibrios. FRI Briefings. University of Wisconsin–Madison: Food Research Institute.

Drake, Frances. 2000. Global Warming: The Science of Climate Change. London: Arnold.

Dressler, William. 1993. Social and Cultural Dimensions of Hypertension in Blacks: Underlying Mechanisms. In Pathophysiology of Hypertension in Blacks. J. Douglas and J. Fray, eds. Pp. 69–89. New York: Oxford University Press.

Dressler, William, and J. Bindon. 2000. The Health Consequences of Cultural Consonance: Cultural Dimensions of Lifestyle, Social Support and Blood Press in an African American Community. American Anthropologist 102:244–260.

Drexler, Madeline. 2007. How Racism Hurts—Literally. Boston Globe, July 15:1.

Dunlap, R. 1996. Public Perceptions of Global Warming: A Cross-national Comparison. Human Dimensions of Global Environmental Change Programme. Report No. 8, Global Change, Local Challenge. Geneva: World Health Organization.

Dunphy, Bill. 2006. City Takes Heat for Ending Alerts. Hamilton (Ontario) Spectator, July 31:1.

Easterling, W., P. Aggarwal, P. Batima, K. Brander, L. Erda, S. Howden, A. Kirilenko, J. Morton, J-F. Soussana, J. Schmidhuber, and F. Tubiello. 2007. Food, Fibre and Forest Products. In Climate Change 2007: Impacts, Adaptation and Vulnerability. Contribution of Working Group II to the Fourth Assessment Report of the Intergovernmental Panel on Climate Change. M. Parry, O. Canziani, J. Palutikof, P. van der Linden, and C. Hanson, eds. Pp. 273–313. Cambridge: Cambridge University Press.

Easton, Delia. 2004. The Urban Poor. In Encyclopedia of Medical Anthropology, vol 1. Carol Ember and Melvin Ember, eds. Pp. 207–213. New York: Kluwer.

Ebi, Kristie, Nancy Lewis, and Carlos Corvalan. 2006. Climate Variability and Change and Their Potential Health Effects in Small Island States: Information for Adaptation Planning in the Health Sector. Environmental Health Perspectives 114(12):1957–1963.

Egan, Timothy. 2006. The Worst Hard Time: The Untold Story of Those Who Survived The Great American Dust Bowl. New York: Houghton Mifflin Company.

Ekejindu, I. M., and G. C. Ochuba. 2004. Cryptosporidum Infection Among Young Children in Onitsha Urban Area in South-Eastern Nigeria. Tropical Journal of Medical Research 8(1):17–20.

Elperin, Juliet. 2005. Scientists Link Global Warming, Disease. Hartford (Connecticut) Courant, November 17:2.

Engel, Jeffery. 2007. Pandemic Influenza: The Critical Issues and North Carolina's Preparedness Plan. North Carolina Medical Journal 68(1):32–37.

Engelthaler, D., K. Lewis, S. Anderson, S. Snow, R. Hammond, R. Ratard, S. Straif-Bourgeois, T. Sokol, A. Thomas, L. Mena, J. Parham, S. Hand, M. McNeill, P. Byers, B. Amy, G. Charns, J. Rolling, A. Friedman, J. Romero, T. Dorse, J. Carlo, S. Stonecipher, L. Gaul, T. Betz, R. Moolenar, J. Painter, M. Kuehnert, J. Mott, D. Jernigan, P. Yu,

T. Clark, S. Greene, A. Schmitz, A. Cohn, and J. Liang. 2005. Vibrio Illnesses After Hurricane Katrina—Multiple States, August–September 2005. Morbidity and Mortality Weekly Reports 54(37):928–931.

Environment Canada. 2003. Natural Disasters on the Rise. Science and the Environment Bulletin, April/March. Electronic document, http://www.ec.gc.ca/science/sandefeb03/a3_e.html. Accessed February 4, 2007.

———. 2004. The Heat Is On. EnviroZine: Environment Canada's Online Newsmagazine 45, August 5. Electronic document, http://www.ec.gc.ca/EnviroZine/english/issues/45/feature1_e.cfm. Accessed February 4, 2007.

Environmental Justice and Climate Initiative. N.d. Ten Principles for Just Climate Change Policies in the U.S. Electronic document, http://www.ejcc.org. Accessed August 6, 2008.

Environmental News Network. 2007. Global Warming May Pose Threat to Heart. Electronic document, http://www.enn.com/health/article/22750. Accessed January 3, 2008.

Epstein, Paul R. 2000. Is Global Warming Harmful to Health? Scientific American, August. Electronic document, http://www.sciam.com/article.cfm?articleid=0008C7B2-E060-1C73-9B81809EC588EF21. Accessed January 12, 2008.

———. 2002a. Choking on Climate Change. Boston Globe, August 4.

———. 2002b. Climate Change and Infectious Disease: Stormy Weather Ahead. Epidemiology 13:373–375.

———. 2005. Climate Change and Public Health. New England Journal of Medicine 353(14): 1433–1436.

———. 2007. Chikunguny Fever Resurgence and Global Warming. American Journal of Tropical Medicine and Hygiene 76(3):403–404.

Epstein, Paul, E. Chivian, and K. Frith. 2003. Emerging Diseases Threaten Conservation. Environmental Health Perspectives 111(10):A506.

Epstein, Paul R., and Greg Guest. 2005. International Architecture for Sustainable Development and Global Health. In Globalization, Health, and the Environment: An Integrated Perspective. Greg Guest, ed. Pp. 239–258. Walnut Creek, CA: Altamira Press.

Epstein, Paul R., and Evan Mills, eds. 2005. Climate Change Futures: Health, Ecological and Economic Dimensions. Boston: Center for Health and the Global Environmental, Harvard Medical School.

Epstein, Paul, and Christine Rogers. 2004. Inside the Greenhouse: The Impacts of CO_2 and Climate Change on Public Health in the Inner City. Boston: The Center for Health and the Global Environment.

Escrui, F., A. Fraile, and F. Garcia-Arenal. 2007. Constraints to Genetic Exchange Support Gene Coadaptation in a Tripartite RNA Virus. PLoS Pathogens 3(1):e8.

Ethridge, Robbie. 2006. Bearing Witness: Assumptions, Realities, and the Othering of Katrina. American Anthropologist 108(4):799–813.

Fagan, Brian. 1999. Floods, Famines, and Emperors: El Niño and the Fate of Civilization. Cambridge: Cambridge University Press.

———. 2004. The Long Summer: How Climate Changed Civilization. New York: Basic Books.

Farmer, Paul. 1995. Social Inequalities and Emerging Infectious Diseases Emerging Infectious Disease 2(4):259–269.

Finkel, Michael. 2007. Bedlam in the Blood: Malaria. National Geographic 212(1):32–67.

Finley, Mary Lou. 2007. Shaping the Movement. In Ignition: What You Can Do to Fight Global Warming and Spark a Movement. Jonathan Isham, Jr., and Sissel Waage, eds. Pp. 33–56. Washington, DC: Island Press.

Firor, John, and Judith Jacobsen. 2002. The Crowded Greenhouse: Population, Climate Change, and Creating a Sustainable World. New Haven, CT: Yale University Press.

Fitz, John. 2007. What's Possible in the Military Sector? Z Net, April 30. Electronic document, http://www.zmag.org/content/showarticle.cfm?SectionID=57&ItemID=12705. Accessed March 23, 2008.

Flannery, Tim. 2005. The Weather Makers. New York Atlantic Monthly Press.

Fluger, Jeffery. 1995. Global Warming: The Culprit. Time, October 3:43.

Foster, John Bellamy. 1994. The Vulnerable Planet: A Short Economic History of the Environment. New York: Monthly Review Press.

———. 2000. The Ecological Tyranny of the Bottom Line: The Environmental and Social Consequences of Economic Reductionism. *In* Reclaiming the Environmental Debate: The Politics of Health in a Toxic Culture. Richard Hofrichter, ed. Pp. 135–153. Cambridge, MA: MIT Press.

———. 2002. Ecology Against Capitalism. New York: Monthly Review Press.

———. 2005a. The Renewing of Socialism: An Introduction. Monthly Review 57(3): 1–18.

———. 2005b. Organizing Ecological Revolution. Monthy Review 57(10):1–10.

———. 2007a. The Ecology of Destruction. Monthly Review 58(9):1–14.

———. 2007b. The Imperialist World System: Paul Baran's Political Economy of Growth after Fifty Years. Monthly Review (May):1–16.

Foster, John Bellamy, and Brett Clark. 2004. Ecological Imperialism: The Curse of Capitalism. *In* Socialist Register 2004: The New Imperial Challenge. Leo Panitch and Colin Leys, eds. Pp. 186–201. Monmouth, Wales: The Merlin Press, LTD.

Foster, Mary. 2006. New Orleans Gets a Taste of Real Wildlife. MSNBC, October 3. Electronic document, http://www.msnbc.msn.com/id/15251721. Accessed November 3, 2007.

Foucault, Michel. 1975. The Birth of the Clinic: An Archaeology of Medical Perception. New York: Vintage.

Fountain, Henry. 2000. Observatory: Threat to Rice Crops. New York Times, December 12: F-5.

Frank, Steven. 2003. Canada. Time, April 27. Electronic document, http://www.time.com/time/magazine/article/0,9171,447173,00.html?iid=chix-sphere. Accessed July 25, 2008.

Franks, Peter, Peter Muennig, Erica Lubetkin, and Haomiao Jia. 2006. The Burden of Disease Associated with Being African-American in the United States and the Contribution of Socio-economic Status. Social Science and Medicine 62:2469–2478.

Freudenberg, N., M. Fahs, S. Galea, and A. Greenberg. 2006. The Impact of New York City's 1975 Fiscal Crisis on the Tuberculosis, HIV, and Homicide Syndemic. American Journal of Public Health 96(3):424–434.

Fried, B., T. Gracyk, and L. Tamang. 2004. Food-borne Intestinal Trematodiases in Humans. Parasitology Research 93(2):159–170.

Gallagher, Maureen, Indu Malhotra, Peter Mungai, Alex Wamachi, John Kioko, John Ouma, Eric Muchiri, and Christopher King. 2005. The Effects of Maternal Helminth and Malaria Infections on Mother-to-Child HIV Transmission. AIDS 19(16): 1849–1855.

Geger, Michael. 2006. Bird Flu: A Virus of Our Own Hatching. New York: Lantern Books.

Gelbspan, Ross. 2004. Burning Point: How Politicians, Big Oil and Coal, Journalists, and Activists Are Fueling the Climate Crisis—and What We Can Do to Avert Disaster. New York: Basic Books.

Gennari-Cardoso, M., J. Costa-Cruz, E. de Castro, L. Lima, and D. Prudente. 1996. Cryptosporidium sp. in Children Suffering from Acute Diarrhea at Uberlândia City, State of Minas Gerais, Brazil. Memorial Institute Oswaldo Cruz 91(5):551–554.

Gibbs, Barnett, and Diane Johnson. 2006. Naegleria Infection. eMedicine. Electronic document, http://www.emedicine.com/med/topic1582.htm#section~author_information. Accessed June 23, 2007.

Gielen, A., R. Ghandour, J. Burke, P. Mahoney, K. McDonnell, and P. O'Campo. 2007. HIV/AIDS and Intimate Partner Violence: Intersecting Women's Health Issues in the United States. Trauma, Violence and Abuse 8(2):179–198.

Glantz, Michael H. 2003. Climate Affairs: A Primer. Washington, DC: Island Press.

Glick, Patty. 2006. Fueling the Fire: Global Warming, Fossil Fuels and the Fish and Wildlife of the American West. Washington, DC: National Wildlife Federation.

Global Health Watch. 2005. Global Health Watch, 2005–2006: An Alternative World Health Report. New York: Zed Books.

Goldfeld, A., and J. Ellner. 2007. Pathogenesis and Management of HIV/TB Co-infection in Asia. Tuberculosis. Electronic document, http://www.ncbi.nlm.nih.gov/sites/entrez? Db=pubmed&Cmd=ShowDetailView&TermToSearch=17606407&ordinalpos=13& itool=EntrezSystem2.PEntrez.Pubmed.Pubmed_ResultsPanel.Pubmed_RVDocSum. January 23, 2008.

Gong, Ke Wei, Wei Zhoa, Ning Li, Berenice Barajas, Michael Kleinman, Constantionos Sioutas, Steve Horvath, Aldons Lusis, André Nel, and Jesus Araujo. 2007. Air Pollutant Chemicals and Oxidized Lipids Exhibit Genome Wide Synergistic Effects on Endothelial Cells. Genome Biology 8:R149. Electronic document, http://genomebiology.com/2007/8/7/ R149. January 29, 2008.

Gonzalez, George A. 2005. Urban Sprawl, Global Warming and the Limits of Ecological Modernisation. Environmental Politics 14:344–362.

Goodell, Jeff. 2007. The Prophet of Climate Change. Rolling Stone, October 11. Electronic document, http://www.rollingstone.com/politics/story. February 12, 2008.

Gore, Al. 2006. An Inconvenient Truth: The Planetary Emergency of Global Warming and What We Can Do About It. London: Rodale.

Gorz, Andre. 1973. Socialism and Revolution. Boston: South End Press.

———. 1980. Ecology in Politics. Boston: South End Press.

Graham, Andrea, Tracey Lamb, Andrew Read, and Judith Allen. 2005. Malaria-Filaria Coinfection in Mice Makes Malarial Disease More Severe unless Filarial Infection Achieves Patency. The Journal of Infectious Diseases 191:410–421.

Graham, N., S. Wilson, S. Jennings, N. Polunin, J. Bijoux, and J. Robinson. 2006. Dynamic Fragility of Oceanic Coral Reef Ecosystems. National Academy of Science 103:8425–8429.

Grange, John. 1997. The Global Burden of Tuberculosis. In Tuberculosis: An Interdisciplinary Perspective. John Porter John and John Grange, eds. Pp. 3–32. London: Imperial College Press.

Grange John, and A. Zumla. 2002. The Global Emergency of Tuberculosis: What Is the Cause? The Journal of the Royal Society for the Promotion of Health 122(2):78–81.

Gray, Denis. 2007. Some Say Thailand's Capital at Risk. Hartford (Connecticut) Courant, October 21: A6.

Greaves, T. 2006. Water Struggles of Indigenous North America. In Globalization, Water & Health. L. Whiteford and S. Whiteford, eds. Pp. 153–184. Sante Fe: School of American Research Press.

Grimes, Peter, and Jeffrey Kentor. 2003. Exporting the Greenhouse: Foreign Capital and CO_2 Emissions, 1980–1996. Journal of World-Systems Research 9(2):261–275.

Grogan, H., and P. Hopkins. 2002. Heat Stroke: Implications for Critical Care and Anaesthesia. The British Journal of Anaethesia 88(5):700–707.

Grothmann, Torsten, and Anthony Patt. 2005. Adaptive Capacity and Human Cognition: The Process of Individual Adaptation to Climate Change. Global Environmental Change 15:199–213.

Guillot, Craig. 2006. New Orleans Enlists Fish to Fight Mosquitoes in Swimming Pools. National Geographic News, July 25. Electronic document, http://news.nationalgeographic.com/news/2006/07/060725-katrina.html. Accessed February 23, 2008.

Gupta, Ekta, Lalit Dar, Geetanjalia Kapoor and Shobha Broor. 2006. The Changing Epidemiology of Dengue in Delhi, India. Virology Journal 3. Electronic document, http://www.pubmedcentral.nih.gov/articlerender.fcgi?artid=1636631. Accessed March 1, 2008.

Guthmann, J. 1995. Epidemic Cholera in Latin America: Spread and Routes of Transmission. Journal of Tropical Medicine and Hygiene 98(6):419–427.

Guzman-Tapia, Y., M. Ramirez-Sierra, J. Escobedo-Ortegon, and E. Dumonteil. 2005. Effect of Hurricane Isidore on *Triatoma dimidiata* Distribution and Chagas Disease Transmission Risk in the Yucatan Peninsula of Mexico. American Journal of Tropical Medicine and Hygiene 73:1019–1025.

Hamilton, Clive. 2001. Running from the Storm: The Development of Climate Change Policy in Australia. Sydney: UNSW Press.

———. 2003. Growth Fetish. Crows Nest, NSW: Allen and Unwin.

———. 2007. Scorcher: The Dirty Politics of Climate Change. Melbourne: Black Incorporated.

Hansen, James. 2007a. Climate Catastrophe. New Scientist, July 28: 30–34.

———. 2007b. Huge Sea Level Rises are Coming—Unless We Act Now. New Scientist.com News Service, July 25.

Hardy, John T. 2003. Climate Change: Causes, Effects, and Solutions. Hoboken, NJ: John Wiley & Sons.

Hartman, Chester. 2005. Report from New Orleans. Poverty and Race 14(5):3–5.

Hatch, Michael T. 2003. Chinese Politics, Energy Policy, and the International Climate Change Negotiations. *In* Global Warming and East Asia: The Domestic and International Politics of Climate Change. Paul G. Harris, ed. Pp. 43–65. London: Routledge.

Harvell, Drew, Charles Michell, Jessica Ward, Sonia Altizer, Andrew Dobson, Richard Osteld, and Michael Samuel. 2002. Climate Warming and Disease Risks for Terrestrial and Marine Biota. Science 296:2158–2162.

Hayden, Mary, Christopher Uejio, Kathleen Walker, Frank Ramberg, Rafael Moreno, Linda Mearns, Cecilia Rosales, Mercedes Gameros, Emily Zielinski-Gutierrez, and Craig Janes. 2007. Microclimate and Human Housing Factors in the Re-Invasion of Aedes aegypti along the Arizona/Mexico Border. Unpublished manuscript. CU Trauma Center/NISSC, University of Colorado.

Hayden, M., E. Zielinski-Gutierrez, M. Fonseca-Ford, E. Navarro, L. Nava, and S. Waterman. 2005. Knowledge, Attitudes, and Practices Concerning West Nile Virus on the California/Baja California Border. Presented at the National West Nile Virus Conference. San Jose, CA, February 8–9.

Hayes, E., N. Komar, R. Nasci, S. Montgomery, D. Oleary, and G. Campbell. 2005. Epidemiology and Transmission Dynamics of West Nile Virus Disease. Emerging Infectious Diseases Journal 11:1167–1173.

Helfand, R., W. Moss, R. Harpaz, S. Scott, and F. Cutts. 2005. Evaluating the Impact of the HIV Pandemic on Measles Control and Elimination. Bulletin of the World Health Organization 83(5):329–337.

Helman, C. 2007. Culture, Health and Illness. 5th edition. London: Hodder Arnold.

Henson, Robert. 2006. The Rough Guide to Climate Change: The Symptoms, the Science, the Solutions. London: Penguin.

———. 2007. The Rough Guide to Weather. London: Penguin.

Herring, D. Ann, and Lisa Sattenspiel. 2007. Social Contexts, Syndemics, and Infectious Disease in Northern Aboriginal Populations. American Journal of Human Biology 19(2):190–202.

Hertsgaard, Mark. 2005. Climate and the G-8. Nation, July 18/25: 4–8.

Hillman, Mayer. 2004. How We Can Save the Planet. London: Penguin.

Hoerauf, A., S. Mand, K. Fischer, T. Kruppa, Y. Marfo-Debrekyei, A. Debrah, K. Pfarr, O. Adjei, and D. Buttner. 2003. Doxycycline as a Novel Strategy Against Bancroftian Filariasis—Depletion of Wolbachia endosymbionts from Wuchereria bancrofti and Stop of Microfilaria Production. Medical Microbiology and Immunology 192(4):211–216.

Hoff, Erica. 2003. Global Warming Threatens Food Security. Marist News Watch. Electronic document, http://www.academic.marist.edu/mwwatch/spring03/articles/Environment/environmentfinal.html. Accessed May 2, 2008.

Hoffman, S. 1980. Plague in the United States: The "Black Death" Is Still Alive. Annals of Emergency Medicine 9:319–322.

Hollingsworth, J., S. Kleeberger, and W. Foster. 2007. Ozone and Pulmonary Innate Immunity. Proceedings of the American Thoracic Society 4(3):240–246.

Holmberg, S., J. Stewart, A. Gerber, R. Byers, F. Lee, and P. O'Malley. 1988. Prior Herpes Simplex Virus Type 2 Infection as a Risk Factor for HIV infection. Journal of the American Medical Association 259:1048–1050.

Horstmann, Britta. 2004. Glacial Lake Outburst Floods in Nepal and Switzerland: New Threats Due to Climate Change. Berlin: Germanwatch.

Hossay, Patrick. 2006. Unsustainable: A Primer for Global Environmental and Social Justice. London: Zed Books.

Hota, Bala, Charlotte Ellenbogen, Mary Hayden, Alla Aroutcheva, Thomas Rice, and Robert Weinstein. 2007. Community-Associated Methicillin-Resistant Staphylococcus aureus Skin and Soft Tissue Infections at a Public Hospital. Archives of Internal Medicine 167:1026–1033.

Hotez, Peter. 2003. The Hookworm Vaccine Initiative. Washington, DC: Sabin Vaccine Institute, Georgetown University.

Hotez, Peter, David Molyneux, Alan Fenwick, Eric Ottesen, Sonia Ehrlich Sachs, and Jeffrey D. Sachs. 2007. A Comprehensive Pro-Poor Health Policy and Strategy for the Developing World: Incorporating a Rapid-Impact Package for Neglected Tropical Diseases with Programs for HIV/AIDS, Tuberculosis, and Malaria. PloS Medicine. Electronic document, http://medicine.plosjournals.org/perlserv/?request=get-document&doi=10.1371/journal.pmed.0030102. Accessed January 23, 2008.

Houghton, John. 2004. Global Warming: The Complete Briefing. 3rd edition. Cambridge: Cambridge University Press.

Howard, John. 2002. Media Release, Dec. 9. Electronic document, http://www.pm.gov.au/news/media_releases/2002/media_release%202025.htm. Accessed November 22, 2007.

Hsueh, Po-Ren, Ching-Yih Lin, Hung-Jen Tang, Hsin-Chun Lee, Jien-Wei Liu, Yung-Ching Liu, and Yin-Ching Chuang. 2004. Vibrio Vulnificus in Taiwan. Emerging Infectious Diseases, August. Electronic document, http://findarticles.com/p/articles/mi_m0GVK/is_8_10/ai_n6158532. Accessed January 24, 2008.

Huang, J., C. Dai, S. Hwang, C. Ho, M. Hsieh, L. Lee, Z. Lin, S. Chen, M. Hsieh, L. Wang, S. Shin, W. Chang, W. Chuang, and M. Yu. 2007. Hepatitis C Viremia Increases the Association with Type 2 Diabetes mellitus in a Hepatitis B and C Endemic Area: An Epidemiological Link with Virological Implication. American Journal of Gastroenterology 102(6):1237–1243.

Huckle, John, and Adrian Martin. 2001. Environments in a Changing World. New York: Pearson Education.

Hughes, D. H. 1975. The Ecology in Ancient Civilizations. Albuquerque: University of New Mexico.

Huntington, Henry, and Shari Fox, et al. 2004. The Changing Arctic: Indigenous Perspectives. In Arctic Climate Impact Assessment. Carolyn Symon, Lelani Arris, and Bill Heal, eds. Pp. 61–98. Cambridge: Cambridge University Press.

The Independent. 2006. United Kingdom: Temperature Set to Hit 100 Degrees—and Global Warming Is to Blame. July 19. Electronic document, http://www.heatisonline.org/contentserver/objecthandlers/index.cfm?id=6005&method=full. Accessed June 3, 2007.

Indian Climate Forum. 2002. Delhi Climate Justice Declaration.

Intergovernmental Panel on Climate Change (IPCC). 2007a. A Report of Working Group I of the Intergovernmental Panel on Climate Change: Summary for Policymakers.

———. 2007b. Contribution of Working Group II to the Fourth Assessment Report of the Intergovernmental Panel on Climate Change: Summary for Policymakers.

International Indian Treaty Council. 2001. The Bonn Declaration—The Third International Forum of Indigenous Peoples and Local Communities on Climate Change, July 14–15. Electronic document, http://www.treatycouncil.org.

Jamil, Bushra, Rumina Hasan, Afia Zafar, Kevin Bewlev, John Chamberlain, Valerie Mioulet, Moira Rowlands, and Roger Hewson. 2007. Dengue virus serotype 3, Karachi, Pakistan. Emerging Infectious Disease 13(1). Electronic document, http://www.cdc.gov/ncidod/eid/13/1/182.htm. Accessed January 24, 2008.

Jayachandran, Seema. 2006. Air Quality and Early-Life Mortality: Evidence from Indonesia's Wildfires. Electronic document, http://www.stanford.edu/~jayachan/indo_fires.pdf. Accessed June 25, 2007.

Jennaway, Megan. 2006. Reflections on an Economy of Fluids: Ecology, History and Health in East Timor. Paper presented at the Australian Anthropological Society. James Cook University–Cairns Campus, Queensland, September 26–29.

Johansen, Bruce E. 2006a. Global Warming in the 21st Century, vol. 2: Melting Ice and Warming Seas. Westport, CT: Praeger.

———. 2006b. Global Warming in the 21st Century. vol. 3: Plants and Animals in Peril. Westport, CT: Praeger.

Johnson, S., and R. Martin. 2005. Chlamydophila pneumoniae and Mycoplasma pneumoniae: A Role in Asthma Pathogenesis. American Journal of Respiratory and Critical Care Medicine 172(9):1078–1089.

Kahn, Chris. 2007. Scientists Warn of Lethal Amoeba. The Hartford (Connecticut) Courant, September 29:6.

Kalkstein, Laurence, and J. Scott Greene. 2007. The Development of Analog European Heat Waves for U.S. Cities to Analyze Impacts on Heat-related Mortality. Electronic document, www.as.miami.edu/geography/climatology/Analog_Final.pdf. Accessed January 22, 2008.

Karbuz, Sohbet. 2007. U.S. Military Oil Pains. Energy Bulletin, February 17. Electronic document, http://www.energybulletin.net/26194.html. Accessed March 25, 2008.

Kiely, Ray. 2007. The New Political Economy of Development: Globalization, Imperialism, Hegemony. New York: Palgrave MacMillan.

Kempton, Willet, James S. Boster, and Jennifer A. Hartley. 1995. Environmental Values in American Culture. Cambridge, MA: MIT Press.

Keatinge, W., and G. Donaldson. 2004. The Impact of Global Warming on Health and Mortality. South Medical Journal 97(11):1093–1099.

Kenworthy, J. R., and F. B. Laube. 1999. An International Sourcebook of Automobile Dependence in Cities 1960–1990. Boulder: University Press of Colorado.

Kenya Environment and Political News. 2007. African Farmers Need a Financial Umbrella Says World Bank. Electronic document, http://kenvironews.wordpress.com/2007/10/29/african-farmers-need-a-financial-umbrella-says-world-bank. Accessed June 3, 2008.

Killick-Kendrick, R. 1996. Leishmaniasis—An English Disease of the Future. Bulletin of Tropical Medicine and International Health 4(3):5.

Kinmouth, William. 2004. Climate Change: A Natural Hazard. Brentwood, Essex, UK: Multi-Science Publishing.

Klare, Michael T. 2006. The Coming Resource Wars. TomPaine.com, March 7. Electronic document, http://TomPaine.com. Accessed May 8, 2008.

Klevens, R. Monica, Melissa Morrison, Joelle Nadle, Susan Petit, Ken Gershman, Susan Ray, Lee Harrison, Ruth Lynfield, Ghinwa Dumyati, John Townes, Allen Craig, Elizabeth Zell, Gregory Fosheim, Linda McDougal, Roberta Carey, Scott Fridkin, and the Active Bacterial Core surveillance (ABCs) MRSA Investigators. 2007. Invasive Methicillin-Resistant Staphylococcus aureus Infections in the United States. Journal of the American Medical Association 298:1763–1771.

Klinenberg, Eric. 2002. Heat Wave: A Social Autopsy of Disaster in Chicago. Chicago: Chicago University Press.

Klotzbach, Philip, and William Gray. 2006. Extended Range Forecast of Atlantic Season Hurricane Acitivity, Individual Monthly Activity and U.S. Landfall Strike Probability for 2006. Electronic document, http://tropical.atmos.colostate.edu/Forecasts/2006/aug2006/index.html. Accessed June 15, 2007.

Kluger, Jeffrey. 2005. Global Warming: The Culprit? Time magazine, September 26. Electronic document, http://www.time.com/time/magazine/article/0,9171,1109337-5,00.html. Accessed August 8, 2008.

Knobloch, Bruce, and Tom Barnes. 2006. A Stern Warning But No Solutions. Socialist Worker [Australia], November 10:4.

Knowlton, Kim, Joyce Rosenthal, Christian Hogrefe, Barry Lynn, Stuart Gaffin, Richard Goldberg, Cynthia Rosenzweig, Kevin Civerolo, Ku Jia-Yeong, and Patrick Kinney. 2004. Assessing Ozone-Related Health Impacts under a Changing Climate. Environmental Health Perspectives 112(15):1557–1563.

Kolko, Gabriel. 1994. Century of War: Politics, Conflict, and Society Since 1914. New York: New Press.

———. 2002. Another Century of War? New York: New Press.

———. 2006. The Age of War: The United States Confronts the World. Boulder, CO: Lynne Rienner Publishers.

Komar, Nicolas, and G. Clark. 2006. West Nile Virus Activity in Latin America and the Caribbean. Panamerican Journal of Public Health 19:112–117.

Kovel, Joel. 2007. The Time Has Come: And Now for the Good News about Global Warming. Capitalism Nature Socialism 18(3):1–7.

Krieger, Nancy. 2001. Theories for Social Epidemiology in the 21st Century: An Ecosocial Perspective. International Journal of Epidemiology 30:668–677.

———. 2003. Does Racism Harm Health? Did Child Abuse Exist Before 1962? On Explicit Questions, Critical Science, and Current Controversies: An Ecosocial Perspective. American Journal of Public Health 93:194–199.

———. 2006. Researching Critical Questions on Social Justice and Public Health: An Ecosocial Perspective. In Social Injustice and Public Health. Barry Levy and Victor Sidel, eds. Pp. 460–479. Oxford: Oxford University Press.

———. 2007. Why Epidemiologists Cannot Afford to Ignore Poverty. Epidemiology 18(6):658–663.

Krieger, Nancy, and Stephen Sidney. 1996. Racial Discrimination and Blood Pressure: The CARDIA Study of Young Black and White Adults. American Journal of Public Health 86:1370–1378.

Kuhn, Katrin. 1999. Global Warming and Leishmaniasis in Italy. Bulletin of Tropical Medicine and International Health 7(2):1–2.

Lahsen, Myanna. 2005a. Seductive Simulations: Uncertainty Distribution Around Climate Models. Social Studies of Science 35(6):895–922.

———. 2005b. Technocracy, Democracy, and U.S. Climate Politics: The Need for Demarcations. Science, Technology, & Human Values 30(1):137–169.

Lang, Guenter. 2007. Where Are Germany's Gains from Kyoto? Estimating the Effects of Global Warming on Agriculture. Climatic Change 84:423–439.

Lalonde, Marc. 1974. A New Perspective on the Health of Canadians. Ottawa: Minister of Supply and Services.

Lawless, Daphne. 2006. Vast Cemetery or Socialist Victory? Special Issue on "System Change, Not Climate Change." Unity: A Marxist Journal for All Grassroots Activists [Auckland, New Zealand], December.

Leatherman, Thomas, and Alan Goodman. 1998. Expanding the Biocultural Synthesis Toward a Biology of Poverty. American Journal of Physical Anthropology 101(1):1–3.

Lee, M., R. Hallmark, L. Frenkel, and G. Del Priore. 1998. Maternal Syphilis and Vertical Perinatal Transmission of Human Immunodeficiency Virus Type-1 Infection. International Journal of Gynecology and Obstetrics 63(3):247–252.

Lefevere, Juergen. 2005. The EU Greenhouse Gas Emission Allowance Trading Scheme. *In* Climate Change and Carbon Markets: A Handbook of Emissions Reduction Mechanisms. Farhana Yamin, ed. Pp. 75–149. Sterling, VA: Earthscan.

Leggett, Jeremy. 1990. Global Warming: A Greenpeace Perspective. *In* Global Warming: The Greenpeace Report. Jeremy Leggett, ed. Pp. 457–480. Oxford: Oxford University Press.

Leichenko, Robin, and Karen O'Brien. 2006. Is It Appropriate to Identify Winners and Losers? *In* Fairness in Adaptation to Climate Change. W. Neil Adger, Jouni Paavola, Saleemul Huq, and M. J. Mace, eds. Pp. 97–114. Cambridge, MA: MIT Press.

Leiserowitz, Anthony. 2005. American Risk Perceptions: Is Climate Change Dangerous? Risk Analysis 25:1433–1442.

———. 2006. Climate Change Risk Perception and Policy Preferences: The Role of Affect, Imagery, and Values. Climatic Change 77:45–72.

Lewis, Jori. 2006. Early Signs: Reports from a Warming Planet. Living on Earth. Electronic document, http://www.loe.org/shows/segments.htm?programID=06-P13-00012& segmentID=8. Accessed July 25, 2007.

Liberatore, Angela. 1995. Facing Global Warming: The Interactions Between Science and Policy-Making in the European Community. *In* Social Theory and the Global Environment. Michael Redclift and Ted Benton, eds. Pp. 190–204. London: Routledge.

Lillard, Susan. 2007. Mold—What Is It all About? Mold-Help. Electronic document, http://www.mold-help.org/content/view/478/. Accessed June 26, 2007.

Linden, Eugene. 2006. Winds of Change: Climate, Weather, and the Distraction of Civilizations. New York: Simon & Schuster.

Lindsay, James M. 2001. Global Warming Heats Up. Brooking Review (Fall):26–29.

Lingappa, J., and C. Celum. 2007. Clinical and Therapeutic Issues for Herpes Simplex virus-2 and HIV Co-infection. Drugs 67(2):155–174.

Litsios, Socrates. 1996. The Tomorrow of Malaria. Nampa, ID: Pacific Press.

Little, P., M. Hussein, and D. L. Layne Coppock. 2001. When Deserts Flood: Risk Management and Climatic Processes Among East African Pastoralists. Special Issue on Anthropological Perspectives and Policy Implications of Climate Change Research. Climate Research 19(2):149–159.

Liverman, D. 1990. Vulnerability to Global Environmental Change. *In* Understanding Global Environmental Change: The Contributions of Risk Analysis and Management. R. Kasperson, K. Dow, D. Golding, and J. X. Kasperson, eds. Pp. 27–44. Worcester, MA: Clark University.

Loewy, Michael. 2006. Eco-Socialism and Democratic Planning. *In* Coming to Terms With Nature: Socialist Register 2007. Leo Panitch and Colin Leys, eds. Pp. 294–309. London: Merlin Press.

Lohmann, Larry. 2006. Carbon Trading: A Critical Conversation on Climate Change, Privatisation and Power. Development Dialogue, No. 48, September. Uppsala, Sweden: Dag Hammarskjoeld Centre.

Louisiana Department of Health and Hospitals. 2005. 155 West Nile Cases for Louisiana So Far This Year; Still No Significant Increase Because of Hurricanes. News release, November 17. Electronic document, http://www.dhh.louisiana.gov/news. asp?ID=145&Detail=742. Accessed June 25, 2008.

Loureiro, E., A. Linhares, and L. Mata. 1990. Cryptosporidiosis in Children from 1 to 2 Years of Age with Acute Diarrhea in Belém, Pará, Brazil. Memorial Institute Oswaldo Cruz 84(1):117–122.

Lowe, Ian. 2005. Living in the Hothouse: How Global Warming Affects Australia. Melbourne: Scribe.

Lusso, P., R. Crowley, M. Malnati, C. Di Serio, M. Ponzoni, A. Biancotto, P. Markham, and R. Gallo. 2007. Human Herpesvirus 6A Accelerates AIDS Progression in Macaques. Proceedings of the U.S. National Academy of Science 104(12):5067–5072.

Lutes, Mark W. 1998. Global Climatic Change. *In* Political Ecology: Global and Local. Roger Keil, David V. J. Bell, Peter Penz, and Leesa Fawcett, eds. Pp. 157–175. London: Routledge.

Lynas, Mark. 2004. High Tide: The Truth About Our Climate Crisis. New York: Picador.

——. 2007. Six Degrees: Our Future on a Hotter Planet. London: Fourth Estate.

MacKenbach, J., V. Borst, and J. Schols. 1997. Heat-Related Mortality among Nursing-Home Patients. Lancet 349:1297–1298.

Maddison, Angus. 2001. The World Economy: A Millennial Perspective. Paris: Organization for Economic Cooperation and Development (OECD).

Makunde, William, Leo Kamugisha, Julius Massaga, Rachel Makunde, Zakana Savael, Juma Akida, Fred Salum, and Mark Taylor. 2003. Treatment of Co-infection with Bancroftian Filariasis and Onchocerciasis: A Safety and Efficacy Study of Albendazole with Ivermectin Compared to Treatment of Single Infection with Bancroftian Filariasis. Filaria Journal 2. Electronic document, http://bmc.ub.uni-potsdam.de/1475-2883-2-15/1475-2883-2-15.pdf. Accessed August 3, 2007.

Mamdani, Mahomood. 1972. The Myth of Population Control: Family, Caste, and Class in an Indian Village. New York: Monthly Review Press.

Maree, Cynthia, Robert Daum, Susan Boyle-Vavra, Kelli Matayoshi, and Loren Miller. 2007. Community-Associated Methicillin-Resistant Staphylococcus aureus Isolates Causing Healthcare-Associated Infections. Emergent Infectious Diseases 13(2). Electronic document, http://www.cdc.gov/EID/content/13/2/236.htm.

Marshall, Mac. 2005. Carolina in the Carolines: A Survey of Patterns and Meanings of Smoking on a Micronesian Island. Medical Anthropology Quarterly 19(4):354–382.

Martens, Willem, Louis Niessen, Jan Rotmans, Theo Jetten, and Anthony McMichael. 1995. Potential Impact of Global Climate Change on Malaria Risk. Environmental Health Perspectives 103:458–464.

Maslin, Mark. 2004. Global Warming: A Very Short Introduction. Oxford: Oxford University Press.

Maternowska, M. Catherine. 2006. Reproducing Inequalities: Poverty and the Politics of Population in Haiti. New Brunswick, NY: Rutgers University Press.

McCarthy, Michael. 2006. Temperature set to hit 100 degrees—and global warming is to blame. The London Independent, July 19. Electronic document, http://findarticles.com/p/articles/mi_qn4158/is_20060719/ai_n16541201. Accessed December 3, 2007.

McCarthy, James J., Osvaldo F. Canziani, Neil A. Leary, David J. Dokken, and Kasey White S. White, eds. 2001. Climate Change 2001: Impacts, Adaptation and Vulnerability. Intergovernmental Panel on Climate Change. Cambridge: Cambridge University Press.

McCright, Aaron M., and Riley E. Dunlop. 2000. Challenging Global Warming as a Social Problem: An Analysis of the Conservative Movement's Counter-Claims. Social Problems 47:499–522.

——. 2003. Defeating Kyoto: The Conservative Movement's Impact on U.S. Climate Change Policy. Social Problems 50:348–373.

McClelland, R., L. Lavreys, C. Katingima, J. Overbaugh, V. Chohan, K. Mandaliya, J. Ndinya-Achola, and J. Baeten. 2005. Contribution of HIV-1 Infection to Acquisition of Sexually Transmitted Disease: A 10-year Prospective Study. Journal of Infectious Diseases 191(3):333–338.

McCullers, Jonathan. 2006. Insights into the Interaction Between Influenza Virus and Pneumococcus. Clinical Microbiology Reviews 19(3):571–582.

McCullough, Peter, Claudine Jurkovitz, Pablo Pergola, Janet McGill, Wendy Brown, Alan Collins, Shu-Cheng Chen, Suying Li, Arjay Singh, Keith Norris, Michael Klag, and George Barkris. 2007. Independent Components of Chronic Kidney Disease as a Cardiovascular Risk State: Results From the Kidney Early Evaluation Program (KEEP). Archives of Internal Medicine 167:1122–1129.

McGeehin, Michael. 2007. CDC's Role in Addressing the Health Effects of Climate Change. CDC Conference: Safer Healthier People, May 4-5, Atlanta, Georgia.

McKie, Robin. 2003. A Mountain of Trouble as Matterhorn Is Rocked by Avalanches. The Observer International. Electronic document, http://observer.guardian.co.uk/international/story/0,,1001674,00.html. Accessed November 3, 2007.

McLaughlin, Andrew. 1990. Ecology, Capitalism, and Socialism. Socialism and Democracy 10:69–102.

McMichael, Anthony J. 1993. Planetary Overload: Global Environmental Change and the Health of the Human Species. Cambridge: Cambridge University Press.

———. 1995. The Health of Persons, Populations, and Planets: Epidemiology Comes Full Circle. Epidemiology 6:633–636.

———. 2001. Human Frontiers, Environments and Disease. Cambridge: Cambridge University Press.

McMichael, Anthony, H. Campbell-Lendrum, C. Corvalan, K. Ebi, A.K. Githeko, J.D. Schwraga, and A. Woodward, eds. 2003. Climate Change and Human Health: Risks and Responses. Geneva: World Health Organization.

McMichael Anthony, Tord Kjellström, and Kirk Smith. 2001. Environmental Health. In International Public Health: Disease, Programs, Systems, and Policies, Michael Merson, Robert Black, and Anne Mills, eds. Pp. 379–437. Gaithersburg, MD: Aspen Publishers, Inc.

McQuaig, Linda. 2004. It's the Crude, Dude: Big Oil and the Fight for the Planet. New York: Doubleday.

Medina-Ramón, Mercedes, and Joel Schwartz. 2007. Temperature, Temperature Extremes, and Mortality: A Study of Acclimatization and Effect Modification in 50 United States Cities. Occupational and Environmental Medicine. Published online ahead of print at http://www.ncbi.nlm.nih.gov/sites/entrez?Db=pubmed&Cmd=ShowDetailView&TermToSearch=17600037&ordinalpos=17&itool=EntrezSystem2.PEntrez.Pubmed.Pubmed_ResultsPanel.Pubmed_RVDocSum. Accessed July 23, 2008.

Meegan, J., and C. Bailey. 1989. Rift Valley Fever. In The Arboviruses: Epidemiology and Ecology. T. Monath, ed. Pp 51–76. Boca Raton, FL: CRC Press, Inc.

Melia, Michel. 2007. Dengue Fever Surges in Latin America. Associated Press. Electronic document, http://news.aol.com/story/ar/_a/dengue-fever-surges-in-latin-america/20070930122409990001?ncid=NWS00010000000001. July 21, 2008.

Meng, Y., M. Wilhelm, R. Rull, P. English, and B. Ritz. 2007. Traffic and Outdoor Air Pollution Levels Near Residences and Poorly Controlled Asthma in Adults. Annals of Allergy, Asthma, and Immunology 98(5):455–463.

Mertig, A., and R. Dunlap. 1995. Public Approval of Environmental Protection and Other New Social Movement Goals in Western Europe and the United States. Journal of Public Opinion Research 7:145–156.

Messer, Ellen. 1989. Seasonality in Food Systems: An Anthropological Perspective on Household Food Security. In Seasonal Variability in Third World Agriculture: The Consequences for Food Security. D. Sahn, ed. Pp. 151–175. Baltimore, MD: Johns Hopkins University.

Milanovic, Branko. 2002. True World Income Distribution, 1988 and 1993: First Calculation Based on Household Surveys Alone. Economic Journal 112(47).

Milstein, Bobby. 2001. Introduction to the Syndemics Prevention Network. Atlanta: Centers for Disease Control and Prevention.

———. 2004. Syndemics. In Encyclopedia of Evaluation. S. Mathison, ed. Pp. 404–405. Thousand Oaks, CA: Sage Publications.

———. 2008. Hygeia's Constellation Navigating Health Futures in a Dynamic and Democratic World. Atlanta: The Centers for Disease Control and Prevention.

Mittelstaedt, Martin. 2007. How Global Warming Goes Against the Grain. The Globe and Mail, February 23. Electronic document, http://www.theglobeandmail.com/servlet/story/RTGAM.20070223.wclimatestarve0224/BNStory/ClimateChange/home/?pageRequested=1. Accessed July 1, 2008.

Molina, R., L. Gradoni, and J. Alvar. 2003. HIV and the Transmission of Leishmania. Annals of Tropical Medicine and Parasitology 97(Supplement No. 1):S29–S45.

Monastersky, Richard. 1996. How Would Global Warming Affect Humans? Science News, April: 1.

Monbiot, George. 2006. Heat: How to Stop the Planet Burning. Camberwell, Victoria, Australia: Allen Lane.

Montet, Virginie. 2007. Smithsonian Toned Down Global Warming Exhibit to Please Officials. Seed. Electronic document, http://www.seedmagazine.com/news/2007/05/smithsonian_toned_down_global.php. Accessed July 3, 2008.

Moran, Emilio F. 2006. People and Nature: An Introduction to Human Ecological Relations. South Malden, MA: Blackwell Publishing.

Morton, J. 2007. The Impact of Climate Change on Smallholder and Subsistence Agriculture. Proceedings of the National Academy of Sciences of the United States of America 104(50):19680–19685.

Moscatiello, S., R. Manini, and G. Marchesini. 2007. Diabetes and Liver Disease: An Ominous Association. Nutrition, Metabolism and Cardiovascular Diseases 17(1):63–70.

Mott, Ron. 2006. Cleaning Up New Orleans, One Piece at a Time. MCNBC, August 25. Electronic document, http://www.msnbc.msn.com/id/14517716/. Accessed July 18, 2008.

Mugambi, Jessee. 2006. A Statement from the World Council of Churches (WCC) to the High-Level Ministerial Segment of the UN Climate Conference in Nairobi, November 17. Electronic document, http://www.oikoumene.org. Accessed June 9, 2007.

Murphy, Katherine. 2007. Carbon Trading by 2012. The Age (Australia), June 1:1.

Murray, K., P. Selleck, P. Hooper, A. Hyatt, A. Gould, L. Gleeson, H. Westbury, L. Hiley, L. Selvey, and B. Rodwell. 1995. A Morbillivirus that Caused Fatal Disease in Horses and Humans. Science 268:94–97.

Murry, Henry, Jacques Pépin, and Adel Mahmoud. 2000. Recent Advances in Tropical Medicine. British Medical Journal 320(7233): 490–494.

Mycoses Study Group. 2007. Aspergillosis. Electronic document, http://www.doctorfungus.org/mycoses/human/aspergillus/aspergillosis.htm. Accessed January 11, 2008.

Myers, Norman, and J. Kent. 2001. Food and Hunger in Sub-Saharan Africa. The Environmentalist 21(1):41–69.

Nandan, G. 1994. Troops Battle to Contain India's Outbreak of Plague. British Medical Journal 390:827.

NASD (National Ag Safety Database). 2002. Cantaloupe Picker Dies of Heat Stroke. Summary: Case 191-002-01. Electronic document, http://www.cdc.gov/nasd/docs/d000001-d000100/d000037/d000037.html

National Cancer Institute. 2002. Factsheet: Improving Methods for Breast Cancer Detection and Diagnosis. Electronic document, http://www.cancer.gov/cancertopics/factsheet/Detection/breast-cancer. Accessed July 1, 2007.

National Geographic. 2004. Global Warming: Bulletins from a Warmer World. September.

National Science Foundation. 2003. Lake Ecosystem Critical to East African Food Supply Is Threatened by Climate Change. Electronic document, http://www.nsf.gov/od/lpa/news/03/pr0383.htm. Accessed July 12, 2006.

Natural Resources Defense Council. 2006. Deadly Heat Waves and the Spread of Disease. Electronic document, http://www.nrdc.org/globalWarming/fcons.asp. Accessed March 1, 2007.

Newell, Peter. 2000. Climate for Change: Non-State Actors and the Global Politics of the Greenhouse. Cambridge: Cambridge University Press.

Newman, R., C. Sears, R. Moore, J. Nataro, T. Wuhib, D. Agnew, R. Guerrant, and A. Lima. 1999. Longitudinal Study of Cryptosporidium Infection in Children in Northeastern Brazil. Journal of Infectious Disease 180:167–175.

New Orleans Department of Public Property. 1947. Records, 1912 (1925–1929) 1947. Electronic document, http://nutrias.org/inv/pubprop.htm. Accessed February 12, 2008.

Nguku, P., S. Sharif, A. Omar, C. Nzioka, P. Muthoka, J. Njau, A. Dahiye, T. Galgalo, J. Mwihia, J. Njoroge, H. Limo, J. Mutiso, R. Kalani, A. Sheikh, J. Nyikal, D. Mutonga, J. Omollo, A. Guracha, J. Muindi, S. Amwayi, D. Langat, D. Owiti, A. Mohammed, J. Musaa, J. Sang, R. Breiman, K. Njenga, D. Feikin, M. Katz, H. Burke, P. Nyaga, M. Ackers, S. Gikundi, V. Omballa, L. Nderitu, N. Wamola, R. Wanjala, S. Omulo, J. Richardson, D. Schnabel, S. Martin, D. Hoel, H. Hanafi, M. Weiner, J. Onsongo, T. Kojo, M. Duale, A. Hassan, M. Dabaar, C. Njuguna, M. Yao, T. Grein, B. Telfer, R. Lepec, H. Feldmann, A. Grolla, S. Wainwright, E. Lederman, E. Farnon, C. Rao, B. Kapella, and H. Gould. 2007. Rift Valley Fever Outbreak—Kenya, November 2006–January 20. Morbidity and Mortality Weekly Reports 56(4):73–76.

Nielsen, N., H. Friis, P. Magnussen, H. Krarup, S. Magesa, and P. Simonsen. 2007. Co-infection with Subclinical HIV and Wuchereria bancrofti, and the Role of Malaria and Hookworms, in Adult Tanzanians: Infection Intensities, CD4/CD8 Counts and Cytokine Responses. Transactions of the Royal Society of Tropical Medicine and Hygiene 101(6):602–612.

Nogues-Bravero, D., M.B. Araujo, M.P. Errea, and J.P. Martinez-Ricaet. 2007. Exposure of Global Mountain Systems to Climate Warming during the 21st Century. Global Environmental Change 17:420–428.

Nora, Tamara, Charlotte Charpentier, Oliver Tenaillon, Claire Hiede, Francois Clavel, and Allan Hance. 2007. Contribution of Recombination to the Evolution of Human Immunodeficiency Viruses Expressing Resistance to Antiretroviral Treatment. Journal of Virology. Online in advance of publication at http://www.ncbi.nlm.nih.gov/sites/entrez?Db=pubmed&Cmd=ShowDetailView&TermToSearch=17494080&ordinalpos=6&itool=EntrezSystem2.PEntrez.Pubmed.Pubmed_ResultsPanel.Pubmed_RVDocSum. Accessed July 26, 2008.

Noymer, Andrew. 2006. Studies in the Historical Demography and Epidemiology of Influenza and Tuberculosis Selective Mortality. Ph.D. dissertation, Department of Sociology, University of California, Berkeley.

Nuttall, Mark, Fikret Berkes, Bruce Forbes, Gary Kofinas, Tatiana Vlassova, and George Wenzel. 2004. Hunting, Herding, Fishing and Gathering: Indigenous Peoples and Renewable Resources. In Impacts of a Warming Arctic: Arctic Climate Impact Assessment. Carolyn Symon, Lelani Arris, and Bill Heal, eds. Pp. 649–690. Cambridge: Cambridge University Press.

Nurse, L., G. Sem, J. Hay, A. Suarez, P. Wong, and L. Briguglio. 2001. Small Island States. In Climate Change 2001: Impacts, Adaptation and Vulnerability. Contribution of Working Group II to the Third Assessment Report of the Intergovernmental Panel on Climate Change. Pp. 844–875. Cambridge: Cambridge University Press.

Ocampo, Dan. 2006. 141 Deaths Later, Heat Wave Appears Over. U.S.A. Today, July 29. Electronic document, http://www.usatoday.com/weather/news/2006-07-26-power-problems_x.htm

O'Driscoll, Patrick. 2007. Unseasonable Fever Across Swath of USA Easing Today. USA Today. Electronic document, http://www.usatoday.com/weather/climate/2007-10-08-Weather_N.htm. Accessed February 3, 2008.

Oliver, J., and J. Kaper. 2001. Vibrio Species. In Food Microbiology: Fundamentals and Frontiers. M. Doyle and Larry Beuchat, eds. Pp. 263–300. New York: ASM Press.

O'Reilly, Catherine, Simone Alini, Pierre-Denis Plisnier, Andrew Cohen, and Brent McKee. 2003. Climate Change Decreases Aquatic Ecosystem Productivity of Lake Tanganyika. Nature 424:766–768.

O'Riordan, Timothy, and Andrew Jordan. 1999. Institutions, Climate Change and Culture Theory: Towards a Common Analytical Framework. Global Environmental Change 9:81–93.

Orlove, Ben. 2003. How People Name Seasons. *In* Weather, Climate, Culture. Sarah Strauss and Ben Orlove, eds. Pp. 121–137. Oxford: Berg.

———. 2005. Human Adaptation to Climate Change: A Review of Three Historical Cases and Some General Perspectives. Environmental Science and Policy 8:589–600.

Orlove, B., J. Chiang, and M. Cane. 2000. Forecasting Andean rainfall and crop yield from the influences of El Nino on Pleiades visibility. Nature 403:68–71.

———. 2002. Ethnoclimatology in the Andes: A cross-disciplinary study uncovers a scientific basis for the scheme Andean potato farmers traditionally use to predict the coming rains. American Scientist 90:428–435.

Orlove, B., C. Roncoli, M. Kabugo, and A. Majugu. Under review. Indigenous knowledge of climate variability in Southern Uganda: The multiple components of a dynamic regional system. Climatic Change.

Pachauri, R.K. 2003. Global Climate Change: Indian Perspective Revisited and Restated. *In* India and Global Climate Change: Perspectives on Economics and Policy from a Developing Country. Michael A. Toman, Ujjayant Chakravorty, and Shreekant Gupta, eds. Pp. 341–346. Washington, DC: Resources for the Future.

Pan, Jiuhua. 2005. China and Climate Change: The Role of the Energy Sector. Science and Development Network, June. Electronic document, www.scidev.net. Accessed August 27, 2007.

Pandya, Robert J., Gina Solomon, Amy Kinner, and John R. Balmes. 2002. Diesel Exhaust and Asthma: Hypotheses and Molecular Mechanisms of Action. Environmental Health Perspectives Supplements Volume 110(S1):103–112.

Paolo, Jr., W., and J. Nosanchuk. 2004. Tuberculosis in New York City: Recent Lessons and a Look Ahead. Lancet Infectious Diseases 4(5):287–293.

Parish, R., and D. C. Funnell. 1999. Climate Change in Mountain Regions: Some Possible Consequences in the Moroccan High Atlas. Global Environmental Change 9:45–58.

Parker, Ian. 2006. Birth of a Nation? The New Yorker, May 1:66.

Parsons, H.L. 1977. Marx and Engels on Ecology. Westport, CT: Greenwood.

Patz, J., D. Campbell-Lendrum, T. Holloway, and J. Foley. 2005. Impact of Regional Climate Change on Human Health. Nature 438(7066):310–317.

Patz, Jonathan, Willem Martens, Dana Focks, and Theo Jetten. 1998. Dengue Fever Epidemic Potential as Projected by General Circulation Models of Global Climate Change. Environmental Health Perspectives 106:147–153.

Pearce, Fred. 2006. The Last Generation: How Nature Will Take Her Revenge for Climate Change. London: Transworld Publishers.

Pearse, Guy. 2007. High & Dry: John Howard, Climate Change and the Selling of Australia's Future. Melbourne: Viking.

Pearson, Helen. 2003. West Nile Virus May Have Felled Alexander the Great. Nature. Electronic document, http://www.gideononline.com/reviews/nature.htm. Accessed March 3, 2008.

Pearson, Holly L. 2002. Climate Change and Agriculture: Mitigation Options and Potential. *In* Climate Change Policy: A Survey. Stephen H. Schneider et al., eds. Pp. 307–335. Washington, DC: Island Press.

Pennington, S. 1995. Global Warming and Disease. The Geographic Magazine 67:7.

Pennsylvania State University Press Release. 1998. Climate Change May Impact Waterborne Diseases. May 26. Electronic document, http://www.psu.edu/ur/NEWS/news/crypto.html. Accessed July 19, 2006.

People's Health Movement. 2005. Global Health Watch 2005–2006. London: Zed Books.

Pepper, David. 1993. Eco-Socialism: From Deep Ecology to Social Justice. London: Routledge.

Perez, R.T., R.B. Feir, E. Carandang, and E. B. Gonzalez. 1996. Potential Impacts of Sea Level Rise on the Coastal Resources of Manila Bay: A Preliminary Vulnerability

Assessment. *In* Climate Change Vulnerability and Adaptation in Asia and the Pacific. Lin Erda et al., eds. Pp. 137–147. Dordrecht, the Netherlands: Kluwer Academic Publishers.

Petterson, John, Laura Stanley, Edward Glazier, and James Philipp. 2006. A Preliminary Assessment of the Social and Economic Impacts Associated with Hurricane Katrina. American Anthropologist 108(4):643–670.

Pew Center for Global Climate Change. 2007. Climate Change Mitigation Measures in the People's Republic of China, International Brief, April.

Pimentel, David, Marcia Pimentel, and Mary Lou Guerinot. 2000. To Improve Nutrition for the World's Population. Science 288:1966–1967.

Pittock, A. Barrie. 2005. Climate Change: Turning Up the Heat. Collingwood, Victoria, Australia: CSIRO Publishing.

Platt, A. 1995. Global Warming and Disease. World Watch 8:26–32.

Podobnik, Bruce. 2002. Global Energy Inequalities: Exploring the Long-Term Implications. Journal of World-Systems Research 13:252–274.

Ponting, Clive. 2007. A New Green History of the World: The Environment and the Collapse of Great Civilisations. London: Vintage.

Purse, Bethan, Philip Mellor, David Rogers, Alan Samuel, Peter Mertens, and Matthew Baylis. 2005. Climate Change and the Recent Emergence of Bluetongue in Europe. Nature Reviews 3(2):171–181.

Rabe, Andrew C. 2004. Greenhouse and Statehouse: The Evolving State Government Role in Climate Change. Washington, DC: Pew Center on Global Climate Change.

Rabe, Barry G. 2004. Statehouse and Greenhouse: The Emerging Politics of American Climate Change Policy. DC: Brookings Institution Press.

Ralston, Holley, Britta Horstmann, and Carina Holl. 2004. Climate Change Challenges Tuvalu. Berlin: Germanwatch.

Rapach, Michael R. 2007. Global and Regional Drivers of Accelerating CO_2 Emissions. Proceedings of the National Academy of Sciences, Early Edition. Pp. 1–6.

Ratard, R., C. Brown, J. Ferdinands, K. Dunn, M. Scalia, R. Moolenaar, S. Davis, L. Pinkerton, C. Rao, D. Van Sickle, M. Riggs, and K. Cummings. 2006. Health Concerns Associated with Mold in Water-Damaged Homes After Hurricanes Katrina and Rita—New Orleans Area, Louisiana, October 2005. Morbidity and Mortality Weekly Review 55(02):41–44.

Raupach, Michael R. Gregg Marland, Philippe Ciais, Corinne Le Quéré, Josep G. Canadell, Gernot Klepper, and Christopher B. Field. 2007. Global and regional drivers of accelerating CO_2 emissions. PNAS Early Edition. Electronic document, http://www.pnas.org/cgi. Accessed January 26, 2008.

Ravindran, B., P. Sahoo, and A. Dash. 1998. Lymphatic Filariasis and Malaria: Concomitant Parasitism in Orissa, India. Transactions of the Royal Society for Tropical Medicine and Hygiene 92(1): 21–23.

Ray, Celeste. 2001. Cultural Paradigms: An Anthropological Perspective on Climate Change. *In* Global Climate Change. Sharon L. Spray and Karen L. McGlothin, eds. Pp. 81–100. Lanham, MD: Rowman & Littlefield.

Reay, Dave. 2005. Climate Change Begins at Home: Life on the Two-Way Street of Global Warming. London: Macmillan.

Rees, William E. N.d. Revisiting Carrying Capacity: Area-Based Indicators of Sustainability. Electronic document, http://dieoff.org. Accessed August 8, 2007.

Reinberg, Steven. 2007. Global Warming Poses Health Threats. Washington Post, February 2:1.

Reiter, Paul, Sarah Lathrop, Michel Bunning, Brad Biggerstaff, Daniel Singer, Tejpratap Tiwari, Laura Baber, Amador Manuel, Jaime Thirion, Jack Hayes, Calixto Seca, Jorge Mendez, Bernardo Ramirez, Jerome Robinson, Julie Rawlings, Vance Vorndam, Stephen Waterman, Duane Gubler, Gary Clark, and Edward Hayes. 2003. Texas Lifestyle Limits Transmission of Dengue Virus. Emerging Infectious Diseases. Electronic document, http://www.cdc.gov/ncidod/EID/vol9no1/02-0220.htm. Accessed July 29, 2006.

Remnick, David. 2006. Ozone Man. The New Yorker, April 24. Electronic document, http://www.newyorker.com/archive/2006/04/24/060424ta_talk_remnick. Accessed March 3, 2007.

Resistance. 1999. Environment, Capitalism & Socialism. Sydney: Resistance Books.

Reynolds, S., and T. Quinn. 2007. Developments in STD/HIV interactions: The intertwining epidemics of HIV and HSV-2. Infectious Disease Clinics of North America 19(2):415–425.

Reynolds, S., A. Risbud, M. Shepherd, A. Rompalo, M. Ghate, S. Godbole, A. D. Divekar, R. Gangakhedkar, R. Bollinger, and S. Mehendale. 2006. High Rates of Syphilis among STI Patients Are Contributing to the Spread of HIV-1 in India. Sexually Transmitted Infections 82(2):121–126.

Rickerts, Volker, Hans Reinhard Brodt, Bernd Schneider, Eckhart Weidmann, and Kai Uwe Chow. 2006. Host Factors and Disease Severity in Two Patients with SARS. Laboratorium Medizin 30(1):18–22.

Riordan, Colin, ed. 1997. German Thought in German Culture: Historical and Contemporary Perspectives. Cardiff: University of Wales Press.

Roberts, Anwen. 2007. What Will Become of Tuvalu's Climate Refugees? Spiegel Online International, September 14. Online at: http://www.spiegel.de/international/world/0,1518,505819,00.html. Accessed August 12, 2008.

Roberts, J. Timmons. 1996. Predicting Participation in Environmental Treaties: A World-Systems Analysis. Sociological Inquiry 66:38–57.

Roberts, J. Timmons, and Peter E. Grimes. 1997. Carbon Intensity and Economic Development 1962–91: A Brief Exploration of the Environmental Kuznets Curve. World Development 25:191–198.

Roberts, J. Timmons, Peter E. Grimes, and Jodie Manale. 2003. Social Roots of Global Environmental Change: A World-Systems Analysis of Carbon Dioxide Emissions. Journal of World-Systems Research 9:277–315.

Roberts, J. Timmons, and Bradley C. Parks. 2007. A Climate of Injustice: Global Inequality, North-South Politics, and Climate Policy. Cambridge, MA: MIT Press.

Robinson, Peter. 2001. On the Definition of Heat Wave. Journal of Applied Meteorology 40(4):762–775.

Rogers, David. 1979. Tsetse Population Dynamics and Distribution: A New Analytical Approach. Journal of Animal Ecology 48:825–849.

Roncoli, Carla, and John Magistro. 2000. Global Science, Local Practice: Anthropological Dimensions of Climate Variability. Practicing Anthropologist 22(4):2–5.

Rose, J., P. Epstein, E. Lipp, B. Sherman, S. Bernard, and J. Patz. 2001. Climate Variability and Change in the United States: Potential Impacts on Water- and Foodborne Diseases Caused by Microbiologic Agents. Environmental Health Perspectives 109 (Supplement 2): 211–221.

Rowlands, Ian H. 1995. Explaining National Climate Change Policies. Global Environmental Change 5:235–249.

Ruddiman, William F. 2005. Plows, Plagues and Petroleum: How Humans Took Control of Climate. Princeton, NJ: Princeton University Press.

Rumble, Eric. 2006. Business as Usual: Adbusters: Journal of Mental Environment (July/August): 46–47.

Running, Steven. 2006. Is Global Warming Causing More, Larger Wildfires? Science 313(5789):927–928.

Sachs, Jeffrey D., and Andrew Warner. 1997. Fundamental Sources of Long-run Growth. American Economics Review, May.

Sacks, Lauren, and Cynthia Rosenzweig. 2007. Climate Change and Food Security. Climate.org. Electronic document, http://www.climate.org/topics/agricul/index.shtml. Accessed June 25, 2008.

Sallah, Ann. 2003. Gene Swap Led to Superbug. ABC Science. Electronic document, http:// www.abc.net.au/science/articles/2003/11/28/999126.htm?site=science&topic=tech. Accessed August 2, 2008.

Scenta: Engineering & Technology Careers & News. 2007. Engineering: Who has the biggest carbon footprint? Electronic document, http://www.scenta.co.uk/engineering/ materials/cit/1488560/who-has-the-biggest- carbon-footprint.htm. Accessed March 23, 2008.

Schacker, Timothy. 2001. The Role of HSV in the Transmission and Progression of HIV. Herpes 8(2):46–49.

Schäfer, J., Y. Kawaoka, W. Bean, J. Süss, D. Senne, and R. Webster. 1993. Origin of the Pandemic 1957 H2 Influenza A Virus and the Persistence of Its Possible Progenitors in the Avian Reservoir. Virology 194(2):781–788.

Scheper-Hughes, Nancy. 1995. The Primacy of the Ethical: Propositions for a Militant Anthropology. Current Anthropology 36:409–420.

Schull, Tad. 1999. Redefining Red and Green: Ideology and Strategy in European Political Ecology. Albany: State University of New York Press.

Scott, Daniel, Geoff McBoyle, and Alanna Minogue. 2007. Climate Change and Quebec's Ski Industry. Global Environmental Change 17:181–190.

Secretariat of the Pacific Regional Environment Programme. 1996. Annual Report. Apia, Samoa.

Sellers, R., G. Bergold, O. Suarez, and A. Morales. 1965. Investigations During Venezuelan Equine Encephalitis Outbreaks in Venezuela—1962–1964. American Journal of Tropical Medicine and Hygiene 14(3):460–469.

Sharma, H. 2005. Heat-Related Deaths Are Largely Due to Brain Damage. Indian Journal of Medical Research 121:621–623.

Shearman, David, with Gary Sauer. 1997. Date Greener Gone: Health, Ecology, Plagues. Kent Town, South Australia: Wakefield Press.

Shiva, Vandana. 2005. Earth Democracy: Justice, Sustainability, and Peace. London: Zed Books.

Shope, Rober. 1991. Global Climate Change and Infectious Diseases. Environmental Health Perspectives 96:171–174.

———. 1992. Impacts of Global Climate Change on Human Health: Spread of Infectious Disease. In Global Climate Change: Implications, Challenges and Mitigation Measures. S. Majumdar, L. Kalkstein, B. Yarnal, E. Miller, and L. Rosenfeld, eds. Pp. 363–370. Easton: The Pennsylvania Academy of Science.

Shukla, P. R., Debyani Ghosh, and Amit Garg. 2003. Future Energy Trends and Greenhouse Emissions. In India and Global Climate Change: Perspectives on Economics and Policy from a Developing Country. Michael A. Toman, Ujjayant Chakravorty, and Shreekant Gupta, eds. Pp. 11–35. Washington, DC: Resources for the Future.

Singer, Merrill. 1994. AIDS and the Health Crisis of the U.S. Urban Poor: The Perspective of Critical Medical Anthropology. Social Science and Medicine 39(7):931–948.

———. 1995. Beyond the Ivory Tower: Critical Praxis. Medical Anthropology Quarterly 9:80–106.

———. 1996. A Dose of Drugs, a Touch of Violence, a Case of AIDS: Conceptualizing the SAVA Syndemic. Free Inquiry in Creative Sociology 24(2):99–110.

———. 1998. The Development of Critical Medical Anthropology: Implications for Biological Anthropology. In Building a New Biocultural Synthesis: Political-Economic Perspectives on Human Biology. Alan Goodman and Thomas Leatherman, eds. Pp. 93–123. Ann Arbor: University of Michigan Press.

———. 2006. A Dose of Drugs, A Touch of Violence, A Case of AIDS, Part 2: Further Conceptualizing the SAVA Syndemic. Free Inquiry in Creative Sociology 34(1):39–51.

———. 2007. Ecosyndemics: Global Warming, Disease Spread and Interaction, and the Coming Plagues of the 21st Century. Presented at the Wenner-Gren Conference, Plagues: Models and Metaphors in the Human "Struggle with Disease." Tucson, AZ.

Singer, Merrill. In press. Ecosyndemics: Global Warming and the Coming Plagues of the 21st Century. *In* Plagues: Models and Metaphors in the Human "Struggle" with Disease. Alan Swedlund and Ann Herring, eds. London: Berg.

———. In press. Introducing Syndemics: Toward a New Biosocial Synthesis in Public Health. San Francisco: Jossey-Bass.

Singer, Merrill, and Hans Baer. 2007. Introducing Medical Anthropology: A Discipline in Action. Walnut Creek, CA: AltaMira Press.

———, eds. 2008. Killer Commodities: Public Health and the Corporate Production of Harm. Walnut Creek, CA: AltaMira Press.

Singer, Merrill, and Scott Clair. 2003. Syndemics and Public Health: Reconceptualizing Disease in Bio-Social Context. Medical Anthropology Quarterly 17(4):423–441.

Singer, Merrill, Pamela Erickson, Louise Badiane, Rosemary Diaz, Dugeidy Ortiz, Traci Abraham, and Anna Marie Nicolaysen. 2006. Syndemics, Sex and the City: Understanding Sexually Transmitted Disease in Social and Cultural Context. Social Science and Medicine 63(8):2010–2021.

Sklar, Holly. 2006. It's Boom Time for Billionaires. The Hartford (Connecticut) Courant, October 4: A11.

Skjaereth, Jon Birger, and Tora Skodvin. 2003. Climate Change and the Oil Industry. Manchester, UK: Manchester University Press.

Small, C., and R. J. Nicholls. 2003. A Global Analysis of Human Settlement in Coastal Zones. Journal of Coastal Research 19:584–599.

Smith, A., D. Skilling, J. Castello, and S. Rogers. 2004. Ice as a Reservoir for Pathogenic Animal Viruses. Medical Hypotheses 63:560–566.

Smith, Kevin. 2007. The Carbon Neutral Myth: Offset Indulgences for Your Climate Sins. Amsterdam: Transnational Institute and Carbon Trade Watch.

Smoyer, K., D. Rainham, and J. Hewko. 2000. Heat-Stress-Related Mortality in Five Cities in Southern Ontario: 1980–1996. International Journal of Biometeorology 4:190–197.

Sobhani, Ladan and Simon Rettack. 2001. Fuelling Climate Change. *In* The Case Against the Global Economy and for a Turn Towards Localization. Edward Goldsmith and Jerry Manour, eds. Pp. 224–237. London: Earthscan.

Socialist Alliance. 2007. The Socialist Alliance 10-Point Climate Action Plan. Pamphlet, Climate action now! Australia.

Spence, Christopher. 2005. Global Warming: Personal Solutions for a Healthy Planet. New York: Palgrave.

Stall, Ron, and Thomas Mills. 2006. Health Disparities, Syndemics and Gay Menís Health. Presented at the Center for Health Intervention and Prevention. University of Connecticut. Electronic document, http://www.chip.uconn.edu/lec/Stall percent20-percent20Connecticut percent20Talk.pdf. Accessed August 22, 2007.

Stall, Ron, Thomas Mills, J. Williamson, and T. Hart. 2003. Association of Co-occurring Psychosocial Health Problems and Increased Vulnerability to HIV/AIDS Among Urban men who have Sex with Men. American Journal of Public Health. 93(6):939–942.

Stamm, W., H. Handsfield, A. Rompalo, R. Ashley, P. Roberts, and L. Corey. 1988. The Association Between Genital Ulcer Disease and Acquisition of HIV Infection in Homosexual Men. Journal of the American Medical Association 260:1429–1433.

Stanley, David. 2007. South Pacific Organizer: Tuvalu. Electronic document, http://www.southpacific.org/faq/tuv.html. Accessed August 23, 2008.

Statistics New Zealand. 2007. Tokelauan–Population. Electronic document, http://www2.stats.govt.nz/domino/external/web/nzstories.nsf/092edeb76ed5aa6bcc256afe0081d84e/9054fc57961cc2fecc256ccf0064afe9?OpenDocument. Accessed January 22, 2007.

Steain, Megan, Bin Wang, Dominic Dwyer, and Nitin Saksena. 2004. HIV-1 Co-infection, Superinfection and Recombination. Sexual Health 1(4):239–250.

Stenseth, Nils, Noelle Samia, Hildegunn Viljugrein, and Kyree Kausrud. 2006. Plague Dynamics Are Driven by Climate Variation. Proceedings of the National Academy of Sciences of America 103:13110–13115.

Stern, Nicholas. 2007. The Economics of Climate Change: The Stern Review. Cambridge: Cambridge University Press.

Stevens, D., V. Kan, M. Judson, V. Morrison, S. Dummer, D. Denning, J. Bennett, T. Walsh, T. Patterson, and G. Pankey. 2000. Practice Guidelines for Diseases Caused by Aspergillus. Clinical Infectious Diseases 30(4):696–709.

Stevens, William K. 1999. The Change in the Weather: People, Weather, and the Science of Climate. New York: Delta Trade Paperbacks.

Strauss, Sarah, and Ben Orlove. 2003. Up in the Air: The Anthropology of Weather and Climate. In Weather, Climate, Culture. Sarah Strauss and Ben Orlove. Pp. 3–14. Oxford: Berg.

Striepen, B., A. Pruijssers, J. Huang, C. Li, M. Gubbels, N. Umejiego, L. Hedstrom, J. and Kissinger. 2004. Gene Transfer in the Evolution of Parasite Nucleotide Biosynthesis. Proceedings of the (U.S.) National Academy of Sciences 101(9):3154–3159.

Striepen, B., M. White, C. Li, M. Guerini, S. Malik, J. Logsdon, Jr., C. Liu, and M. Abrahamsen. 2002. Genetic Complementation in Apicomplexan Parasites. Proceedings of the National Academy of Sciences of the United States of America 99(9):6304–6309.

Strom, Robert. 2007. Hot House: Global Climate Change and the Human Condition. New York: Copernicus Books.

Struck, Doug. 2006. Climate Change Drives Disease to New Territory. Washington Post, May 5: A16.

Sturman, Andrew, and Nigel Tapper. 2006. The Weather and Climate of Australia and New Zealand. 2nd edition. Oxford: Oxford University Press.

Sutter, Christop, and Juan Carlos Parreno. 2007. Does the Current Clean Development Mechanism (CDM) Deliver Its Sustainable Development Claim: An Analysis of Officially Registered CDM Projects. Climatic Change 84:75–90.

Symond, Carolyn, Lelani Arris, and Bill Heal, eds. 2004. Arctic Climate Impact Assessment. Cambridge: Cambridge University Press.

Tabb, William K. 2007. Resource Wars. Monthly Review Press, January: 32–42.

Taubenberger, Jeffery, A. Reid, A. Krafft, K. Bjwaard, and T. Fanning. 1997. Initial Genetic Characterization of the 1918 "Spanish" Influenza Virus. Science 275:1793–1796.

Taubenberger, Jeffery, and David Morens. 2006. 1918. Influenza: The Mother of All Pandemics. Emergent Infectious Diseases 12(1). Electronic document, http://www.cdc.gov/ncidod/EID/vol12no01/05-0979.htm. Accessed August 21, 2007.

Thailand Ministry of Public Health. 1999. Annual Epidemiological Surveillance Report. Office of the Permanent Secretary for Public Health, Ministry of Public Health.

Thompson, Alexander, Paul Robbins, Brent Sohngen, Joseph Arvai, and Thomas Koontz. 2006. Economy, Politics and Institutions: From Adaptation to Adaptive Management in Climate Change. Climatic Change 78:1–15.

Thornton, P., P. Jones, and T. Owiyo. 2006. Mapping Climate Vulnerability and Poverty in Africa. Nairobi, Kenya: Report to the Department for International Development: ILRI.

Tidwell, Mike. 2006. The Ravaging Tide: Strange Weather, Future Katrinas, and Coming Death of America's Coastal Cities. New York: Free Press.

Timmons, Robert J., Peter E. Grimes, and Jodie L. Manale. 2003. Social Roots of Global Environmental Change: A World-Systems Analysis of Carbon Dioxide Emissions. Journal of World Systems Research 9(2):277–315.

Townsend, Peter. 1986. Why are the Many Poor. International Journal of Health Services 16:1–32.

Trainer, Ted. 1989. Developed to Death: Rethinking Third World Development. London: Green Print.

———. 1995. The Conserver Society: Alternatives for Sustainability. London: Zed Books.

Tsui, Judith, Eric Vittinghoff, Michael Shlipak, Daniel Bertenthal, John Inadomi, Rudolph Rodriguez, and Ann O'Hare. 2007. Association of Hepatitis C Seropositivity With Increased Risk for Developing End-stage Renal Disease. Archives of Intern Medicine 167:1271–1276.

Turner, Bryan. 2006. Vulnerability and Human Rights. University Park, PA: Penn State Press.

TuvaluIslands.com. 2007. Tuvalu and Global Warming. Electronic document, http://www.tuvaluislands.com/warming.htm. Accessed November 2, 2007.

Umar, K. 2003. Disparities Persist in Infant Mortality: Creative Approaches Work to Close the Gap. Closing the Gap: Newsletter of the Office of Minority Health. Washington, DC: U.S. Department of Health and Human Services.

UNDP. 1999. Human Development Report 1999. New York: Oxford University Press.

UNESCO. 2006. Carbon Emissions—UNESCO-Scope Policy Briefs, October, No. 2.

Union of Concerned Scientists. 2005. Early Warning Signs: Spreading Disease. Electronic document, http://www.ucsusa.org/global_warming/science/early-warning-signs-of-global-warming-spreading-disease.html

United Kingdom Department of Health. 2004. History of Influenza Pandemics. Electronic document, http://www.globalsecurity.org/security/library/report/2005/history2.pdf. Accessed 7/03/07.

United Nations Environment Program. 2007. The Global Outlook for Snow and Ice. Electronic document, http://www.unep.org/Documents.Multilingual/Default.asp?DocumentID=512&ArticleID=5599&l=en. Accessed February 22, 2008.

U.S. Bureau of the Census. 2005. American Community Survey Change Profile, 2001–2002. Electronic document, http://www.census.gov/acs/www/Products/Profiles/Chg/2002/0101/. Accessed June 15, 2006.

U.S. Department of Health and Human Services. 2000. Healthy People 2010 (Conference Edition, vols. 1 & 2). Washington, DC: U.S. Government Printing Office.

Ventura, H., and M. Mehra. 2004. The Growing Burden of Health Failure: The "Syndemic" Is Reaching Latin America. American Heart Journal 147(3):412–417.

Victor, David G. 2004. Climate Change: Debating America's Policy Options. New York: Council on Foreign Relations.

Wackernagel, M., and W. Rees. 1996. Our Ecological Footprint: Reducing Human Impact on the Earth. Gabriola Island, BC: New Society Publishers.

Wager, William. 1992. The Future of History. Chicago: University of Chicago.

Wall, Dennis. 2007. Global Warming a Threat to Alaska Native Communities. Native Voices XIII(4):1 & 3.

Wallerstein, Immanuel. 1979. The Capitalist World-Economy. Cambridge: Cambridge University Press.

———. 2004. World-Systems Analysis: An Introduction. Durham, NC: Duke University Press.

———. 2007. Climate Disasters: Three Obstacles to Doing Anything. Commentary No. 205, March 15. Electronic document, www.binghampton.edu/fbc. Accessed June 16, 2008.

Warner, D. 1991. Health Issues at the US-Mexican Border. Journal of the American Medical Association 265:242–247.

Waters, W. 2001. Globalization, Socioeconomic Restructuring, and Community Health. Journal of Community Health 26(2):79–92.

Watkins, J. 1997. Briefing on Poverty. Oxford: Oxfam Publications.

Watson, Robert, Marufu Zinyowera, Richard Moss, and David Dokken. 1997. Special Report on the Regional Impacts of Climate Change:An Assessment of Vulnerability. Cambridge: Cambridge University Press.

Wayne, P., S. Foster, J. Connolly, F. Bazzaz, and P. Epstein. 2002. Production of Allergenic Pollen by Ragweed (Ambrosia artemisiifolia L.) Is Increased in CO_2-enriched Atmospheres. Annals of Allergy, Asthma and Immunology 8:279–282.

Weart, Spencer R. 2003. The Discovery of Global Warming. Cambridge, MA: Harvard University Press.

Weather Almanac. 2006. How Hot Can It Get? Electronic document, http://www.islandnet.com/~see/weather/almanac/arc2006/alm06jul.htm. Accessed December 21, 2007.

Webb, Dave. 2007. Thinking the Worst: The Pentagon Report. In Surving Climate Change: The Struggle to Avert Global Catastrophe. David Cromwell and Mark Levene, eds. Pp. 59–81. London: Pluto Press.

Webster, Ben. 2001. Boeing Admits Its New Aircraft Will Guzzle Fuel. London Times, June 19.

Wessen, Albert, ed. 1992. Migration and Health in a Small Society: The Case of Tokelau. Research Monographs on Human Population Biology, No. 8. New York: Clarendon Press.

West, Colon Thor. 2003. Testing Farmers' Perceptions of Climate Variability: A Case Study from the Sulphur Springs Valley, Arizona. In Weather, Climate, Culture. Sarah Strauss and Ben Orlove, eds. Pp. 233–250. Oxford: Berg.

West, Colin Thor, and Marcela Vasquez-Leon. 2003. Testing Farmers' Perceptions of Climate Variability: A Case Study from the Sulphur Springs Valley, Arizona. In Weather, Climate, Culture. Sarah Strauss and Ben Orlove, eds. Pp. 233–250. Oxford: Berg.

Westerling, Anthony, H. Hidalgo, Daniel Cayan, and T. Swetnam. 2006. Warming and Earlier Spring Increase Western U.S. Forest Wildfire Activity. Science 313(5789):940–943.

Whitman, S., G. Good, E. Donoghue, N. Benbow, W. Shou, and S. Mou. 1997. Mortality in Chicago Attributed to the July 1995 Heatwave. American Journal of Public Health 87:1515–1551.

Whyte, Ian D. 1995. Climate Change and Human Society. London: Arnold.

Wigley, T. M. 2000. ENSO, Volcanoes, and Record Breaking Temperatures. Geophysical Research Letters 27:451–454.

Wilkie, David, Gilda Morelli, Fiona Rotberg, and Ellen Shaw. 1999. Wetter Isn't Better: Global Warming and Food Security in the Congo Basin. Global Environmental Change 9:323–328.

Willis, David. 2004. Sea Engulfing Alaska Native Village. BBC News, July 30. Electronic document, http://news.bbc.co.uk/2/hi/europe/3940399.stm. Accessed June 2, 2007.

Woods Institute for the Environment. 2007. The Second Annual "America's Report Card on the Environment" Survey. Electronic document, http://woods.stanford.edu/docs/surveys/GW_200709_AP_survey.pdf. Accessed January 38, 2008.

Woolhouse, M. 2002. Population Biology of Emerging and Re-emerging Ppathogens. Trends in Microbiology 10:S3–7.

Working Group on Climate Change and Development. 2005. Africa—Up in Smoke? International Institute for Environment and Development.

———. 2006. Africa—Up in Smoke 2. International Institute for Environment and Development.

———. 2007. Up in Smoke? Latin America and the Caribbean. International Institute for Environment and Development.

World Bank. 2000. Cities, Seas and Storms: Managing Change in Pacific Island Economies, vol. IV: Adapting to Climate Change. Washington, DC: World Bank.

———. 2001. World Development Report 2000/2001: Attacking Poverty. Oxford: Oxford University Press.

World Commission on Environment and Development. 1987. Our Common Future. Melbourne: Oxford University Press.

World Health Organization. 1978. Primary Health Care. Geneva.

———. 1998. Rift Valley Fever. Electronic document, http://www.who.int/mediacentre/factsheets/fs207/en/. Accessed June 5, 2007.

———. 2000. Lymphatic Filariasis. Fact Sheet 102. Electronic document, www.who.int/mediacentre/factsheets/fs102/en. Accessed April 19, 2007.

World Health Organization. 2001. Yellow Fever. Fact Sheet 100. Electronic document, http://www.who.int/mediacentre/factsheets/fs100/en/. Accessed March 9, 2008.

———. 2002. Reducing Risks and Promoting Health Life. Vienna: WHO.

———. 2003. WHO Report on Global Surveillance of Epidemic-prone Infectious Diseases—Cholera. Electronic document, http://www.who.int/csr/resources/publications/cholera/CSR_ISR_2000_1/en/index2.html. Accessed August 14, 2008.

———. 2004. Ten Things You Need to Know about Pandemic Influenza. Electronic document, http://www.who.int/csr/disease/influenza/pandemic10things/en. Accessed July 3, 2007.

World Watch Institute. 2007. State of the World: Our Urban Future. New York: W. W. Norton & Co.

Yamin, Farhana, and Johanna DePledge. 2004. The International Climate Change Regime. Cambridge: Cambridge University Press.

Yanagihara, R. 1990. Hantavirus Infection in the United States: Epizootiology and Epidemiology. Reviews of Infectious Diseases 12(3):449–457.

Yang, J. K., Y. Feng, M. Yuan, S. Yuan, H. Fu, B. Wu, G. Sun, G. Yang, X. Zhang, L. Wang, X. Xu, and J. Chan. 2006. Plasma Glucose Levels and Diabetes are Independent Predictors for Mortality and Morbidity in Patients with SARS. Diabetic Medicine 23(6): 623–628. Electronic document, http://www.ingentaconnect.com/content/bsc/dme;jsessionid=5b1eph31nvuet.victoria. Accessed March 27, 2007.

Yim, Wyss W. S. 1996. Vulnerability and Adaptation of Hong Kong to Hazards and Climatic Change Conditions. In Climate Change Vulnerability and Adaptation in Asia and the Pacific. Lin Erda et al. Pp. 181–190. Dordrecht, Netherlands: Kluwer Academic Publishers.

Young, C. Ann. 2004. A Syndemic Perspective on Whooping Cough Epidemics at York Factory. Presented at the Canadian Association for Physical Anthropology, London, Ontario, Canada.

Zabarenko, Deborah. 2007. Global warming Is Human Rights Issue: Nobel Nominee. Reuters. Electronic document, http://www.reuters.com/article/environmentNews/idUS N0227026920070304?pageNumber=1. February 2, 2008.

Zang, Y., Nakata, K., Weiden, M. and Rom, W. 1995. Mycobacterium Tuberculosis Enhances Human Immunodeficiency Virus-1 Replication by Transcriptional Activation at the Long Terminal Repeat. Journal of Clinical Investigation 95(5):2324–2331.

Zhang, Zhihong. 2003. The Forces Behind China's Climate Change Policy: Interests, Sovereignty, and Prestige. In Global Warming and East Asia: The Domestic and International Politics of Climate Change. Paul F. Harris, ed. Pp. 66–85. London: Routledge.

Ziska, L. 2003. Evaluation of the Growth Response of Six Invasive Species to Past, Present and Future Atmospheric Carbon Dioxide. Journal of Experimental Botany 54(381):395–404.

Ziska, L., D. Gebhard, D. Frenz, S. Faulkner, B. Singer, and J. Straka. 2003. Cities as Harbingers of Climate Change: Common Ragweed, Urbanization, and Public Health. The Journal of Allergy and Clinical Immunology 111(2):290–295.

Index

About the Authors

HANS A. BAER is a Senior Lecturer in the Development Studies Program, School of Philosophy, Anthropology, and Social Inquiry, and the Centre of Health and Society at the University of Melbourne. He earned a PhD in Anthropology at the University of Utah in 1976 and was a postdoctoral fellow in the Medical Anthropology Program at Michigan State University in 1979–1980. He held regular positions at Kearney State College (1972–1973), George Peabody College for Teachers (1976–1979), St. John's University (1980–1981), the University of Southern Mississippi (1981–1983), and the University of Arkansas at Little Rock (1983–2005). He has been a visiting professor at Humboldt University in Berlin; the University of California, Berkeley; Arizona State University; George Washington University; and Australian National University. Dr. Baer has conducted research on the Hutterites in South Dakota; the Levites (a Mormon sect in Utah); African American Spiritual churches; complementary and alternative medicine in the United States, United Kingdom, and Australia; socio-political and religious life in East Germany; and conventional and complementary HIV clinics in a Western U.S. city. He has published 14 books, coedited several special journal issues, and published some 140 book chapters and journal articles. Some of his books include *Recreating Utopia in the Desert*; *African American Religion*; *Encounters with Biomedicine: Case Studies in Medical Anthropology*; *Critical Medical Anthropology* (with Merrill Singer); *Medical Anthropology and the World System: A Critical Perspective* (with Merrill Singer and Ida Susser); and *Biomedicine and Alternative Healing Systems in America: Issues of Class, Race, Ethnicity, and Gender, Toward an Integrative Medicine* and *Introducing Medical Anthropology* (both forthcoming with Merrill Singer). He received the Rudolf Virchow Prize awarded by the Critical Anthropology Caucus in 1994. Dr. Baer has served on the editorial board of *Medical Anthropology* from 1998 to 2000 and *Medical Anthropological Quarterly* from 1996 to 2004. He presently is on the editorial board of *Complementary Health Practice Review* and is conducting an ethnographic study of two natural medicine colleges in Australia.

MERRILL SINGER is a Professor in the Department of Anthropology and Senior Research Scientist in the Center for Health, Intervention and Prevention at the University of Connecticut. Former Director (for 20 years) of the Center for Community Health Research at the Hispanic Health Council in Hartford, CT; he earned a PhD in Anthropology at the University of Utah in 1979 and was a post-doctoral fellow at George Washington University Medical School 1979–1980 and the University of Connecticut Health Center 1982–1983. Dr. Singer has been the Principal Investigator on a continuous series of basic and applied federally funded drinking, drug use, community 20 and interpersonal violence, and AIDS prevention studies since 1984, and currently is involved in studies on second-hand smoking among Puerto Rican children, ethical issues in the public health study of illicit drug users, and patterns of communication and negotiation of sex, contraception use, STI prevention, and reproductive decision-making among young adults in the inner-city. Additionally, Dr. Singer is involved in a study designed to assess the implementation of oral HIV testing among injection drug users in Rio De Janeiro, Brazil and in efforts to expand public health research in Haiti. Dr. Singer has published over 200 articles and chapters in health and social science journals and books and has authored or edited 20 books including *The Political Economy of AIDS* (edited), *Medical Anthropology and the World System* (with Hans Baer and Ida Susser), *Introducing Medical Anthropology* (with Hans Baer), *Unhealthy Health Policy: A Critical Anthropological Examination* (edited with Arachu Castro), *Something Dangerous: Emergent and Changing Illicit Drug Use and Community Health*, and *Drugging the Poor: Legal and Illegal Drug Industries and the Structuring of Social Inequality*. He is the recipient of the Rudolph Virchow Prize, the AIDS and Anthropology Paper Prize, the George Foster Memorial Award for Practicing Anthropology from the Society for Medical Anthropology and the Prize for Distinguished Achievement in the Critical Study of North America from the Society for the Anthropology of North America. Dr. Singer is on the Board=20 of Directors of the Society for Applied Anthropology and the Committee on Ethics of the American Anthropological Association. He has served on the editorial boards of *Medical Anthropology Quarterly, Medical Anthropology, Ethnicity and Substance Abuse*, and the *International Journal of Drug Policy*.